SCREWED

SCREWED
THE TRUTH ABOUT LIFE
AS A PRISON OFFICER

RONNIE THOMPSON

headline
review

First published in 2007
by HEADLINE REVIEW

An imprint of Headline Publishing Group

2

Cataloguing in Publication Data is available from the British Library

ISBN 978 0 7553 1665 6

Typeset in ZapfElliptical by Avon DataSet Ltd,
Bidford on Avon, Warwickshire

Printed and bound in Great Britain by
Mackays of Chatham plc, Chatham, Kent

Headline's policy is to use papers that are natural, renewable and recyclable products and made from wood grown in sustainable forests. The logging and manufacturing processes are expected to conform to the environmental regulations of the country of origin.

HEADLINE PUBLISHING GROUP
An Hachette Livre UK Company
338 Euston Road
London NW1 3BH

www.reviewbooks.co.uk
www.hodderheadline.com

CONTENTS

CHEERS TO

Oasis for being the best band in the world, putting on the most amazing live shows and undoubtedly being the true soundtrack to my life.

The View (my favourite band of recent times), Arctic Monkeys, Kasabian, Kaiser Chiefs, The Enemy, Doves, Kings of Leon, The Prodigy, The Libertines, Sex Pistols, Stone Roses, Paul Weller (pint of), Razorlight, The Kooks, The Charlatans, Bloc Party, Maximo Park, The Streets, Jamie T, Jack Penate, Primal Scream, Jet, Morning Runner, The Kinks, The Beatles, The Killers, Foo Fighters, Ocean Colour Scene and The Verve for all being amazing bands, and for supplying me with burning inspiration through the great vehicle of music.

Chris Moyles, for being an absolute legend and entertaining me with his great show.

Jo Whiley, for having an equally great show, impeccable taste in music and for presenting it with by far the sexiest voice around.

Terry the printer and Fox (early encouragement), drinks are on me.

And finally, cheers to Colin Butts for writing three of my favourite novels (where's the next one, mate?!). And for being a great mentor to me; showing me the rules to this crazy game.

AUTHOR'S NOTE

All the characters in this book are based on real-life individuals; however, their names have been changed for security reasons. HMP Romwell is a fictitious prison that I created to protect the reputations of the Establishments where I have worked and, more importantly, to protect the colleagues who I worked with.

Some of the conversations in the book are, of necessity, imaginary or re-imagined; but they accurately reflect the mood of the times and the way that I felt; and my memory of the events described.

GLOSSARY

ABH – actual bodily harm

bang up – prisoner who is inside his cell

banged up – put inside a prison cell

barnet – (barnet fair – rhyming slang) hair

Basic Regime – minimum entitlements

beasted – worked hard, pushed around, thrashed, got the better of

bent screw – Prison Officer who is trafficking drugs

bent up – prisoner under restraint

bird – time being served in prison; a girl

boat – (boat race – rhyming slang) face

bottler – someone who loses his nerve and backs off

bottling it – *see* **bottler**

brown – heroin

burn – tobacco

C&R – Control and Restraint (techniques used when restraining a prisoner)

CC – cell confinement

cell fabric check – checking locks, bars, general state of cell, and that everything's working

cell spin – cell search

Charlie – cocaine

chase the dragon – smoke heroin

civvy – civilian as in 'non-uniform'; also non-uniform staff member, e.g. teacher, councillor etc

clucking – withdrawing from drugs, going cold turkey

con – a prisoner

cons with keys – bent screws

contract – when someone has been paid to murder someone else

CPS – Crown Prosecution Service

crack – crack cocaine

crackhead – crack-cocaine addict

cuff-carry – the awkward and painful (for the con) procedure of carrying a handcuffed prisoner

Dep – *see* **the Dep**

dojo – padded gymnasium

double bang up – two inmates sharing a cell

dropped; drop – prisoner taken to the floor with force to be placed under restraint; to hit someone to the ground

dummy is spat out – (as when a kid isn't getting what it wants) getting angry, pissed off, kicking off

fabric check – *see* **cell fabric check**

firm – a gang

fraggle – a drug addict detoxing; and a prisoner who cannot cope with prison

Fraggle Wing – Hospital Wing

GBH – grievous bodily harm

gobby – mouthy, over-talkative

grass – informant

Guv – how a prisoner addresses a Prison Officer

Intel – insider info, covert security intelligence

jack up – inject oneself with a drug

jail craft – security and prison awareness

jog on – move on; disregard; **tell someone to 'jog on'** – tell them to 'go away', 'piss off'

jugged – someone who has had boiling water plus sugar thrown over them

junkie – heroin addict

kick off – start trouble; a flare-up of trouble

kit up – get into protective riot clothing worn by Prison Officers

kosher – something that is true; real

locating – taking prisoners to their cells

lock down – out-of-cell movements of all prisoners have ceased, and all are back in their cells and accounted for

minging – drunk, ugly person, unwashed, smelly, disgusting

monkey – £500

MSL – Minimum Staffing Levels

neck; necking – to swallow (something), drink

nick – prison or police station; to arrest

nicked – prisoner placed on report for an offence, and seen by the Governor; arrested by the police

nob; nobhead – idiot, objectionable person

nonce – sex offender

Nonce Wing – Wing for prisoners that are segregated for their own protection

Number One – Governor

Number Two – Deputy Governor

numpty – idiot

nut nuts – criminally insane

old lag – older prisoner who has spent a long time in prison

on the road – outside the prison; freedom

ones, twos, threes etc – *see* **The Ones** etc

op cap – operational capacity of a prison/Wing/unit

OSG – Operational Support Grade: a uniformed grade, a rank below Officer, a non-prisoner-contact role

PE – physical education

PEO – Physical Education Officer

pesting – on the pull for; over-heavy chat-up

pikey – traveller, gypsy

pills – ecstasy

plug – stuff up the arse

PO – Principal Officer

POA – Prison Officer's Association

POELT – Prison Officer Entry Level Training

PSC – Prison Service College

puff – cannabis

rock – crack cocaine

roll check – periodic daily check of prisoners to make sure the numbers match previous checks

rub-down – search whereby the body is frisked

savvy – understanding

Scooby (Doo) – clue

screw – Prison Officer

scroat – a prisoner

serve up – deal in drugs

single bang up – one prisoner in a cell

smack – heroin

smackhead – heroin addict

SO – Senior Officer

Special K – the drug ketamine

spin, spun – *see* **cell spin**

spit his dummy out of his pram – *see* **dummy**

sprog – new Officer

stand-fast roll check – roll check during a rapid response; *see* **roll check**

stave – a truncheon; defensive weapon made out of hard wood

Stella – Stella Artois lager

straight – doesn't participate in criminal activity; not on a criminal path

strip cell – strip conditions cell: no furniture or clothes, just a gown to wear. This is for extremely non-compliant cons and avoids cell harm and the harming of staff

sweatbox – prison van

swinger – prisoner who's found dead from hanging themselves

The Block – The Segregation Unit

The Dep – Deputy Governor, (Deputy in charge of the prison), Number Two Governor

the nuts – the best

The Ones, The Twos etc – various landings, with cells, within a Wing

the road – outside the prison; freedom

The Rule – Rule 45, under which prisoners separated from others for their own protection

the Scrubs – HMP Wormwood Scrubs

The Seg – The Segregation Unit where the dangerous and disruptive are located

The Well – HMP Romwell

toe-rag – despicable git; scrounger; thief; fag (rhyming slang for)

tooled up – prisoner who is armed with a weapon

Tornado Team – riot-response team

touch, a – something extra, over and above, on the side, a bonus, a piece of luck

VO – Visiting Order

VPs – vulnerable prisoners

Wakey – Prison Service College Wakefield

wedge – large bundle of folded banknotes

Wing – one of the different residential areas where prisoners are located

wrap – small package or packet

wrap up – put prisoner under restraint

yardie – Jamaican gang member

STATEMENT OF PURPOSE

Her Majesty's Prison Service serves the public by keeping in custody those committed by the courts.

Our duty is to look after them with humanity and help them lead law-abiding and useful lives in custody and after release.

POWERS OF A CONSTABLE

Every Prison Officer while acting as such has all the powers of a constable.

(*Prison Act 1952 15 & 16 Geo 6 and Eliz 2 Section 8*)

INTRODUCTION

y name is Ronnie Thompson, I'm twenty-seven years old. Being a Prison Officer for Her Majesty's Prison Service was something that I used to be proud to do. I soon realised the truth of what it's like working as a screw. A fucking headache. The pressures, duties, life-wrecking conditions, corruption, danger – none of this is known to the public, but all of it makes up a day in the life of a Prison Officer.

There are many misconceptions of the job. People think that Officers are bully-boy meat heads who unlock and lock doors. I have seen a lot of bullies in the Service and I've seen many abuse their authority – but that's not what we are all like, and that is not exclusive to the Prison Service; there are those types of people in every walk of life. The role of a Prison Officer is the unspoken job, the unspoken service. We continually hear reports of every other service within the public sector: the Fire Service, Police, Nurses and the Armed Forces. We hear of underpayment and overworked staff – all valid and things should be changed. For members of the Prison Service, it is different: always bad reports and never any recognition of the jobs they do. The general understanding is that if a con pisses off a screw, then the Officer will give him a good kicking. Not always the case, and I do stress *not always* the case. I will explain what goes on, the times when force is necessary and used, and when it is unnecessary but still used. Likewise, I will express my downright disgust at Officers with no bollocks, who would rather walk the other way when some poor cunt is getting the shit kicked out of them. These cowards look out for no one.

I will show the underworld of bent screws, the drugs they traffic, the firms they work for and what they get paid for their sins. These screws will traffic anything for the right price, not giving a fuck about the safety of the cons or of the other Officers. Scumbags, the lot of them. The pathetic punishment they get for these activities is something that you have a right to know about.

A dangerous and violent member of the public gets sentenced 'five to ten' (years) on a GBH or attempted-murder conviction. When he's inside, if he seriously assaults another prisoner or puts some screw in hospital, all he gets as punishment is fourteen days' loss of canteen! Get that? The cons get LESS for breaking the law inside than they do on the outside. What is that all about? Some poor bastard screw goes to work on an early shift, with his six-month-old baby and wife at home, and a junkie, fucked out of his head, tears into him. What kind of job is this?

2

Not only, as Officers, do we have to deal with the prisoners, which is what we are paid to do: we have to deal with another type of Prison Service species – the Governor. These people are the bosses who are supposed to know what is going on. They are employed to manage the prison, to make it a safe environment, to deal with serious issues, AND to ensure that their staff's wellbeing is a priority. Bollocks! The overall management that I have been accustomed to is corrupt. I've seen Governors cover up the most outrageous incidents while, on the other hand, using a decent Officer as a scapegoat to further themselves.

Being a good screw doesn't mean always sticking to the rules. If we were to stick to the fluffy human-rights crap we deal with now, then there would be riots every other day. The rules have to be bent to get the job done effectively. You have to give the prisoner the odd extra, allowing that bonus phone call etc, to ensure good rapport, so the environment stays stable. Give that little bit 'over and above' and then the con will trust you. When he trusts you he will give you Intel – insider info, covert security intelligence – which helps to fry the bigger fish, the dealer, the bully or, if you are lucky, the scumbag bent screw.

I'm not going to claim to be whiter than white. I've bent the rules and done shitloads that I shouldn't have, but I am one of the good guys who takes pride in being a screw and who does the job well. I do give my extras, I do favours; but, if any fucker takes liberties with me, I'll go to their cell to have a 'career chat'. I don't condone bully-boy tactics. I always deal with things alone: stopping the problem and educating the dickhead. Of course, this is bending the rules but, nine times out of ten, without an audience the problem can be sorted. If that means a slap, so be it; but most of the time, once they are on their own, they are sound. I'll never forget a prisoner called Ali telling another new con what I was like.

He said, 'Mr Thompson, he's sound, don't fuck him about, do as he asks and you will get your touches. Fuck him about and he will destroy you, simple as that; you will be fucked.'

Violence, corruption. Welcome to my world.

WRONG SIDE OF THE DOOR

My alarm went at 04.45 hrs that morning, the same as every morning that I was on duty. I've never got used to getting up at that unearthly hour. I always have to drag my arse out of my warm bed. I had a large mug of coffee, like I always do, contemplating the two-hour drive I had to negotiate before my day's graft at the prison. Putting on the uniform is never nice first thing in the morning. Itchiest fucking trousers ever known to man. You'd think they would be nice and comfortable, considering the job I was doing. Not a chance; fucking horrible. That, followed by a starchy shitty shirt, epaulettes, clip-on tie, keychain and stave, and I was ready to head to work. The drive always gives me the chance to wake up before I get to the nick. The last thing you want is to be half asleep when you're walking on one of the Wings. That's when things go wrong; someone gets hurt.

The drive in was normal: long and boring, but normal. Roads are always quiet until I get close to the city which is always busy with traffic whatever the time you get there. I pulled into HMP Romwell – known to all as 'The Well' – at 07.05 hrs, just as I do everyday. The car park was busy as always; screws flooding in to face the day's work. I headed to the staff mess for my breakfast. Fucking horrible; it is everyday. Little did I know it was going to be a day that would turn my life upside down.

I'd settled in nicely. I knew all the screws who were geezers and the Officers who did the job well. I had made some really good mates, lads that I could trust with my life. There weren't many of them, but we surrounded ourselves with each other so we could get on with the job – do it well and safely. I knew exactly who the wankers were; I knew who I could trust and who I couldn't. That goes all the way through the ranks. There were a few good Governors but, to be fair, not many. Most of them were out to get you in order to further their own career. But I was in the know; I knew who was good and who was bad. That went for the cons as well. I knew the dealers, the grasses, the gang leaders, the gang followers, the first timers, and the old lags.

There wasn't much that I didn't know. I had become a good screw. I'd found my strengths. I was good at getting the job done efficiently. I was fair, firm and was able to talk to people. Ninety per cent of the job is the ability to communicate. If you can't do that then life is very hard as a Prison Officer. You've got to learn the rules fast because, if you don't know them, the cons will be all over you. Most of them know the rules far better than you do. I was in my early twenties when I joined, and some of the cons I was looking after had been going in and out of prison longer than I'd been alive. Learning quick is a must if you are going to get on. Judging a situation and being aware is the only way. You have to recognise the dangers and have to be able to switch it on instantly. No time for complacency. Thankfully I had my wits about me; I was able to react within a split second and I was good at putting them under restraint, bending them up, if I needed to.

After I'd finished my horrible breakfast, I headed to the Wing for the morning briefing, which is held in the Wing's staff room before duty commences. So, whatever Wing or group you work on, the Senior Officer (SO) conducts a briefing, running through the detail, where you are ordered to work, what activities are due to happen and any intelligence. The Intel for the day could be anything from a prisoner refusing transfer to information suggesting there could be a riot.

The briefing was a formality as usual – except that morning I was detailed to work in the Visits Hall. I was being cross-deployed. That happens when an area of the nick is short of Officers; they then pinch some from a better-staffed area. I say 'better staffed' not 'fully staffed' for a reason. The jail was in shit state, as always. The fucking idiots at the top had no idea. They never employed enough staff. It was bollocks. Fucking dangerous.

I was quite happy to be cross-deployed to the Visits Hall, though. It was normally a nice little number, off the Wing for the day – where you don't even get a chance to shit in peace. Everything there is constant; suffocating. The cons are round you like flies round shit. Don't blame them. There are hundreds of them, with fuck-all staff. All of them wanting a piece of you.

Visits was a nice break. You didn't get any grief. They were on their visits; happy with their visitor but, more often than not, trying to smuggle crack and smack into the place. Drugs do get into the prison through these visits and over the wall. When I say 'over the wall', I mean it literally. But the main way drugs got in was through bent screws. Simple as that.

Your duties, in Visits, are to police the Hall and make sure that no trafficking is going on. You have to stay alert, looking around, keeping your wits about you. Drugs will always get through, that's a fact, but you have to do your best to catch them at it.

The prisoners that have visits are collected from their Wing locations and taken to the holding room next to the Visits Hall. It is one room that all the cons have to wait in before entering the main hall for their visit. They wait there until they are called, one by one, to go through to the search room to be rub-down searched, like you get at a nightclub or an airport. You can have fifty or sixty cons waiting in a room that's not very big at all. Fuck me, does it stink! It's disgusting! The dirty bastards piss in there, spit, smoke (I've even found a turd before now; fucking animal!) It's cramped and hot with scum in the corners of every dirty magnolia wall. There are pieces of broken lino, exposing the concrete underneath. There is one small window, about seven feet up, with bars running down it. The one light it has is useless.

Sometimes tensions can run high in there. When scraps break out, it can be a fucking nightmare. You have to get in there and drag them out, delaying the start of their visits. You rely on the good will of the other cons. A lot of them don't want to scrap in there. They want to have their visit. Some cunt delaying that isn't good; the rest fucking hate it. Assisting the screws happens more often than not in that situation. Saying that, it's also the perfect opportunity for an Officer to be taken hostage. A small room . . . sixty cons . . . a couple of screws; would be easy, but it ain't happened yet. Yet.

One at a time and by name they leave the holding room to go into the search room. Two Officers are there waiting to perform the rub-down search and take away any property, as nothing is allowed in the Hall. They don't need anything other than themselves. The prop (property) they hand over is kept until after the visit. The con is then given a bib to wear to make it easier to identify the prisoner. You'd be surprised how many cons try to get out with their visitors. Some of them are on remand, you see, so they are wearing their own clothes. Even the convicted ones do, most of the time. Rules are lax.

Once they have been searched, prop taken and bib put on, they go up the stairs opposite the search room into the Visits Hall. They are told by a waiting Officer where to sit. This process should take a couple of minutes, at least, per prisoner. Does it fuck, though. You would have a fucking riot if it took that long. Two hours for sixty cons? Yeah right! You are taught one thing on basic training, but expected to do another by the jail's Governors. They don't tell you to break the rules but, if there was a riot, you would be in for it, so they rely on you to speed things up accordingly. When there's an audit, marks could be deducted on the grounds that the searching is taking too long – or that it's not being done correctly. You were in for it, whichever way you looked. The sneaky cunts would cover their arses from the start while the screws take the shit. Once the cons are all in the Hall and seated, the visitors are sent up.

The visitors come in at the front of the prison, through the main gate – the same gate that is used every day by the Prison Officers. Whoever walks in will see, in front of them, the gate

Officers. They deal with visitors, hold the keys for the screws and other members of staff, answer the phone etc. They are behind thick glass, as you would expect at a bank. On entering the prison, Officers go through a door to the left, visitors go though on the right. OK, they are different entries but, fucking hell, it's still security at its poorest. Any visitor can observe the whole process of an Officer going into the establishment. Loads of ex-cons, criminals and all sorts turn up for visits, and it's a fact that prisoners try to escape – and sometimes succeed. So the last thing you want is their fucking visitors seeing exactly how members of staff manoeuvre in and out of the nick, thus giving them the perfect intelligence to plot an escape. The solution? Simply use another entrance for the visitors. Hardly rocket science. It still astounds me that this simple yet critical procedure is so cocked up. Typical Prison Service bollocks.

The visitor has to show the Visiting Order (VO) and identification to the sweaty old Prison Officer sitting at the gate. 'VO? ID?' – moody, rude, not giving you the time of day. They are always miserable old cunts at the gate, coming to the end of their career. They are angry at having spent thirty years working in a prison, angry that their wives are fat old bitches that don't want sex anymore, angry at the world, and angry to still be fucking breathing. It can be intimidating for someone that has not been inside a nick before; the surroundings of the place, and the moody bastard they are greeted with. I've yet to find a nick with a happy young gate screw!

Once the visitor has shown their ID, they go through the security doors to the locker and search room. Every visitor has a locker into which they must put all their belongings. Beverages can be purchased up there from machines which, might I add, don't work half the fucking time; another thing that causes unnecessary arguments. In the search room there are Operational Support Grade staff (OSGs) and Officers waiting to search them: if a visitor has decided to plug drugs up their arse to smuggle them in, they would already have done that. Some of the lowlife cunts have been known to stuff gear in a baby's nappy. Fucking dirty lowlife. The visitor goes through a metal detector as well as having a rub-down search. It's at this point that, if a visitor appears to be pissed out of his or her head, or heavily under the influence of drugs, they are refused a visit. That can result in a kick off and the visitor getting bent up, cautioned and the police called. Providing that doesn't happen, the visitors go up to Hall to their waiting inmates and they have their visits.

Once all the cons and visitors have been searched, and everyone is seated, the screws then patrol the Hall, watching for any drug passes and keeping control of the area. Sometimes fights and arguments start up between visitors and prisoners. That has to be controlled. Most of the lazy screw fuckers just sit there and go to sleep. They can't be arsed to do fuck all. They see working on Visits as a day off, not giving a fuck what comes in. Some see it as 'The security is shit, why the fuck should I bother?' But I always wanted to do the job correctly and catch the drug-passers at it. It was a job to do, something that had to be done. A game. Cat and mouse. I would have a laugh with the cons during their visit, always polite, joking that I would catch them. I would get introduced to the inmate's families, if it was a con I got on with – which I did with quite a few. I'm a normal bloke, with normal values. Besides, it was fucking boring sitting there scratching my bollocks, clock-watching. The day would have dragged on and on. I enjoyed doing the job right, so I was cutting about the Hall, watching them all like a hawk.

If you see a pass, or a potential pass, you attend the table as quick as you can. You terminate the visit instantly – no questions – doing it as quickly and politely as you can. You take the con downstairs to perform a strip-search on him, always watching him closely on the way down to make sure that he doesn't try to plug the gear he has been passed. If he does, or tries to put it in his mouth, you drop him and wrap him up (put him under restraint). If you get him to the strip-search room and he refuses to comply with the search, you drop him. If he doesn't carry out the instructions correctly, you drop him. If he shows any form of aggression or moves when he hasn't been told to, you drop him. It's as simple as that. This is when you adhere to strict guidelines because you have to stop smack and crack getting in the nick through visits. The visitor is held in a holding room outside the Hall, until the prisoner has been searched. If he has contraband on him, the visitor will be cautioned by a Prison Officer and the police called. As a Prison Officer, you have the powers of arrest while you are in the prison. If the visitor kicks off, they get bent up, just as a con would.

After the morning briefing, I attended the Visits Hall. The SO in charge detailed me as a Searcher. That job IDs exactly what it says it is. It was my job to rub them down on their way in, and do the random or targeted (Intelligence-based) strip-searches on their way out. Obviously this would be very confrontational, especially if they had a little present that they didn't want finding. Also, if anyone's visit was terminated, then I would be the one performing the strip-search on the inmate, so it was inevitable that I was going to end up rolling around on the floor with some junkie or other.

I was patrolling the Visits Hall when I noticed a visitor pass something under the table. A pass! I had to get there quick. I ran over, terminated the visit and took the scroat downstairs to strip-search him. When you perform a strip-search, you always have two Officers in with you. This is to ensure the process is carried out correctly, to avoid allegations of sexual assault and to assist in wrapping him up if necessary. You'd be surprised how many cons would say they were touched up by the Officers. You also always have a third Officer standing outside the search room; that way, if you do bend anyone up, you have your third Officer there to confirm that the correct techniques have been used.

I took this con to the search room where I reeled off the speech I'd said a thousand times: 'I have brought you into this room to perform a strip-search as I have a strong suspicion that you may have something that you shouldn't have. I'm going to give you clear instructions from start to finish. I want you to face me and listen. If you raise your voice, look around, move or do anything whatsoever other than what I've asked you to do, I will drop you to the floor and place you under restraint. Do you understand what I've told you?'

'Yes Guv, I'm sweet, I know how it works,' he replied in a nervous voice.

How clear were the instructions? He had just told me he understands but, before I'd even given him his first order, he blasted, 'This is a fucking stitch up, you screw cunt!'

At the same time, he was putting his hands down his pants. So everything that he could do wrong, he did! Bang! I grabbed his head and dropped him to the floor, like a man-sized lead weight. The other screw in there with me grabbed his arm and pulled it out of his pants. He had a fucking huge bag of smack which he was trying to shove up his arse. We radioed through and told them to nick the visitor. We got a pat on the back, and were told it was a good job well done.

It was more of the same in the afternoon. I was patrolling the Visits Hall when I saw an Officer called Bob arguing with a con and calling for assistance. I ran over as quickly as I could. Bob joined the job just before me. He was at Wakey (Prison Service College Wakefield) doing his basic training when I was there. I knew him, but not that well. He was a big unit, a sturdy geezer. Not fat – a solid short and stocky fella in his early thirties. He was a gobby fucker but, nonetheless, he did the job right. He did it well – but he was a little thick. If he got backed into a corner, he would just shout; and, my God, when he did, it was like a fucking foghorn!

I got there and said, 'What's the problem?'

'He's been passed gear, get the little bastard out of here!'

This was not the best way of dealing with it; he could have used more tact but, still, everyone knew where they stood. The con was mouthing his head off. It was plain as day why he was.

Frankie was the other Officer that came to assist. Now, this fella was absolutely bonkers. He had been in the job for fifteen years. He was one of the brutal old school and one of those that the Prison Service wanted rid of. He had joined a very different Service. When he joined, screws got pissed together every day, at lunch and at night, and they brutalised the inmates. If a con looked at them the wrong way, he got bashed up. I disagree with this, but that is how it was.

He didn't look like I would have expected. He was a short man of average appearance, in his late thirties or early forties, who was very well spoken (he spoke the Queen's English perfectly) and was always smartly dressed. But this was a great disguise; he was pissed ninety per cent of the time he was awake. He hated cons and despised how soft the Service had become. That wasn't his fault; the art of being a screw was very different when he was taught it. He had left loads of prisons with trails of allegations and investigations for pissing management off for one reason or another, or for simply being Frankie. But he was a man very much liked by both the screws and the cons (surprising as it may seem). He had a wicked sense of humour that was appreciated by all and the cons knew exactly where they stood with him; he was the boss, they were the prisoners. They respected him. They liked his methods. He would always be fair. But on your head be it if you fucked him off. The management hated him. Fucking despised him.

Bob had made the call; he had seen the drugs being passed to the con. The con was being an abusive little cunt and we had to get him out of there. Aggressive behaviour by a con can sometimes encourage other cons to jump on the bandwagon. Frankie, Bob and I escorted him to the strip-search room. He wouldn't shut up, gobbing off like fuck on the way down. I told him to calm down and, with that, he punched Bob. Just like that, the crazy fucker. No warning, just bang. He was mouthing off before he belted him, but I thought I recognised it as bravado, a show to hide the fear. We all thought that, but sometimes you get it wrong. We got it wrong. Bob went flying; he didn't know what had hit him. I was on him in a flash; I dropped the piece of shit straight to the deck. He was eating the concrete before he had the chance to blink. Frankie dived on an arm like a shot, controlling his violence. There was another screw, called AJ, at the top of the stairs who saw Bob being knocked out so he jumped in quickly to assist, as. It was correct procedure; correct techniques. We got hold of the con and restrained him as we had been taught and had done time and time before. It was second nature, our job, our profession.

AJ was an Officer who had thirteen years in the job and he hated everything about it. He was the most cynical man that I have ever met. He was a tall fella, six foot two in height, and a lump. Like Frankie, he hated the way the Prison Service now operated; he hated what it had become.

Anyway, we bent this wanker up, the alarm was raised and the troops arrived, as they do. Every screw goes running to an alarm because it means an area has lost control and everyone available needs to attend until it is announced over the radio net, 'No further staff required.' Plus everyone wants some action. One of the first people to attend this incident was SO Neil. I had the utmost respect for her; she was good at the job. We had the scroat under restraint, but he was still trying to fight. He was not being compliant on any level.

'Anyone injured?' Neil asked.

'May I get relieved Miss Neil? I have this creature's saliva all over my face,' Frankie answered in his silky smooth tones.

Miss Neil took over from Frankie, relieving him as requested, but the con refused to be compliant to any orders that Neil was giving him. She wasn't shy about getting hands on. She was one of the few females who were actually competent at it. The cuffs were applied and one more compliance opportunity was given. No joy, this idiot wouldn't even walk. Neil, now in charge, said we had no alternative other than cuff-carry him. You only do this to the severely non-compliant prisoner because carrying a cuffed prisoner is extremely hard work for the Officers and painful for the con. It was a good call, though, and the only way. This piece of shit had knocked out a screw and was still giving it. We got him down The Seg (The Segregation Unit – for dangerous or disruptive prisoners), kicking and screaming all the way. We handed him over, and the searches were carried out.

Bob was very shaken up. It didn't last for long, though; he was as tough as old boots.

The con was down The Seg in a strip cell (strip-conditions cell – no furniture or clothes, just a gown to wear). This is for extremely non-compliant cons and avoids self harm and the harming of staff. He was still being aggressive. In his eyes, everyone was wrong except him.

A bald ex-TA cunt went down there to speak to him. This prick was behaving like he was ex-SAS trooper Andy McNab, but we knew the truth – weekend-warrior fuckwit. You might guess that I don't like this bloke. Oh, and he was a Governor. He went into his cell and filled him full of fags and promises. He was keen to point out to him that being mistreated or assaulted by an Officer was serious. The lad looked confused, but the Governor explained that he could get a decent pay-out from the Prison Service, if it was proved that an Officer assaulted him. That was the magic word, pay-out. What junkie wouldn't say they got assaulted by an Officer, especially when a Governor tells them the benefits and politely points out to him that Frankie was a menace and known for assaulting cons.

Frankie had pissed off so many Governors over the years. The TA cunt was just doing the donkey-work. It wasn't long before the con made an allegation against Frankie, saying that Frankie had been punching the shit out of him while he was under restraint. I do not tolerate bully-boy screws who abuse cons when they are under restraint. I deal with these cowards in my own way. But Frankie did fuck all except his duties, using force correctly. He did nothing wrong, no shadow of a doubt. I initiated the force, Frankie assisted. It was done as it should be. This allegation was a joke from the outset.

All of this was going on unbeknown to Bob, AJ, Frankie and me. We didn't have a fucking clue. As far as we were concerned, it was a good job well done. It was a fucking good job well done. We'd done what we were paid to do, and fucking well.

The rest of the afternoon ran smoothly. No more incidents; plain sailing. I was keeping an eye on my watch, waiting for 16.00 hrs. That was the time the visitors left. The group of screws who worked on Visits pissed off home at 16.10 hrs. Wing Officers, like myself, had to stay on the Wing until 18.00 hrs. The Visits staff had it fucking easy. Normally, I found it unfair but, on that day, I was chuffed to fuck: I could piss off early, too. It was Thursday, and I was off after that shift. I could taste the Stella and the vindaloo already. I couldn't wait to get home and relax.

When 16.00 hrs came, we jogged on the visitors and cons in double time. I practically legged it to the gate, threw my keys at the ugly old cunt working there, and sprinted to my motor. It was always amazing when you had a couple of days off, away from the prison.

The journey in sometimes flashes by too quickly. The journey home is a fucker. You get your civvy head on. You want to be home with your family.

That evening, I chilled out with beers and a curry. Handsome. I had a good lay-in the next morning. Always did on my first day off. Gave me a chance to get out of prison mode and back into civvy mode. I had just risen, made a brew and filled a bowl with porridge when my mobile started to ring. It was the Well. I thought to myself, 'What the fuck do they want? Why are they ringing me? They never ring you at home. Not unless there is something wrong.'

'Mr Thompson, we have a problem,' said the gravelly voice at the other end of the phone. It was the Principal Officer (PO) in charge of the Prison Officer's Association (POA). I was fucking worried. There must have been a huge problem if it couldn't wait until I was next on duty.

'Just hello would be nice! Problem with what?' I mumbled in a nervous way, trying to keep my confidence intact.

'That wrap you had yesterday has gone tits up. The con has made an allegation that he was bashed by Frankie, and Frankie's been suspended.'

'Fuck off! Never! He did fuck all! We bent him up textbook!' I shouted defensively. You see, I thought nothing of that incident; there was no abuse of force, nothing. It was just a straightforward wrap-up of a trafficking junkie who belted a screw.

'All you've got to do is tell the truth. Don't lie about anything, or you will be fucked. I will leave you the weekend to think about what happened and what is important to you. I'm in Monday.' With that, he hung up.

I had the whole weekend to let the seriousness of my situation sink in. Surely nothing could come of it?

My girlfriend Danielle asked me what was wrong. She knew that something was bothering me. She knew that I had a secret. I wasn't up to sharing it so I told her nothing. Simple; not having to answer to anyone. I had got the PO's call at midday on the Thursday. I called my pal Jim at 12.30 pm and was in the pub half an hour later. Jim was, and still is, a mentalist. The man is a fucking Duracell. He can party for a week straight without sleep. His heart is in the right place, too. I grew up with him, so I knew that I could trust him – and that he was a sure thing for a top night; someone I can let my hair down with. That's what I needed, something to take my mind off it. I needed a laugh, friends to piss it up with. Jim and I got bang on it straight away: a pint and double-vodka Red Bull. He asked me what the problem was. I told him that it was a work issue and could be serious. So he did what any good mate would do: rang the rest of the lads and organised a three-day bender! We got on it big time. Danielle was ringing me, concerned, worried. I couldn't face telling her. I didn't want to explain it – didn't have the energy to do it. I needed to survive till Monday and then deal with my fate. I spent the rest of the weekend in a pissed haze, not really sleeping, just ending up back at one of the lad's places, getting minging. Sunday came and I had to go home. I had to face Danielle. Quite rightly, she wanted to smash my head in. She asked me again what was wrong, but I didn't tell her anything; just that I would sort it. I knew that I'd done fuck-all wrong but I didn't trust anyone. I knew how a lot of them stitch-up cunts operated.

Monday came round quicker than I thought. It could have been a nightmare, but as I was pissed the whole weekend, I felt no pain. I got into work and went straight to the mess for my normal bacon sandwich and mug of coffee. Today, I needed the coffee more than normal. My head was banging, my mouth dry and chin unshaven. When I got there, I felt everyone's eyes burning into me. I could feel the whispers. I tried to ignore it, ordering my breakfast. I was shitting it big time. The rumours were spreading like wildfire, with my mates telling me what they'd heard and offering advice. Frankie had been suspended already, that was true. Then there were all the people 'in the know' coming up to me telling me that I was going to be suspended. I couldn't believe it. I'd done fuck-all wrong, none of us had. The rumours were suggesting that we were all fucked. 'How could that be?' I thought to myself. I wanted to see the union. I wanted to know what the fuck was going on.

I was sitting there eating my bacon sandwich when Mike Thurston came and spoke to me. He was a Union rep. He was also a Control & Restraint (C&R) instructor. He taught Officers the techniques used for self-defence and for placing an inmate under restraint. He was a popular guy with both screws and the management. He told me that Frankie had been suspended and that I wouldn't be, but he did say that was subject to change. I never knew where I stood. The Governors had permanent PMT: indecisive, moody and always fucking wrong! This was all at seven in the morning. I had my sandwich, downed my coffee, put on my brave face and headed for the Wing. Mike was great at calming nerves, but my anxiety was still burning a hole in the pit of my stomach. I carried on hearing rumours of what was going to happen. Some said I was going to be suspended, some said I wasn't. I tried not to listen to anyone. My mask was slipping, though: I was struggling to protect my fear from everyone and was only just managing to hold it all together. I desperately wanted this feeling to pass; I was in despair. Mike came up to me and said that he needed a chat. I knew what was coming. He told me that I was going to be suspended.

Some more evidence had come to light. SO Neil had put forward a statement saying that, when she arrived on the scene of the incident, Frankie was punching the con repeatedly in the face.

That did not fucking happen. I don't know what she thought she saw, but that certainly didn't happen. I wouldn't have tolerated it. A con held under restraint, while another one bashes him – not where I was fucking working. This SO, who I used to look up to, had turned into a horrible piece of shit, as far as I was concerned. It did not happen. If it did I would have sorted Frankie out. And if Frankie had been punching the con directly in the face while he was under restraint, then why weren't there any injuries to his face? There was fuck-all. 'A joke – it must be,' I thought to myself. She was saying she'd seen the inmate seriously assaulted – but in that case, cuff carrying was surely the last thing that should have been ordered; but that's exactly what she did. Something didn't ring right. And why didn't she put her statement in on the day of the incident?

The Governors had made their decision. I was to be removed from the premises and suspended from duty, from the job I was proud to do. My livelihood . . . mortgage . . . family . . . thoughts were blasting around my head like a hurricane. All this and we had done nothing wrong. We were just doing our fucking jobs. What we were paid to do.

I told Mike everything about the incident and he believed me. I went from start to finish, detailing it all. It was still fresh in my mind. It was all so quick. *They* knew I wasn't covering for him; they knew I was telling the truth. Mike spoke to me about the terms of my suspension and how I should conduct myself. He was giving me sound advice. He told me that there could be a chance of media coverage, and that I should keep a low profile when I left the prison. Talk about extra pressure. Not only was this corrupt and wrong, but the media could get hold of it. I tried to be every inch the man I was brought up to be. I stayed

22

confident and strong. I looked everyone in the eye and kept my handshake firm. I was staying proud. But on the inside, I was dying.

Accompanied by Mike, I was taken to Governor Keenan's office for him to issue my suspension papers. When I entered his office, he was clearly uncomfortable. Looking at him, deep in his eyes, I sat down. I didn't take my eyes off him for a second, staring into the back of his head. He couldn't look at me. Fucking spineless cunt. He then read my suspension papers. I was being suspended on allegations of assault and conspiring to assault a prisoner. Fucking hell. One minute I'm doing my job, the next I'm being suspended for assault. This was serious; this was bad. I was told that the matter had been handed over to the police and they would be in touch with me to carry out a full investigation. I was then told to hand over my ID card, keychain and key tally. At this point, I felt my world had caved in. I was being stripped of my integrity, my pride, and the job I was proud to do. He told me that Frankie was a menace, and that 'He no longer had a place in the Service.' Keenan had it in for him and he wanted him out. This wasn't fair. Frankie had done fuck all, but he was condemned by reputation. Keenan then explained my terms of suspension. I had to ring in at 09.00 hrs every Monday. I had to say that I was ready for duty. Provided I rang in, and co-operated with the investigation, I would receive full pay. The internal investigation would be placed on hold until the criminal investigation had finished. That's right, two investigations, one charge. Dangerous, very dangerous indeed. I signed the papers and received my copy.

After the suspension speech, and telling me that Frankie was a wrong'un, he said I should go home and enjoy my garden. The wanker. I was then given the number of the solicitor who was going to represent me. That was provided by the POA. A fucking solicitor? Mike was straight with me. He said that if getting Frankie meant getting me and the others, then so be it; that's what they would do.

I'm not in the business of wallowing in self-pity or telling tales of woe about how hard my life is. I have lived a life that many would envy but, at that point, I was about to go through a whole load of shit that I wouldn't wish on a mongrel.

AJ and Bob had suffered the same fate. Bob gets knocked out, then suspended. Fucking bastards. Mike walked me to the gate. He shook my hand and said, 'Chin up! Keep yourself occupied and try not to worry.' But it was impossible.

I phoned my solicitor and had a brief chat. He wouldn't go into too much detail; he wanted a meeting first. I dragged out of him what the worse-case scenario was for me. If charged, a prison sentence. A fucking prison sentence. It was a nightmare. It had to be. My world had crumbled before my eyes. 'Gutted' was an understatement. I'd never felt so low. How was I going to tell my family? How the fuck did it get to this?

ONE MAN, ONE LIFESTYLE

I was up really early. It was the day of my selection tests and interviews to become a Prison Officer. The recruitment process was an absolute joke. I understand that joining a service like the Prison Service will take a lot more time than a normal job – there is a lot of vetting and security-clearing to do – but this crowd take the piss, they take forever! Everyone could have travelled round the world seven fucking times before they hear back from the Service's recruitment cowboys. And then they wonder why they struggle to recruit!

You must, of course, pass the vetting (not have a criminal record etc) and a series of selection tests before you are accepted. The selection tests and interview were all on the same day. It's different now, but that's how it was when I joined.

I'd not had much sleep the night before. I was invited to do my selection tests at an assessment centre at HMP Wormwood Scrubs (usually known as 'the Scrubs'). I had to be there at 09.00 hrs for a day of assessments. In true Ronnie style, I went out with my mates and got pissed out of my head the night before. I only went out for a cheeky pint to relax myself so I could get to sleep. A pint turned into two, then three, then eight, which turned into doubles, nightclub, kebab, home! Even though I was pissed, I still couldn't get to sleep; I was worried that I'd oversleep.

Being up long before my alarm clock went off, I had plenty of time to get into my suit. I made sure I was dressed smart as fuck. Had to make a good impression. (I should have thought of that before tipping all that booze down my neck the night before!) I had plenty of coffee, breakfast, mouthwash and chewing gum. I was as ready to make my way to the Scrubs as I ever would be. My brother Mark gave me a lift to the station. Fuck paying their prices to park!

I am the youngest of three kids. There is Sarah, my sister, Mark, my older brother, and me. Sarah is the oldest, then my brother and then me. Obviously, when we were kids, I was the annoying little brother but, as we got older, the years seemed to thin out and the age gap closed. Mark and I are good mates who share a lot of friends. Sarah is a lovely lady whom I really get on with. My Mum and Dad are still together. Dad is eighteen years older than my Mum. That's a big gap, but it works.

Mark dropped me off at the station and wished me good luck. He couldn't understand why I wanted to be a screw. He thought that wearing a suit, not a uniform, was the way forward. Most people thought I was fucking nuts to be going for a job like that. I was already working in a suit. I worked in a contact centre for a bank for which you had to look smart, look professional, but the money was shit. Bear that in mind when you see a suit. Most of them are not high-flyer stockbrokers. They are wannabes on twelve grand a year. What a place that bank centre was, though: about six hundred employees and most of them were birds! I had a couple of office flings, as you do, but nothing serious. Then I met Danielle. I thought that she was a lovely-looking girl with a great personality and a gorgeous smile. I managed to get her to go out with me and the rest became history.

I said goodbye to Mark, got on the train and headed to the prison for my selection day.

I turned up there at the gate; time to take the tests and see if I was good enough. I still felt minging from the night before. Mouth dry, tummy bloated, shirt damp. I walked up to the gate, observing the aggressive stance of the building. Fuck me, did it look intimidating! I'd never been to a prison before. I'd never needed to. I came from a good working-class family from whom I learned good values and principles. I wasn't sheltered from the real world; I was taught from an early age how to look after myself. Don't get me wrong, I've done my fair share of bad things and I'm no angel, but none of my family had been banged up so I'd only seen prisons on the TV or in the paper.

I was directed to a building that was outside the main gate. I walked inside and was faced with the biggest fucking Prison Officer I'd ever seen! He was sitting at a desk waiting to tick the names off of the potential recruits as they arrived. I was the first. I was always early for first meetings such as job interviews. Got to make that lasting impression. He asked me my name and the prison of choice that I was applying for.

'Ronnie Thompson. HMP Romwell, sir.' I made sure I

addressed him as 'sir', and any female as 'ma'am'. Giving respect; gaining respect.

Originally, I hadn't even considered joining the Prison Service. I was green to it like the majority of the general public. I, too, thought that they were bullies who unlocked and locked doors while giving the cons a good kicking. But I was wrong. I had been in a couple of jobs, but I always had a direction that I wanted to go in. The plan was to work for a few years to build up some valuable life experience. Once I had that, I would join the Fire Service. The Fire Service was my first choice but my eyesight wasn't good enough, so that was out the window. Then I thought of the Old Bill. Seemed interesting and not fucking boring, not sitting on your arse all day. I liked the security of a service – the excitement, the pay and the pension seemed good. I was naughty and had enjoyed my teenage years. I did some fucking dangerous things but I was always switched on, thinking about the direction I wanted to go in. Security ... money ... It's the way I was brought up. I've always worked, never just sat on my arse.

A friend of my Dad suggested the Prison Service. He was an Officer and had been for years. He told me of the opportunities to specialise. You could train to become a Hostage Negotiator, or maybe train to be a member of Operation Tornado, which is a riot-response team. I'd worked as a gym instructor before; he told me that I could use my experience of working in a gym to specialise as a Physical Education Officer (PEO).

I looked on the Prison Service website and requested an application pack. It turned out that the Prison Service was the better option for me. It appeared to offer the challenges I was looking for, giving me the chance to use my personality and skills in a career I could flourish in. Danielle was supportive from day one. She was happy with whatever I wanted to do. She agreed that it would give me more money and appeared to be a better career move. *Appeared* to be a better career move . . .

I applied. It was a bit of a trek for me as there wasn't a prison in my home town, but it made sense. I was young, I could manage the travel and the extra money was a good incentive. I chose HMP Romwell. That was the easiest prison for me to get to and the shifts seemed OK. It was a nasty fucking prison, but I was told that if you start in a hard, shit place, you gain respect. If you decide to transfer later on, then you will be a good option – having worked in the shit of the shit. The Well (HMP Romwell) was the shit of the shit.

After I'd told the screw at the desk my details, he directed me to a waiting room. The others began to turn up. My hangover was getting a bit better; fuck me, was I thirsty, though. I couldn't believe some of the bloody losers that had been invited to the selection day. One dickhead was wearing a tracksuit. Fancy turning up like that; you just wouldn't do it! But this geezer turns up for his job interview, wearing a tracksuit and with an 'I'm a dumb cunt' expression slapped across his unshaven, pock-marked ugly head. This wasn't just any old job interview, either. It was for a service, which surely prides itself on smartness and etiquette. What a prick.

The massive screw came into the waiting room once everyone had arrived. He briefed us on how the day would go. He was emotionless, professional. It was very organised. A good cover for what a shit state the Prison Service is really in. First, there was an English and maths test which, if I'm honest, you didn't need to be a rocket scientist to pass. After that it was your medical. Bog-standard stuff: height, weight, eyesight, squeeze of your bollocks. One or two then fucked off straight away – having failed the medical.

What followed was a series of role plays dealing with different scenarios. You were given a brief to read before you went into the room. You had to deal with a situation as you saw appropriate. You don't know what they wanted to hear, so you had to use your common sense. All the role-play rooms had video cameras set up, recording each session. It was obvious that you had to be as politically correct as you could. Fucking politically-correct-gone-mad society.

It was like a conveyor belt: from one test to another; no break whatsoever. My mouth was so dry; the kebab was repeating on me. Report writing followed the role plays. We were giving a scenario that was written down. We had to write a report on it, giving our recommendations and reasons. I was having brain fry by this point. I was knackered. Once that test was finished we were taken for our final one: the fitness test. That was fucking pathetic. A snail could have passed it. It was a joke. It should be much tougher. Some useless cunts failed it, though.

Then we got changed and were thanked by the staff for attending. We were told we would hear our results in due course and be given a start date if successful. All of this process lasted about six or seven hours without as much as a cup of tea. My hangover had disappeared but my tongue was like sandpaper. I needed a drink. A strong drink.

On the way back, I bought a few cans from the off-licence to have on the way home. Hair of the dog and all that. I was pleased it was over. My mobile went mad with everyone asking how I'd got on. I didn't have a Scooby. I did my best, and said what I think they wanted to hear.

Days, weeks, months went by. I heard nothing at all. A year and a half, and still I had heard nothing. I assumed that I didn't get in. Anyone would think the same, after that length of time. I was gutted. They hadn't even bothered to contact me with feedback. I was sure I had been switched-on enough to pass the tests. Obviously not. I knew that it would take a long time to get through the selection process, but a year without any noise was the loudest message they could have sent.

I couldn't just sit there and stay stuck in a rut. I decided to go for something else; something better. I went for an interview for a job with a bank. I was still ambitious, always looking for a direction in which to better myself. I got the job, and it was better money than I was earning in the contact centre. I hoped the bank would be a new challenge, something to get my teeth into. Working in the contact centre bored me. Working for a bank would also most probably bore me, but at least I was trying to make the best of things. I always had plans to reach the top in something. I wanted the big house, nice motor and good fucking holidays! I wasn't the sort of person to settle for any less. You get people who are content to stay in the same job, same routine. Boring breakfast, boring suit, shit work, shit bog-standard saloon in the drive of a boring shit house. The same cheese sandwich and bag of Walkers for lunch. Knock off at the same time everyday, same packet lasagne for dinner, *Corrie* and *EastEnders* overload. No fucking way, I wanted more. I was always striving to get something better. I needed to keep interested; I had to or I would have given up.

The day after I got the job in the bank, I was at work when I got a phone call from Danielle. She told me that the Service had phoned my Mum's house to say that I'd got through the selection process. I'd moved since my selection tests; my Mum's was the only contact they had for me. They wanted me to report to the Well to start my basic training – or Prison Officer Entry Level Training (POELT), as they like to call it. Just like that. All that time, no contact or letter or anything to say I'd got in. Nearly two years after my selection, they phoned, out of the blue, asking me to start! Danielle told me that my mum had said not to tell me, and to let me take the bank job. Mum didn't want me to be a Prison Officer; she wanted me to have a regular job; but deep down she knew that I couldn't do 'nine to five'. However, Danielle knew it was what I wanted. She wouldn't have been able to live with herself had she not told me. Danni and I discussed it for a minute or two, but we both knew that I was going to take the job in the Service.

I had got into the Service! I was chuffed. I was so proud that I had finally got the opportunity to be someone and to do a job that was important. Start a career; be somebody – it was just the beginning that Danielle and I wanted and needed. I was twenty-one when I got that call, and joined the Service. It was far more 'me' than a bank. We were on a good path to better things. Or so we thought . . .

BASIC TRAINING AND
MY PAL HENRY

I was told to report to the Well on the Monday morning wearing smart attire. They had phoned me the Tuesday before, thereby not even giving me a week's notice. It was lucky that my boss at the contact centre was a lad I used to go drinking with. He let me take leave, pulled a few strings and let me go early; fucking early, as I should have given a month's notice. I had a goodbye lunch at the contact centre: a Chinese buffet, all you can eat for £4.99, a glass of shandy and plenty of giggles. I didn't give a shit about leaving the contact centre. I'd made a couple of good pals, but nothing I was too bothered about.

I had the weekend to celebrate. Out for a meal with the missus on the Friday, on the piss with the lads on the Saturday, family lunch on the Sunday. It was a good weekend. I was excited.

33

I wanted to crack on with the new job. I was nervous; of course I was. It's nerve-racking when you start any new job. But this wasn't any new job. I didn't know how I was going to react. What if I couldn't handle it? It was the unknown.

I got up bright and early on the Monday. I decided to get the train – it was easy; I couldn't get lost. If I did, I was a doughnut! I made sure I didn't get minging the night before. A few cans of bitter with my family, a roast dinner and that was it. The train journey flew past. I was there in no time. I got out of the station, and walked towards the prison. I was greeted with a fucking great wall with razor wire all the way around it. I could see great big buildings towering above the wall. All had metal bars covering the windows. They were the Wings – the residential area where the cells were. I was surprised at how close to the wall and main road they were. As I got closer, I could hear some prisoners shouting out the window. 'Real-life prisoners!' I thought to myself. Little did I know what I was letting myself in for.

A sign on the prison wall directed me to the entrance. From there, I was directed to a building inside the grounds but outside the main prison. It was a bit like the assessment centre at the Scrubs: an outer building where all training happened, so you had screws in there doing courses, and new-Officer intakes.

I walked into the building. I felt a ball of sweat on my forehead. I didn't know what to do. There was a group of screws standing chatting. I went up to them to ask where I should go. Their conversation stopped and all of them looked at me like I was the shit on their shoes. New Officers always get shit from the old screws. That's how it is. I could take it, but some took liberties with it. I didn't like any cunt taking liberties with me.

They reluctantly told me where to go, adding the 'He won't last' comments. Fucking wankers didn't know me from shit. Pricks.

I went into the waiting room; helped myself to the coffee, tea and digestives. There were about twelve of us on my intake. We sat there nervously, making small talk. Then 'Mr Prison Service' walked in. He had already served thirty-two years and had reached the rank of PO. His father before him had served forty years. If there was something about the Service that man didn't know, it wasn't worth knowing. He was our trainer. He gave us the talk about the Service, telling us what we had to look forward to! He answered all of our questions in a tired yet experienced way. He didn't try and paint a pretty picture. He told how it was. No bullshit. He knew the job; he knew fucking everything. He was a great big fat bastard with a huge gut and grey hair sort of swept back. He looked tired, with a terribly pockmarked face. He was like the legendary 'Fat Controller'. He was also head of the POA at The Well. This was the first time I met Rumpole. Little did I know he would be the one ringing me two years later, telling me, 'We have a problem.' He is a man you want on your side.

After the talk, Rumpole told us it was time for our tour. I was about to go into a nick for the first time. As we left the classroom, everyone was whispering to each other in anticipation of how the tour would be. The lads were sticking their chests out, trying to be macho, the birds were clutching note pads and pens, pretending this was just an education process they had to go through. The truth was, everyone was shitting it.

The walk to the main gate was one or two hundred metres away from the training centre. The gate was a huge, intimidating structure. Being Victorian, the design of this place suited its fear factor. We walked into the gate area to be faced with the gate Officers, staring at us, grinning, knowing we were 'new meat' and that we didn't have a fucking clue what we were letting ourselves in for. The gate screws operated the huge electric gates. These opened at an alarmingly slow pace, squeaking with every inch. We walked through the first gate, squeezing into the tight space between it and the second so that it could close behind us. Silence fell over all of us. Nerves were getting the better of everyone. Rumpole had lit a Superking the minute we'd left the training room. We were only a couple of hundred metres away, and the fat fucker was already lighting his second. He did nothing to relax us. New screws were something he dealt with day in, day out. He knew how we were feeling but he didn't give a shit. He saw it as 'Deal with it or fuck off.' He was right, but it would have been nice to have one or two pleasantries, the miserable fat bastard!

Once the gate behind us had shut, the one in front of us began to move. Yet again, slow and noisy. We walked through the second security gate where the keys were collected. There was a bit more room but it was still tight. We weren't allowed any keys. We were sprogs (new Officers) so we weren't allowed keys.

Going into a prison without keys isn't nice. You feel like a con yourself, not having the keys you need to move around the jail. If someone were to attack, you wouldn't be able to retreat. You're locked in.

The anticipation was building. The silence deafening. Rumpole had collected his keys. The main gate is a part of the outer perimeter wall. Once you have gone through the security doors and collected your keys, you go through the next door, which takes you inside the perimeter wall. We now stepped through that door, so we were all inside the perimeter. We were in the open air again. There is a road that goes all around the inside of the perimeter wall. It's there so that vehicles are able to manoeuvre, and so that the wall can be patrolled. It also provides a gap between the prison and the wall for extra security and the prevention of escapes.

We looked around, seeing prison vans and Officers running about. I was shitting myself and I'd not even got inside the nick yet! We moved into the main building and this took us to the Governors' corridor – called that because it is where all the Governors are based, office next to office, all filled with plain-clothed Governors. I noticed there and then how many chiefs there were. Surely there was no need for that many bosses? No there fucking wasn't. More foot soldiers less cunts, is what I say.

We made our way towards the other end of the corridor, Rumpole was still sucking hard on his fag, not giving a toss about the no-smoking signs everywhere, and daring the Governors to say anything. But Rumpole was left well alone, by them. I could sense straight away that Rumpole was a powerful man who knew his shit. I could tell the Governors wouldn't bother him, and I could see he was a handy man to get on with, even then.

There was a gate there that Rumpole needed to unlock. It was the entrance to the main prison. This was it, the moment of truth, we all thought. I was excited as well as nervous. He unlocked the gate and we all walked through. Fucking hell. Fucking hell it was massive, noisy, old and dirty. It was so much bigger than I anticipated. Rumpole locked the gate behind us. We were standing at the centre of the main jail. We all huddled together, watching the chaos. In front of us were the entrances to the four main Wings. A Wing on the left, then B, C and D Wing on the right. There were gates locking off the Wings from the centre. Standing at the centre, you could see down every Wing. They were all fucking huge, with most of them too big to see to the other end.

I could see the madness on the Wings. The thing that shocked me the most was the amount of prisoners roaming about on them. Fucking loads of them and hardly any screws. It looked out of control. It *was* out of control. The regime dictates that the cons have time 'out of cell'. The Governors didn't give a fuck about security or safety. On paper, the more the prisoners are out of the cell, the better the regime. Supposedly, this is more constructive. If 'constructive' is cons kicking fuck out of each other, Officers getting attacked and smack and crack being dealt, then that's exactly what it is. In reality, it's merely a paper exercise for the prison audits.

Each Wing had five floors, known as landings. Each landing had cells running down both sides of the Wing from one end to the other. From either side, you could look down the centre 'well' to see the ground level. There was suicide netting around these centre wells to prevent any dickhead from jumping off. Each landing was called by the number of its level: ground level was The Ones, first floor was The Twos – working up to the top floor being The Fives. The Fives were fucking high up. I was in awe at the sheer size of the place. Each level had a landing that ran around the centre and joined all the Wings at that same height. So you could, say, leave B Wing on The Threes and come to the centre 'Threes' landing from where you could see – and move round on to – any other Wing on The Threes level.

While we were standing there, screws were walking back and

forth from one Wing to another, some of them escorting cons to other areas of the nick. Everyone was looking at us laughing, as if they knew something we didn't.

Rumpole pointed out each Wing to us, like he'd done to others a thousand times before. He led us towards A Wing. Fuck, we were actually going on to a Wing. In prison! Rumpole unlocked the gate, and ushered us through. He had to stand at the gate and lock it once we had gone through. Lack of keys seemed to annoy Rumpole. Night following day seemed to annoy Rumpole. He was only happy eating fry-ups and chain-smoking. Together preferably. He knew we couldn't have any keys, but it still pissed him off.

The first thing I noticed was the stench. It smelt like a mixture of sweaty bollocks and dead people. The first time you enter a prison like that, you lose all functions of the brain. You stand there while a gate's unlocked, obviously for you to walk through, but you don't walk through, your brain doesn't register. You are too fucking scared and stupid! The whole place intimidates you. On that first tour, we were like a group of children being shown a new nursery. It frustrated Rumpole having a dozen wide-eyed, brain-dead chimps to show around.

Once on the Wing, it was unbelievable. Fucking prisoners everywhere, walking about unsupervised with hardly any Officers. A sea of heads with hardly any white shirts. Funny that, loads of suits down the corridor, fuck-all shirts on the Wing where it counted.

'Where are all the Officers?' I asked in amazement.

Rumpole, puffing away on a fag as always, replied in his dull tones, 'Get used to it son, *the scroats run the nick, we are just visitors.*'

I should have left there and then. We got abuse from the cons as we walked about the prison wearing our suits and our 'Oh my God what the fuck have I let myself in for?' faces.

'Look at the big cunt, bet he fancies himself as a handy fucker,' one con said to another, talking about me.

'Don't worry, we'll wipe that smarmy look off the fucker's face once he's in a shirt,' he replied to his mate.

Rumpole was an old fat bastard, but he was still game. He grabbed the mouthy cunt by his throat: 'What the fuck did you say, you little tosser?'

'Nothing, Guv, nothing,' he mumbled.

'That's what I thought. Any more of that and I will have you down the fucking block,' Rumpole warned.

I couldn't believe the authority the man commanded. We were all in awe of him. This man was about fifty-eight, overweight, out of breath and with a fag in his mouth. And, fuck me, was he ugly. But he didn't give a second thought to grabbing this thirty-something tasty-looking bastard. To make it even better, the con shat himself! He looked a right prat in front of his pals, and in front of us.

Rumpole took another puff and said, 'Sorry about that but I won't have these wankers trying to intimidate my staff. Even if they are a big cunt like you, Mr Thompson.'

Everyone tried not to laugh! He had a wonderful way with words. He took us round the whole prison. We went through every Wing, tip-toeing as we looked on, taking abuse, watching Rumpole. He took us to the gym next. It had a class full of cons in there as we entered. I'd never seen so many Olympic bars and benches in one room before. Only three treadmills and a couple of bikes: these fellas weren't interested in cardiovascular exercise, they wanted to lift weights and get big.

We left the gym and headed towards the Education Unit. I was surprised how much they could do there; but I could also tell that most of the cons used it as a doss to get out of their cells and out of their fucking heads. They had everything from music to art, and basic reading to A-levels. We went to the Hospital Wing next – or the Fraggle Wing, as it's better known. Fucking horrible place that was. It was full of junkies detoxing and the criminally insane nut nuts who couldn't handle prison. A lot of them played the game of pretending to be a fraggle, trying to get nutted off to a secure hospital. Better facilities there, and an easier time. I noticed a geezer come out of his cell, wearing a surgical mask.

'What's he wearing that for?' I asked Rumpole.

'TB,' he answered in between a lug of his fag, still smoking on a Hospital Wing. God love him!

Fucking TB! I thought that was something out of the dark ages. I thought it was a disease of Third World countries. How wrong I was. The place was rife with it. The Fraggle Wing would laugh at MRSA. The whole stinking place was filthy, disgusting.

As we walked round, I was watching the screws. I could already see who was good and who was bad; who hid behind the shirt and who did the job well.

It was a long tour, but it went quickly. The Well is a fucking huge place. We didn't get comfortable, just used to it. We finished the tour and went back to the training centre. We were told exactly how our basic training would go and were given a breakdown of our whole timetable. It was exciting stuff; all of us were eager to get down to business and start pounding them landings. Well, not all of us. Some were so horrified by what they saw on the tour, they never came back.

41

The timetable was as follows:

Week One: HMP Romwell. Induction week

Week Two: PSC (Prison Service College) Wakefield. Residential training

Week Three: PSC Wakefield. Residential training

Week Four: HMP Romwell. Establishment training.

Week Five: HMP Romwell. Establishment training.

Week Six: PSC Wakefield. Residential training

Week Seven: PSC Wakefield. Residential training

Week Eight: HMP Romwell. Establishment training

Week Nine: HMP Romwell. Establishment training

Week Ten: PSC Wakefield. Residential training

Week Eleven: PSC Wakefield. Residential training. (Final-assessments week)

So, we had three periods away from home, learning the trade. That's how Rumpole told us it would work. Two weeks' learning, then back to the establishment for two weeks putting the knowledge into practice. I was well excited. It seemed awesome.

Rumpole took us to the stores, next, to collect the uniforms and Prison Service kits required for our residential training. Great! A uniform at last! At least I would blend in next time I went into the prison. Fuck walking around looking a bunch of knobheads like we did on the tour.

I went home full of beans. I was so excited by it all. The journey home was a pain in the arse. Fucking train delays. I got home and blurted it all out to Danielle. I couldn't stop talking about it. I couldn't wait to get back there the next day. I wasn't tired; I was too excited.

I got up at silly o'clock again in the morning – this time putting on my uniform. Fucking trousers were itchy as fuck.

I didn't care. I looked the part. I felt a part of something. I got on the train, and started my journey. I wore a civvy jacket, which we had been told to do if using public transport. It was for our safety. Even though I was wearing my civvy coat, I was paranoid that people were staring. You couldn't see the shirt or epaulettes, but the horrible trousers and magnum boots were instantly recognisable. Worst still, they might have thought I was a pig!

I got to the Well unscathed. There was an Officer waiting for me at the training centre. It happened that he and another Officer lived in the same town as me – and they drove in. They'd heard about my starting at the Well and wondered if I wanted to join. It was cheaper, more comfortable and normally a bit quicker. That suited me down to the ground. I didn't fancy going on the train again. Next, I went to the training room to meet up with the other sprogs. We were all a bit more relaxed, now, but the group of twelve had dropped to eight. Four had decided not to come back; it wasn't for them.

The rest of the week was spent on more history lessons to give us a thorough introduction to the Service and the Well. We had talks by all the Group Governors, who were basically telling us how good they were and how big their cocks were. We also spent time getting beasted – worked hard and pushed around – in the gym by the PEOs. We were doing circuit training, bleep tests and running and I loved it. I've always enjoyed circuits, running and weight training, so I was in my element. Craig David and I were the two fittest in the group. Not the real Craig David, just a guy that looked like him! These gym sessions were to gear us up for Wakey where we would have PE and C&R training, both of which were demanding for the average slob. Craig David and I hit it off: we had a lot in common. He was a few years older but, like me, he had a missus and a kid at home. I pretty much stuck with him for the rest of the week, which was cool.

I started coming in with the screws from my home town. We went round all the back roads. I thought I'd never fucking remember the route. They had both been in the job for over ten years. They used to give me their 'war stories' on the journey in. Funny, but scary. They were always telling me, 'It ain't like it used to be.'

There was a bloke we nicknamed Dad. He was a top Scouse lad who kind of looked after us all. He was old enough to be our dad, and he hated being reminded of that, but he was still one of the lads. There were two females on the course. One was a common thing called Kay who seemed cock-hungry and up for anything that came her way. We'd been there under a week and already we'd heard rumours about her fucking around with every half-decent Officer that worked in the nick. She was working as an Operational Support Grade (OSG) – which was a rank below Officer and a non-prisoner-contact position – before being accepted to Officer grade, so she had the time to get to know the lads around the nick. Then there was also Miss Crowe the Graduate. I thought that she was up herself.

It was an exhausting week. Parts of it were boring as fuck, but generally it was good. It was Monday to Friday during training so we had every weekend off.

I got home after the first week, looking forward to Monday and the start of my Wakey training. I had a chilled-out weekend, making sure I was switched on for Monday. Wakey was a good four-hour drive; three-and-a-half if I was toeing it. We had to be there for 13.00 hrs on the Monday. That gave us time to travel.

I pulled into the car park of the college. I knew I had the right place; it had a fucking great Prison Service Emblem at the front. I noticed some of the others from the Well. There were also loads of people I didn't recognise. This was a training centre attended by Officers from all over the country, so it wasn't just us from the Well; and there are other courses for people at different stages in their training, so it was busy. There were groups of Officers who were running and being beasted by the PEO, and other groups in full riot kit heading to the dojo (padded gymnasium) for C&R lessons. I liked what I saw. I wanted to be part of it.

I saw Craig David and Dad and we walked in together. We were issued with our room keys and told to report to the lecture theatre at 13.30 hrs, in uniform, of course. We went upstairs to our rooms: single rooms with a sink, but communal showers. Men and women in different areas. At least, men and women were supposed to be in different areas.

We got changed into our uniforms and headed to the lecture theatre. We were all nervous. It seemed so professional. I thought, 'This course is gonna be tough.' The lecture hall filled quickly. There were hundreds of us there for training. And still there's not enough – prisons or staff. The college Governor and PO came in to give us our 'Introduction to PSC' talk. Even though it was a college, the ranking structure was the same as a prison.

They showed us videos that spoke of how professional the training was. We were told about all the learning we had to do. Security awareness, cell searching, communications, diversity, C&R. Fucking hell, it sounded good. We left there feeling worried we might not pass.

We were broken up into sections (classes) that mixed everyone together. Taking you out of your comfort zone. I had security-awareness first lesson. Security awareness is your basic jailcraft. They teach you to look for signs of security being breached, i.e. potential break outs, drug deals, bullying etc. Fucking boring in the classroom – it is something that can only be learnt with experience, pounding the landings. It was still essential to the course, apparently. The day finished quickly. We went back to our rooms, got changed and had our dinner. The Governor did say he didn't mind us drinking in the evening, but not to go overboard. We had to be fit for class the next day.

After dinner, everyone went down to the bar to mingle and have a beer . . . or ten! I was surprised at how many fit birds were there. I'd thought it would be all hairy-arsed geezers with tattoos. Everyone was very nervous, staying in their safety nets, only talking to people from their own prisons. There was a class of Officers who were four weeks further into their training. They all came into the bar and, I tell you something, there was no fucking around with that crowd. They were relaxed, confident and, above all, looked as though they were a bunch of mates on holiday. They were bang on the doubles, snogging and groping each other, having a right ball. I couldn't believe my eyes. They didn't give a fuck who saw, either. From the first lecture, I thought they would be harsh on people drinking too much. Not on your fucking Nelly.

I left my safety net straight away; I needed no encouragement. I love a drink and love to socialise. I got talking to the lads in the course above. They told me where to drink, party, and damn well have it large! That's when I properly met Henry. He was the main man. I gave him the nickname Henry because the lad drinks like a fucking Hoover! Pint after pint, double after double, he just never stops. He is cross-eyed, so the poor bastard looks pissed before he has even started. He was also from the Well. I thought he was a geek in my first week there. I had no time for him. But the minute we were at the bar in Wakey, he came up to me with a pint in his hand and started talking. He could sense what I was all about, so he quickly told me that he was the same. I told him that I'd spoken to the lads in the class above about where to go in the town. Before I could finish my sentence he said, 'Shall I book a taxi?!'

I fell in love with Henry there and then. First night there and he wanted to get bang on it. Our friendship became a match made in heaven! We arranged to meet the lads from the course above in a bar in town. It was called Mustang Sally's. What a bar! They had a *U2* tribute band playing, it was packed from wall to wall, and it was only Monday. That's what I love about northerners. They love to go out on the piss regardless of whether it's a school night. They put us southerners to shame, I'm sorry to say! Henry and I got talking to a guy called Mac from another nick. He was in our class and was a top lad, so we recruited him fast. We got to town, meeting the group from the class above. At Prison Service College, people lose inhibitions. When we got back to the college in the early hours, we noticed two people going at it in the car park! Unbelievable, getting paid to get hammered and to shag; 'Thank you, Your Majesty!' Unbelievable. This wasn't training, it was worse than fucking Ibiza. I thought that it was going to be very militant and strict; boy, was I wrong. Inside the college there were groups of people playing strip poker, sleeping in each other's rooms and having bloody orgies. This place was crazy, and it was only my first night. I was happy that I could go out and get pissed every night, though. I love a beer with the lads.

First thing in the morning, I had to report to class wearing my PE kit. We went on a five-mile run, which would normally be fine for me. Not that morning, after only three hours' sleep, no breakfast and a head that felt like it had been hit with a sledgehammer.

The classes were conducted professionally. C&R was my favourite class. Learning self-defence; learning how to use force. Lessons took place in a dojo where we were taught the techniques which we practised on one other. The moves are all Ikedo-based, and are very effective. It is not a matter of simply battering people; it is a highly professional, safe and efficient way of using pain compliance. That crap you see the Old Bill using downtown, or on the telly, is embarrassing. They have not got a clue how to restrain people; it's a joke how useless they are at it. Any decent Prison Officer will tell you the same.

That's how the next two weeks went: a work-hard but fuck-me play-hard culture. Getting pissed every night and beasted doing PE and C&R in the morning, and then falling asleep in class in the afternoon. After that initial two weeks away, we were sent back to our establishments for two weeks. This was to enable us to shadow an Officer and see what actually happens on the job. We all missed Wakey, the holiday camp! Getting home after two weeks away was a culture change. I was starting to become a Prison Officer; starting to get into the culture. I told Danielle what went on but I didn't tell her I was on the piss every night, and what people got up to.

While back at the Well for two weeks, I was trying to watch everything the screws did. I wanted to see how different Officers reacted to different situations. Everyone develops their own style. What works for one might not work for another. It was quite an experience when I first saw a con getting bent up. It was a frightening experience. I'm someone who has been in enough scraps over the years – after school, downtown and on the rugby pitch – but it was different in a prison: the whole place was so very dirty, old, loud and intimidating.

Some of the experienced screws were wankers to us new Officers. What they did was give us the cold shoulder, or be really rude and, in some cases, just as intimidating as the cons. I had this from this one bloke who was a right cunt to me. He was Scottish and sounded just like Mrs Doubtfire, so it's obvious what his nickname was. It sounds strange that someone who sounds like that can be intimidating, but he was. He gave me loads of shit the first week that I was back at the Woll: dropping comments, being rude and always trying to make a cunt of me. By the second week, I'd had a fucking gutful of him.

'You lanky streak of piss, put the fucking kettle on instead of standing there like a paperweight with eyes,' Doubtfire said to me in front of an audience of screws.

Embarrassed and angry I snapped quickly, 'At least I don't stink of piss, you ginger cunt. I might be a paperweight with eyes, but at least I'm in shape and can see properly, you four-eyed prick!'

I was as stunned as everyone else that I had come out with that so quickly. Doubtfire and I got on great after that, he said that I'd got balls.

The one place Rumpole didn't show us on our initial tour was the Officers Club. I don't think that he wanted to show us the dark side too early. It was situated round the back of the nick. After my fracas with Doubtfire, he took me round there at lunchtime to buy me a pint. That was good; I was being accepted early on.

We got round there. It was a dark, smoky bar with a pool table and Sky sports on. It was jam-packed. Loads of screws ordering pints with large brandies. Doubtfire didn't even ask what I wanted; he slapped a pint and brandy in front of me. Rumpole had told us that drinking on duty was not permitted. But people didn't take one bit of notice of that.

I was sitting there sipping my drink, when I heard this loud bastard with a thick Scouse accent. He was pissing about, being Jack the lad.

Doubtfire called him over. 'This is Horrible Scouse!'

'Alright kidder!' Scouse said to me, smiling, being hectic. They called him Horrible Scouse because he was, well, horrible! In a good way. A top bloke, just had ants in his pants. He never slept, just worked, got pissed and went to the gym. Not necessarily in that order. We hit it off straight away. He was a diamond geezer.

The club was the place where screws let their hair down. Some days it was like the Wild West. Screws would also come to sort their differences in there. It could be full of activity at times. You would get screws in there every night, pissing it up until the early hours. It was a great place!

We managed to get through the next two weeks. It was boring; all we wanted to do was get back up to Wakey. We couldn't do much on our two weeks back at the Well except observe. We had time slots in every department; going from Wing to Wing, Visits, reception (where cons enter and leave the prison, e.g. on transfer, out on bail, off to court), the Fraggle Unit etc. All we could do was watch. It was frustrating. We couldn't get hands on; we weren't trained yet. I noticed how clinical things were at the college: straightforward, never really making it realistic. Back at the nick, in the real world, it wasn't rosy like training made it seem. At last it was time to go back up to Wakey. Henry and I couldn't wait to get on the piss, practise our C&R, and learn the trade the best we could.

Henry is a cracking bloke. He was twenty-eight at the time we joined. The lad is like a caged animal because, quite simply, his missus is a nutter. As I got to know him, I soon realised that his missus didn't know him at all. He was a complete pisshead who loved going out and enjoying himself, but his missus only let him have a couple of beers a month. Or so she thought. He got on it every time her back was turned, and when he was pissed he would fuck anything with a pulse. Now, we were back at Wakey, going out every night and training hard, and I was struggling to keep up with the man Hoover! Henry wanted to grasp it all with both hands while he was away.

One night when we were out on the piss up there, Henry pulled a complete rotter. He took this bird back to the college but these jobs-worth fuckwit security guards wouldn't let him take her to his room. They were acting like Governors! Fucking twats. Henry wasn't giving up that easy. He wanted to empty his sack, so the desperate sod took her to a hotel. He couldn't go to hers, you see; that would have upset her husband. He took her to this hotel at a ton a night and paid on his debit card. He's not the brightest of sparks, as his lunatic wife checks his bank statements, wallet, car, everything. So, instead of cancelling the statement, or hiding it, he left it on the kitchen table, nice and neatly, for her to inspect. The thick bastard told her that I robbed his card to pay for a room so I could shag a bird. She believed him! So then she fucking hated me. Not that I'm bothered, I wanted nothing to do with her.

Being away was taking its toll on a lot of new Officers' home lives and relationships. Also the Service's culture was beginning to change people, making them very different. Their partners were seeing the change and, in some cases, not liking it. Danielle, too, was affected. She could see that this was more than a job; it was a way of life. Even during these early stages, she could see the job was beginning to be the most important thing in my life. It was a weird time being on training. You just felt detached from reality, like nothing else mattered. I am someone who took my partner for granted, thinking that she would always be there. I began to let her down and go back on my word, putting the job first, social life second, and her and my boy third.

In Wakey, there is a police college and a nurses' college as well as the Prison Service College, so there were regular 999 nights for mixed 'service' personnel. They were always good, but there was hostility between the coppers and us. They thought we weren't as good as them, and we thought they were cunts.

It was near the end of our second stint at Wakey. We were out on the piss as usual. There was a 999 night organised, so we went along. We walked into the bar all half pissed. It was pretty busy already. There was a group of lads from 'the Filth College'. We knew who they were, we'd seen them loads of times. I don't really remember how it started, but the inevitable happened. I saw some shoving going on, drinks getting spilt. Before I knew it, there were punches being thrown and we were all kicking fuck out of each other. It was like a fucking riot! It spilled out on to the street and over to the kebab house.

This one lad, about my height, was trying to punch me. I was managing to deflect his fists. I grabbed him by his Gary-boy shiny shirt and nutted him. He went down; he didn't try to hit me again, the cunt. Everyone was kicking the shit out of each other.

Someone called the Old Bill, and yes, I am talking about the ones that were actually on duty! We thought that was it, all nicked, all sacked. We had a result, though, because they knew that we were all coppers and screws so they let us off. It got back to the college, though; fuck knows how.

The Governor called a meeting to give us a bollocking. It was first thing, before any classes. All of us were still pissed; some with black eyes and fat lips. We walked into the lecture hall, giggling like kids. We should have been seriously worried but, like I said, we were still pissed and we'd had fuck-all sleep. We all sat down. The Governor came in with a face like thunder.

'You are Prison Officers representing Her Majesty's Prison Service! What the fuck do you sorry lot think you are doing, getting pissed and fighting? Hey? With policemen! I should sack every last one of you. This place is not a fucking holiday camp,' he screamed.

I couldn't resist it; still pissed up from the night before, I yelled, 'Don't be like that, sir, it's better than Benidorm around here!'

Three hundred screws roared; it was hysterical!

'GET OUT THOMPSON!' bellowed my section SO.

I left the room and waited outside the Governor's office, as ordered by my SO, for my personal bollocking. The SO made it clear to me I would do well to hold on to my job after that. I sat outside the office, sweating, waiting, stinking. The Governor finished his lecture and headed to his office and to me. He was a big fat bastard. He looked like Rumpole, but with a beard. Standard service procedure: get old, ugly and fat. He ordered me into the office. Jack Daniels and Stella were oozing out of my skin. I was struggling to focus on him. I needed sleep. He gave me a bollocking, but wasn't too harsh. He saw the funny side. He said that I was 'a character'. He wanted me to calm it, though, or I would be in trouble. I was lucky, very lucky. But his advice went in one ear and out of the other.

The weeks of training were excellent from start to finish. We all made some brilliant mates. The Prison Service does some real strange things to people. False reality sets in more for some than others. I watched people walk out of their marriages for other Officers they had only known for ten weeks. A true example of this is Bob and Alison. Alison had been married for five years when she joined the Service. She hit it off with Bob so she split up with her husband, just like that. Alison and Bob are both decent people who are still together. Sometimes, holiday – or should I say Prison Service College – romances do last. I knew who Bob was during training. When he and I were suspended together a couple of years later, I got to know him a lot better.

Soon it was time to go home. It was Friday, and time to head back to do our two-week stint at the Well. We were all gutted about having to leave. We loved it there more than anything. We'd made some good mates from other nicks and now we wouldn't be seeing them for a while.

I got about thirty miles away from Wakey when I had to pull over at a service station to get my head down. I was fucked. I woke up, a lot later than I intended. Three cans of Red Bull and I was on my way again. When I got home, I said I'd been stuck in a traffic jam. Danielle was pleased to see me; she wanted to hear all about everything, but I needed my bed. My relationship was struggling to say the least. I had my missus and young son at home, but all I was interested in was being a screw and one of the lads. I was a young lad, with a baby that wasn't planned, doing a job that I loved with a load of mates. When I was at Wakey, I was in my prime, enjoying the course and learning new skills and having a laugh. When I was home I wanted to sleep, and when I woke I wanted to go out with the lads. As you can imagine, we had a lot of rows about how I was neglecting my family and putting the job and my mates first.

While I was back at the Well for my two weeks, I concentrated hard, watching, listening learning. You could see who was keen. I didn't see much of Danni or my boy; I didn't see enough of them.

Soon enough, it was time to head back up to Wakey for the last time for our final assessment. That consisted of a written exam and, even more important, the final C&R assessment. That had to be passed. You weren't allowed to deal with prisoners unless you were signed off as 'C&R trained and competent'.

We were told to go easy on the drink. Did we fuck, we were hammered every night. The schedule wasn't as gruelling as for our first two trips up. Initially, there had been a lot to get through, but this final trip was all revision, gearing us up for the exam and the assessment. We saw it as less to do, more time to drink. The first of the final two weeks was a pissed haze. Before we knew it, the tests were upon us.

The exam came first. It took fucking ages. It was a bit of a head fuck but, surprisingly, I'd absorbed a lot of what I'd been learning. If you failed that, you could re-sit it before the end of the week. If you failed again, you got the chance of a second re-sit back at your establishment. You are not told that, of course. I learnt it later. They would pretty much walk you through it, if necessary; so badly do they need Prison Officers on the landings.

I didn't need to re-sit it. I passed it. I actually got a good mark.

I did pretty shit at school. I passed my GCSEs with three C grades being my highest. I was switched-on, though. I hated exams. I was pleased that I passed my final at Wakey; I thought if I failed anything, it would be that part.

The C&R assessment followed. For this, you are taught how to use the correct techniques to take down a refractory prisoner. We took it in turns to play the con. I liked that. I got to bash up the fuckers who were trying to learn. I laughed at the useless cunts that flapped and couldn't do it.

For the final assessment, we had to enter a cell, restrain the prisoner, remove him under control, and relocate him to another cell. I was good at it. I could do the job well, fast and hard. Some people couldn't get to grips with it at all. They didn't have a clue about co-ordination, technique or how to apply force. That's fine; but then being a Prison Officer is not for them. Right? Not right. No chance! They passed everybody. *EVERYBODY!* They passed dickheads with the authority and power of a pussycat. I couldn't believe it. I asked the Instructors why. The simple answer was – numbers. They had to pass everyone because they needed the screws on landings. Staff were leaving quicker than they joined. That was the first time I saw the Service do what suits them instead of doing what was right. Fucking wankers. They make it unsafe for everyone.

But I'd finished, I'd passed. We all had.

Training was now complete. It had given me a little insight into the Prison Service and how prison works, but it taught me jack shit about how to be a screw. What it did do, though, was build confidence and strength of mind. It encouraged camaraderie. It welcomed you into the Prison Service lifestyle. It made you feel a part of something, like you were doing something important. We had a little ceremony where the college Governor gave us our pass certificates and Officer ID cards. This was followed by a final piss-up, of course.

You were normally given a week off after training. Not at the Well.

I got a call from Rumpole who told me what Wing I would be working on. D Wing: the hardest, roughest Wing in the jail. I was up for it. I wanted it.

I got home and slept, got up then slept some more. A few beers on the Sunday and now Monday had come round. I was about to start work on one of the biggest Wings in Europe. I had passed the course and was ready to be a Prison Officer. I was ready to face the prisoners. So I thought. But it hadn't even begun; I didn't have a fucking clue.

WELCOME TO THE WELL, MEET THE PRISONERS

Being a Prison Officer was not the job I'd always dreamed of having. Like everyone else, I had greater aspirations. I would have loved to be Liam Gallagher on stage in front of eighty thousand people, putting attitude, meaning and hope into people's worlds. Or perhaps a hot-shit surgeon saving the lives of the needy. Or maybe the ultimate, Tony Blair's successor! But, like the masses, I got something different. All the same, it was a job I was proud of doing, and I did it to the best of my ability. It paid the mortgage, looked after the family and gave me beer tokens.

Now that I'd done the training; it was time to start doing. I needed to know what was what and who was who.

There are four different Categories of prisoners and prisons. I, like many, thought the prisoner was banged up and dealt with in the strictest conditions. That turned out to be yet another misconception. The four different Categories are A, B, C and the hotel, Cat D.

Cat A prisoners are the ones that are a high risk of escape, have a life sentence or are extremely dangerous. These types are your murderers, serial rapists, drug barons and gangland bosses. They live in Cat A establishments like HMP Wakefield, Whitemoor and Belmarsh.

Now, you would think that these prisoners, being Cat A, would live in completely basic conditions and serve hard time so as to be punished for their severe crimes. Well that's bollocks. For instance, Ian Huntley, that piece-of-shit scumbag child-killer, lives the life of Riley in a mini self-contained flat with the use of a kitchen, a PlayStation and a state-of-the-art gym. So the kind of things that we pay for out of our hard-earned cash, this murdering nonce cunt gets for free. Where is the justice? How can this be serving the innocent victims? Within a Cat A nick, there is always a unit that is like a prison within a prison. This is for the nut nuts. Complete mad fuckers in there. Put into perspective, this is a unit that holds four to six cons with twenty Officers to look after them, in comparison with, for instance, ten Officers to four hundred cons, which were the conditions I was about to work in on D Wing.

These nut-nut cons are so dangerous – to themselves, each other and the Officers – that they have a whole unit to them- selves. They are in there, instead of in a secure hospital, quite simply because hospitals can't handle them. A perfect example of this is the prisoner Charles Bronson. I'm sure you know who I mean, a big lump with a shaven head and a tache. He is always in the papers for one reason or another. He has been passed back and forth from the Prison Service to the NHS for years and years. The Service will nut him off, saying that he is unfit for prison due to his mental state. The secure hospitals will have him for a while, then say he is bad not mad and pronounce him fit for prison, because they can't handle him. This man lived a 'twenty-eight-day lay down' for years, which means that every twenty-eight days he was moved to another prison, due to being such a strain on staff.

Cat A nicks have loads of Officers on duty. Let's say that in a unit of forty-five cons, you will have between twelve and twenty screws. This is because these are the most dangerous conditions to work in, right? Wrong. The most dangerous conditions aren't where the most dangerous prisoners are; they are in prisons where the staff are so badly outnumbered by the cons that they are accidents waiting to happen. Which leads me on to the Cat B prisons.

Every person who is sent to prison goes to a Cat B first. Establishments such as HMP Chelmsford, Pentonville, Wandsworth, Bedford and, of course, my personal favourite, Romwell are all local Cat B establishments. No matter what the crime is – fraud, drink-driving, assault, paedophilia or murder – they will all be sent to a local Cat B initially. Unless, of course, they are 'high profile' and in the papers. The idea is, the prisoner gets sent to a local Cat B to be categorised and then sent on to an appropriate prison, but that seldom happens. You get prisoners staying at local Cat Bs for years, mainly due to lack of beds elsewhere.

These locals are dangerous, dirty, horrible places. They have bugger-all money, so the regime is crap and staff levels are extremely low. Quite simply, there is no control. Because it's so rubbish, there are loads of kick offs. For instance, in a Cat A prison, you might get two or three kick offs a week, if you are busy. Remember, they have a shitload of staff to deal with them. A Cat B can have ten kick offs a day. I know what you are thinking: 'Twenty Officers for forty-five prisoners in a Cat A jail, ten screws for four hundred at the Well. Is the head of the Prison Service mental!?' The logic is, Cat A cons are more dangerous so they need more staff. But all of these dangerous cons started at a local Cat B. So on D Wing, there could be, potentially, fifty, sixty, a hundred or however many Cat A prisoners roaming around a Wing of four hundred with only ten screws on there!

They say that they monitor the Cat As who are in custody at a Cat B, but that's bollocks. They should do, but they don't. It boils down to the fact that the Government doesn't want to give money to shit-hole local prisons. They are happy for Officers to put their lives in unnecessary danger every day – and, of course, you accept the risk when you take the job – but there is a difference between risk and downright endangerment. Local prisons exist on neglect. It really is like taking the lambs to the slaughter. Rumpole's words, that 'the scroats run the nick' while the screws are 'just the visitors', are the truest I've ever heard. A local prison is an extremely dangerous, stressful place to work.

Cat C is what the majority get categorised to. These inmates include your run-of-the-mill junkie who got done for thieving, your ABH, drink-drivers and, in a lot of cases, your nonce. These prisons are more open than a Cat B, with the inmates being out of their cells an awful lot. There is plenty of education, gym and work for them to do. In prison, there are lots of opportunities for the cons to learn new skills of some sort, either through education or by working. There are many businesses that use the prisons to do work, as it is very cheap. For instance, the next time you are on a flight that serves you a meal, the chances are some scroat has packed the cutlery you are using to stuff you face. Nice thought, hey? Just after he's scratched his unwashed bollocks.

HMP Highpoint, Edmunds Hill and the Mount are all examples of a Cat C prison. Some Cat C jails are better than others. Some run certain courses, so they have an entry require-ment for the prisoner to get there – like being drug free, for instance. Some of these better prisons are single bang up (one prisoner in a cell) with en-suite showers – and that is punishment . . . ?!

I do believe in the cons doing something constructive, but sometimes I think that it is just too easy for the career criminal. These regimes are no deterrent to stopping people re-offending. If it were harder, perhaps people wouldn't want to come back; but, how it is at the moment, they don't give a fuck. The average person would find prison hard to deal with at first, of course, but most of them settle into it. It is daunting, to begin with: the surroundings, the noise. It goes back to the circles you mix in . . . Most of the cons know the other cons from the road. In the way that most people's circle of mates goes to work, most cons' mates go to prison. For the career criminal or junkie, doing bird is a piece of piss. They all know each other, they have as much drugs as they want and find the discipline a joke. The first timer will struggle at the beginning. If nothing else, the sheer sur-roundings of a Victorian prison are horrible and intimidating. They will struggle with having their liberty taken away. Then, the bullying will start. They will get bullied for their burn (tobacco) and canteen – and to drug run. Sometimes, they will get bullied into taking drugs so they develop a habit. Some people, who would normally know fuck all about drugs, go inside and become smackheads. This introduces them to the criminal underworld, so they then transfer from being a person with one minor offence into a career criminal. Sometimes people come in once, then never again, but that doesn't happen very often. Once someone has done a bit of bird, they normally come back for another stay. It must be the food or the exceptional waiter service that is provided. Some people don't ever get used to the prison and end up getting nutted off to healthcare where they get jabbed up as they simply break down.

Cat D, or, as it's also known, Open Prison, is the lowest-risk prison. These prisoners are not banged up – they have room keys. Their accommodation, I kid you not, is better than the accommodation I had up in Wakey. A disgrace. More and more cons are getting downgraded to Cat D because of lack of spaces in other nicks. I've got a good idea about that: *Build more fucking prisons, you thick cunts!* You have lunatics roaming around who should be locked up.

These establishments are designed for cons who pose little risk to the general public and are at low risk of absconding. However, they can be in for violent crimes, driving crimes or theft, or be a lifer coming to the end of his sentence. These prisons are open in every aspect. A well-known Cat D is HMP Hollesley Bay, the place where perjury-convicted Lord Jeffrey Archer served most of his time. And, as a rule, cons don't generally fuck around in a Cat D. The last thing they want is to be sent back to a real prison.

You can now see that the local Cat B is the shit of the shit.

*

The Monday had come round for me to start my first day on D Wing as an Officer; a real screw. I was live, on active duty.

I drove in on my own on, that day, for the first time. I was fucking worried I'd get lost! I knew one way in and one way out. If there were any road works or anything, then I was buggered.

But I made my way in OK. I got out of the car, although this time I headed for the gate, not the training centre. As I walked past it, I saw Rumpole standing outside sucking on his fag. Even in his moodiness, I could tell he liked me. Liked is probably too strong a word. Tolerated me more than most is probably more accurate.

I went through the gate, and for the first time was given my set of keys. That made me feel good; professional. It was a big thing to get your keys. I headed towards D Wing, my new place of work.

Romwell is what you would imagine a prison to look like, outside and in. It is a Victorian prison that is absolutely huge. Whatever you are thinking, multiply it by ten and you might have an idea. It is absolutely massive. The average Cat B – such as Chelmsford or Bedford – holds around four or five hundred cons. The Well's op cap (operational capacity) is nearly one thousand three hundred. It is very old and very dirty, in poor condition with poor facilities. It has a severe problem with mice, cockroaches and has a smell of decaying meat.

It was all double bang up (two inmates to a cell) and the cells were small. They had a toilet in their cell, with a TV and a kettle. These are two lovely objects that the cons like to throw at you when you unlock the door. Most prisons have alarm buttons to push on every landing. Not the Well; it's about thirty years behind everywhere else. You carry a whistle at the Well. Having

65

to blow your whistle to get help is just great when you have some junkie with his hands around your neck, trying to choke you to death. As well as the four main Wings at The Well – A Wing, B Wing, C Wing and, last but not least, D Wing – you also have the Fraggle Wing, the Nonce Wing (which houses prisoners separated for their own protection) and the Block (the Segregation Unit).

When 'new' cons come into the prison, they are brought to A Wing. They may be first-time prisoners or they may have been transferred in from another nick. Whatever they are, they have an induction and spend their first night there.

The nonces are the only ones that don't stay on the first-night centre. Those dirty cunts get more protection than the Queen.

B Wing is the Remand Wing. When I started, I didn't have a clue what remand was, or what it meant. Remand is when a judge decides that it is not safe to let you out on bail while waiting for your case to be brought to court. Remands are un-convicted prisoners.

You could be on remand for, say, two years, have your trial and then walk free. You get nothing back for the days you served. So, on B Wing, you tend to have nearly four hundred 'innocent' people who have been 'stitched up'. Of course, the reality is that the majority are guilty as sin. As you can imagine, those bastards can be a right handful. Remands do have more entitlements, but with most scroats it's never enough; they think everyone owes them something, nothing is their fault. That gets on my tits so much.

C Wing is 'Detox Wing', so it's full of junkies coming down. There is a massive problem in this country with drugs but most people are not aware of its true extent. I had no idea until I joined the Prison Service. The amount of people in this country who are smack and crack addicts is astonishing.

I'm a young lad who goes out regularly to clubs, pubs, concerts and festivals, so it's fair to say that I'm regularly surrounded by people who are under the influence of Charlie and pills. However, I'd never come into contact with anyone under the influence of the rock or the brown. Not until I became a screw, that is.

Charlie and pills are used recreationally by thousands of people at the weekend. It is something that many choose to do. There are many who use these drugs recreationally without robbing or hurting people. They take it when they are partying, like other people drink. They don't want it all the time and they don't get stressed if they don't get it. I'm not condoning the use of these drugs – I'm just being realistic and honest, because that is how it is in the real world. When you are in a pub on a Saturday night, a lot of people in that pub are not just pissed but pissed and coked up. Until I became a Prison Officer, I thought that was the extent of drug abuse in this country.

I thought the days of jabbing a vein with heroin were long gone. I thought that was the eighties. How wrong I was. Crack and smack are the biggest problem this country has. Some people will be disgusted to know people pop pills and snort Charlie at the weekend, as it is something they don't see or understand. Some people will be disgusted that students in their bed-sits get stoned every day. Or that pissheads binge-drink three times a week. Some of you are like me, in your twenties, you've got a bit of savvy, you go out and you know what is going on. You think that is all that is going on, but the underworld of crack and heroin is huge.

These addicts would rob their own mother for a ten-quid wrap. If they jack up, it's even worse. A lot of addicts smoke crack and smack, but those who inject it take their addiction and habit to another level. These people will inject every vein in their body until all their veins have collapsed. They end up injecting into their groin. All of this goes on in flats and houses all over the country but most of you are unaware of it. That's how big the problem is. As a result, most of the crime in this country is drug-related.

Our Detox Wing held ninety prisoners. Pathetic. Are these people fucking stupid or what? I honestly think that sometimes the Governors must sit there and think of ways to make it as hard as possible for the staff. Obviously, there are loads of junkies who need detox, but the pathetic size of the Detox Wing doesn't even touch the surface. So these junkies are thrown on to a normal Wing when they are clucking to the max. Dealing with people who are clucking is not a nice thing to do. They are violent, incoherent, experiencing hallucinations and are not fit to be on a normal Wing location. So it's nurse-and-Officer Thompson now. Only, I did eleven weeks' basic Officer training, not three years, or whatever nurses do at college.

I made my way towards D Wing, apprehensive about my first day. Would I get in trouble? Would I know the answers to whatever the cons would ask? They like to ask fuckloads of questions and, if you don't know the answers, they make you look a cunt.

D Wing is for convicted prisoners. That means that they have been to court and are now serving the sentence that was awarded them. Again, they are supposed only to stay on D Wing until they have been categorised. They should then be shipped out to an appropriate prison. Never happens correctly, though. They can be put on medical hold, or they may be doing one of them arty-farty courses that are supposed to help them face up to their crimes. That is bollocks, if I've ever heard it. The truth is, they try and get on these courses so they get put on hold. They will have some bent screw in their pocket who is trafficking gear to them. This feeds their habit and makes them a ton of cash dealing on the Wing. This in turn will make them popular on the Wing, so they will soon have loads of lads who will look after them. They then become the number one dealer on the Wing. The bent bastard screw is also earning a fortune. That's why they do these poxy courses, and if the powers that be want to kid themselves that these scroats are doing it to better themselves, then they are fools.

I knew D Wing was an extremely dangerous place to work; I'd been on it loads of times during training and I'd seen enough bend ups taking place there. We were told early on that it was the roughest Wing. I had to keep my wits about me. Try and keep my confidence. Get on it and see what I could do.

I went in to the office for the morning briefing. I sat down nervously. Soon there were eight other Officers in the room. We were one under the MSL (Minimum Staffing Level). The SO told us we would have another Officer from B Wing coming over to make up the numbers. Make up the numbers?! There was fuck-all of us to make up! Even though I knew what the MSL was, it still shocked me the first time I was one of the counted screws. It was fucking crazy. The Wing was so big, so many convicts. Nearly four hundred. Ten screws. One SO. This was my new job. My new career . . .

'Mr Thompson, you are on The Threes today. Any questions?'

'No, sir.'

That was it. My introduction to being a qualified Officer. The briefing was finished so we took up our posts. I left the room, took a deep breath and walked to my landing. The craziness was about to begin.

LIFE ON THE LANDING

That first day on the landing was hard. I couldn't say no to a prisoner. 'Can you do this, can you do that.' I ran around like a right tit. The cons always go to the new Officers: they don't know the rules; they say yes to everything.

On D Wing, there are five landings, with four having capacity for one hundred prisoners on each. One of the landings had less. With the smaller landing, and with cells out of action due to being smashed up, that made the numbers around four hundred altogether. There are two Officers per landing to carry out all of the duties. So, imagine – if you are teamed up with a fucking idiot, you are left to run a landing of approximately one hundred cons on your own.

I was working with a guy called Eddie on that first live shift. Eddie was a top bloke. He had ten years in. He was in his late thirties with swept-back hair and plenty of Brylcreem; very eighties. I liked his style of working. He took the job in his stride.

Our first job was to unlock the landing and send them downstairs for exercise on the yard. I put my key in the first cell door on the landing. I was nervous. I wanted to look the part; not look new. I unlocked the door. I was faced with the two prisoners. I was thinking hard, trying to remember what I was taught.

'Morning, Guv.' They both said.

I had psyched myself up, ready for anything, and all they said was good morning!

I carried on unlocking my side of the landing, while Eddie unlocked his. We ushered them downstairs and out on the yard. I watched Eddie's confidence in how he was handling himself. He was being asked questions about release, probation, visits. Fucking everything. He was calm and collected. Highly knowledgeable and well respected. We had to keep on the backs of all the cons, ushering them on the whole time to make their way downstairs. Two of us, nearly a hundred of them.

We managed to get them down without any dramas. Eddie took me into the office – after he had sent me to make the tea, that is. Sprogs always make the tea. He sat me down and gave me his words of wisdom:

'Be fair, be firm. Do what you can and don't bullshit them. If they play the game, reward them. If they fuck up, give them a chance. If they fuck you around give them fuck-all. If you feel threatened in any way, shape or form, drop them.'

Straightforward, no messing. That was Eddie. He stuck to those simple principles and they worked. They were the principles I was going to adopt. Eddie was a geezer. He got on with the cons. But if they stepped out of line, he would fuck them up. He wanted an easy life for everyone. His rules were simple, and provided that easy life.

We did the cell fabric checks next. That was making sure everything was working OK – locks, bars, necessary items – and no one had anything that they shouldn't have. It wasn't a full cell spin (cell search), just a quick look. The fabric checks should be done every day but they don't get done, hardly at all. You have too much other paperwork and shit to do. Not enough screws and not enough hours in the day.

The cons came back in from exercise. We had to bang them all up. That went plain sailing until one little cunt came up to me with attitude.

'I want a phone call in the office. Now!' he said to me, aggressively.

I knew that we weren't officially allowed to give phone calls in the office. Eddie told me the screws' rules, though. Calls were given to the good lads who behaved themselves. A treat, a goodwill gesture to encourage them to continue acting that way.

But this guy was not acting how he should be. He was acting like a cunt. I told him that no calls were allowed.

'Please go back to your cell,' I said, looking him in his eyes.

'You fucking move me, you cunt.'

I didn't know what to do. You are told how to react to an incident where the use of force is being used, but no one teaches you when it is correct to initiate the use of force. So I had this little prick who was half my size, gobbing off at me but, because I was new in the job and didn't know how to react, he was getting away with it. If it had been on the road, outside the prison,

I would have put the little prick on his arse but, for an Officer, there are rules.

Eddie came over and told him either to move on his own or be dragged down the block. He moved. The rest of the day went OK. I was learning.

A couple of days went by and then I faced my first challenge. I was working on The Threes when I had this con who wanted a cell move. It was out of the question, there were no spaces. Some of them cunts think it's a hotel. If they don't get what they want, then the dummy is spat out.

'Guv, I want a cell move.'

'Out of the question, place is full.'

'I want a fucking cell move now, you cunt,' he shouted.

He was becoming aggressive. I knew that if he didn't back off, I would have to drop him.

'I don't know who the fuck you think you're talking to. But I will repeat myself again. No fucking cell moves.'

He stepped up to me, with a clenched fist. Before he knew it, I grabbed the back of his head and dropped him to the floor. I smashed him down hard; fucking hard. He didn't know what hit him. I heard someone blow their whistle. It was Eddie. He jumped on, helping restrain him. I'd done it. I dropped my first con. I had found my level of intimidation, how much I was prepared to take before dropping a con. And I had acted on it. The training had taken over. It worked.

Eddie had been watching from a distance, seeing if I could handle myself, handle the situation. He said that I was fucking good. He said I acted like someone who had been in the job for years. That was a big compliment. I was the talk of the jail. I'd only been live for a few days and I'd dropped someone! The use of force is a big part of the job as a Prison Officer, and it is something that bullies take advantage of – and get away with, the gutless bastards.

Sometimes I would have to bollock a geezer old enough to be my Dad, which I found very embarrassing at the start. A lot of new screws suffer this way, suffer from being young. Of course, some of the inmates would see this as a weakness; they'd abuse it and intimidate the young members of staff. I would be lying if I said that I was never intimidated when I first started. But it didn't take me long to settle into things and get a grip of them cunts. Like many, I was taught to respect my elders but I quickly realised that most of these older lads had the mentality of a toddler.

These fellas had to have their lives organised by screws, some of them young enough to be their grandchildren. When I first started, I used to be sympathetic to the old geezers, but that didn't work; they took advantage of me. So in the end I thought, 'Fuck it, I will treat them all the same, regardless of their age.' They were all banged up, so I had to have some consistency. I had to forget their age.

I also found I could communicate with the cons well. A lot of times I could joke them into doing what I asked. I always did it like that, but made sure they knew they couldn't take liberties with me. I made it quite clear that if I had to, I would turn it on. That's the respect I built up with the cons, too. They knew they could have a laugh and a joke with me, and that I would do anything to help if they were decent, but they also knew not to cross the line.

'Roy, can you go to your cell now, mate; association has finished,' I said politely to an inmate who was in his forties, covered in tattoos, thickset and quite a lump. He was OK, but he would get a bit too familiar and try and manipulate you. He would use his age, stature and confidence to do this.

'I'm gonna make a call first, Guv,' he replied firmly, but keeping a relative politeness in his language.

'Not now, Roy, time is up. You will have to do it tomorrow. You had plenty of time to do it.'

'Who the fuck are you telling what to do, you cunt?' he said, aggressively leaning towards me.

'You, you cunt! You ain't making no fucking call now. You forget who the screw is and who the con is. Now, go to your fucking cell and mind your manners.'

He stopped for a second and stared at me closely. He knew what I was saying. I was saying, 'I don't give a fuck who you are or how old you are, I will do my job, and I will not let anyone walk all over me.'

'Sweet, Guv, tomorrow is sound. See you in the morning, Mr Thompson.' With that he walked off back to his cell. I was twenty-two. I was young but not stupid. After that, I never looked back, and I had the confidence to deal with people and forget their ages.

It didn't take me long to work out the good screws from the bad ones. I could see the bullies and the scared. It was plain to me who the workers were compared to the lazy bastards. There were many, like Doubtfire, who tried it on with me, treating me like shit for being a sprog. I took it to a degree, it's all part of being in a service, but some wankers took liberties with it. Some new Officers got it so bad they quit the job. But most of them knew not to push too hard with me. There were a couple I had to see in the car park to educate them as to who I am and what I'm about, but generally I got on with most. Well, I got on with the screws who wanted to do the job, and do it no matter what it takes. You see, there are four types of Prison Officer: the Officer, the con with keys, Mr No and the screw.

The Officer is a human-rights lover, or shall I say a real fucking care bear. They are the ones who truly believe that we can change, or 'rehabilitate', each and every one of those cons. They are the most naïve idiots you could ever have the misfortune to pound the landings with. They have no idea of security awareness: there could be a drug deal in front of their dumb fucking eyes but they are too busy trying to hug everyone to notice. Some scroat would jug someone (scald with boiling sugared water) in front of them, and all they would want to do is counsel the scroat and psychoanalyse the reasons why they did it. Never mind the poor cunt next to him who is screaming on the floor with his face melted. These Officers can be lethal people to work with. You could have some lunatic threatening to bite your throat out. You start fighting with this nutter, trying to wrap him up, and care bear just stands there with an 'Oh, my God! What is happening?' look on their stupid face. They say to both of you, 'Stop fighting,' instead of doing what they are paid to do which is to assist and restrain the mental bastard. These fuckers are a nightmare. They call the inmate 'Mr' when, as far as I'm concerned, they gave up their title once they were sent to prison for committing a crime severe enough for a custodial sentence. Care bears run around for the cons like waiters. It never occurs to them that the inmates would lie to them. They seem to forget that some of the scroats are criminals who would rob an old people's home. Most of the old lags hate these weak bastards. They have seen the Service change; they can see this new breed create problems instead of controlling them. For obvious reasons, the others tend to go to these wimps when they want something, realising these idiots are the easiest to manipulate.

The Officer is what the Prison Service wants. They want the waiter service and prisoner hugging – no disciplinarians.

Then there are the cons with keys. These are the trafficking bent scum that bring in any type of contraband for money. This is a huge problem within the prisons. These bastards don't give a fuck what it is; if they can get paid for it, they will bring it in. Nor do they give a fuck about staff or prisoner safety.

Then there is Mr No. This type of Officer is just plain lazy. They can't be arsed to do anything at all. They have similarities to the screw in a sense that they see it as 'us and them': we're the goodies and they are the baddies. But they simply don't want to do anything about it. They say 'No' to everything that a con asks them. They see it as 'They are banged up, so they should get nothing at all and should be banged up all day'. That is a popular public view, too. I think that there should be less fluffy bullshit, but I do know that we must have a constructive regime. Not the destructive waiter service we have now but not what the Mr Nos want either. They are only interested in going into work, doing as little as possible, giving the scroats absolutely nothing and then going home.

The next type is the screw. This is the type I fell into. The screw is someone who also sees it as 'us and them' – we're the good guys and they are the bad guys. Don't get me wrong, I have forged many great relationships with cons who, on the other side of the gate, could easily have been friends of mine. A couple of my very close friends have been banged up, too. There were probably more cons that I got on with than Officers. That said, you always have to keep a professional distance. The good-guy-bad-guy method is not always the correct way of looking at it, but it is a way you can keep that professional distance. It stops the career criminal, who knows the system inside and out, from manipulating you. I've fallen into that trap. It's easy to relax too much. It's something you become aware of as you build more experience.

The screw is someone who has a bit of savvy and who knows what is going on. A screw is someone who lives in the real world, who is not phased by a con making threats or becoming violent, unlike the useless care-bear type. They understand and know exactly what is happening on the Wing. They know who the dealers are, the drug runners, the smackheads, the bullies, the grasses, the jailhouse poofs, the hard bastards, the weak cunts, the old lags, the new bosses, the yardies, the pikeys, the Asians, the skinheads. There is very little that a screw misses.

The Prison Service has a fluffy way of wanting to deal with inmates. The screw still wants to police these criminals, putting some law and order in their lives, even if the Governors want the Officers to act like waiters. Screws can distinguish between the shit rules and the good ones, and know what it takes for the cons and screws to live together in harmony. They know how to keep a balance. For the Governors, having their freedom taken away is the inmates' punishment and there is no need to add to that. What a load of bollocks. I'm sure their victims feel the same – not! Freedom loss is enough? Wrong!

The biggest part of doing the job successfully is having discretion. If the con is playing the game well, then he is always polite and does what he is asked. In exchange, the screw will bend the rules a little bit. Maybe he will unlock this con for an extra phone call or shower. This is not an entitlement, but he will be given a little reward for being decent. On the other hand, if there is some wanker who is constantly abusive, violent, and plain horrible, a screw will deal with that inmate accordingly to adjust his behaviour.

I will give you an example. A con is violent so he gets bent up. He's nicked, that is, he's placed on report and then seen by the Governor. The Governor's verdict? Three days' cell confinement. The con laughs at it; he does not see this as punishment at all. The result is he does not change his ways, or his violent behaviour. The screw, however, is resourceful and will find a way to make this con fall into line with everyone else. First of all, this piece of shit's daily newspaper keeps going missing. On top of that, he always manages to be the last to be let out for a shower and first to be banged up again. He never gets what he ordered for his dinner, and his mail constantly goes astray. Believe you me, this cunt will soon start to conform to the regime and what is expected of him.

Now, don't misunderstand me: this type of thing doesn't go on for the amusement of the screw, it goes on to keep some sort of law and order. Prisoners will complain about how hard they have it and how 'screw cunts' do that sort of thing for fun. This is all shit. If a screw does do it to someone who doesn't deserve it, then they are a cunt. I certainly wouldn't do it for fun, and screws I surrounded myself with wouldn't do it for fun. But, like every job in the world, you have your wankers. The picture painted is that the cons have tough lives and the screws are bullies. It's a load of old bollocks, it really is. The cons rely on the screws – the good screws, that is. There are some very good relations between prisoners and screws. There are bad ones, too, of course.

If need be, a screw will go to a prisoner's cell to give him a personal lesson, so he knows exactly what the score is. I'm not talking about a load of screws going to a cell to give a scroat a good kicking. A decent screw is not a bully or an animal. I do stress the word 'decent'. Sometimes, if all else fails, a bit of man-to-man can sort it. I live in the real world. I don't say things to be politically correct. I say things that I think are right. If people don't like it, they can fuck off. Sometimes, if you take the piece of shit away from his audience, and you tell them how it is, when there are just the two of you, most of the time he will crumble like a cake. Sometimes he won't and there will be a scrap in the cell. No alarm bell, no whistles, it gets sorted there and then between the two of you. The problem is then rectified, and he stops acting like a cunt.

Whichever way it goes – chat, fight, win or lose – what happens in the cell stays in the cell. His papers and mail start to arrive again, he always gets his meal of choice, and he has plenty of time for showers and phone calls. The problem is dealt with, and the problem is now controlled. You see, a screw wants to do the job well, and the job is keeping control of the Wing so that it is safe for the staff and the cons. If a screw is good at his job, he will have control of the Wing while at the same time keeping the respect of the inmates. To be good, you must be fair. Always do what you say you are going to do, never make promises you can't keep and, when you say no, mean it.

Screws who gain the respect of cons also gain their trust. They can then forge close relationships with these inmates, which helps the Wing run well. You rely heavily on these relationships to get the information that you need. Once a con trusts you, and the relationship is good, he will grass on his own fucking brother! When you receive Intel, you have to be very discreet. You mustn't tell another screw because you never know who is bent. I am normally a good judge of character and have an idea who is bent, but I have been fooled more than once. Always make sure you look after a grass. If he wants a transfer to another nick, you sort it. If you find him with puff, you don't nick him. Treat him well and he will give you more and more Intel. Hopefully this will lead to the big fish, the bent screw. Good screws do the job how it should be done.

And lastly, there is a final type of Officer – the ones that get through training, but simply can't cope with the job. They may join the job and get bullied by other screws. Or the cons see that these Officers have the backbones of jellyfish, so they take advantage. This kind of Officer ends up quitting or, in some cases, developing mental problems. There is a huge problem with suicide and stress among Prison Officers because there is no support for staff. The Governors wouldn't notice an Officer walking into work with a fucking noose around his neck. But if a con has a pillow that is a little hard then, fuck me, they *are* worried.

I was taking to my work like a duck to water. I was gaining respect from the inmates, and the experienced and good screws were treating me like one of their own. The management was fifty-fifty with me. Some of them liked my methods and were starting to rely on me to deal with things that needed sorting. Others found me a bit dangerous. Not politically correct enough. And I was outspoken. If the bosses said things that I thought were shit, I would say. I had a voice. The Governors didn't like anyone with a voice, especially not a cock-sure-of-himself bloke in his early twenties. Fuck them.

But the months were passing, and my rapport with the cons was good.

'I need a word, Guv.'

'Go on, I'm listening.'

'Nah, a private word.'

I took him to my landing office. He went on to tell me that his cellmate was receiving drugs from a particular screw. I knew the con telling me was a junkie cunt, who was in with one of the firms on the Wing. So I knew the info wasn't for moral reasons. When you receive Intel from a con you have to put it in a report and hand it to the security department. They collate the info and act accordingly. This info seemed good so I put it in. I fucking hate bent cunts. Hate them.

Gang culture in prisons is rife because of the drugs. Everyone is in competition to be the number one on the Wing. Because of this, there is some horrific violence between gangs. There was a prisoner called Ajar on my landing. He was a big dealer on the Wing. He was always polite, always did what was asked of him, so he played the game well. We all knew he was a dealer, he knew we knew, but we could never catch the little bastard. We would spin his cell nearly every day but never found anything. He used to find it hilarious. He was connected big time on the road and worth a lot of money. On the inside, he worked for Jake's firm. Jake was a nasty fucker. He was the boss of bosses if you like. He was richer and more powerful than most of the scroat dealers. He had bent screws in his pocket.

'Ajar, why are you so happy all the time? Is your cellmate knocking one up you of a night time!?' I jokingly said to him.

'Mr Thompson, I earn four times more in here than I do on the road, and I get a break from my fat missus! It's hard not to smile!'

Cheeky bastard! That's how he always was; completely open about what he was doing. But I will give him his due; he was bloody good at it.

I was having a shit morning. I was working on The Threes with a right useless cunt. I had two bend ups before it was even 09.00 hrs. I'd not been back on the landing for long since my last bend up. The numpty I was working with had done fuck-all. I went into the office for a well-deserved brew. I heard the whistle go. I jumped up, ran out of the office and saw numpty standing outside a cell, looking as useless as ever. I sprinted over. When I got there I saw something that I will never forget. Ajar was lying on his bed screaming uncontrollably. I've never heard anything like it. He was bare-chested; his body was swollen where it had been beaten so severely. Then I looked at his face. This will haunt me for the rest of my life. He had been jugged with hot water, bleach and sugar. They put the bleach in for added damage, but the sugar sticks to the skin and keeps in the heat from the boiling water. They had completely covered his face and neck in it. Ajar was a black fella, but his face had turned completely white with lots of blood stains on it. The skin on his face had literally fallen off like orange peel. It was horrendous. He was completely unrecognisable. I almost vomited there and then.

I screamed for a medic. He wasn't making much noise, now, just shaking violently. Shock had set in. He was taken straight to hospital. I never saw him again after that. That's what happens when you mix in those circles and get involved in that type of thing; you have to accept the risks involved. You are either straight or not. It's certainly a life I've had no interest in living – mainly because I like living. The lad who did it to Ajar was a nobody trying to be a somebody. He spent the rest of his bird living on Rule 45. That means he was segregated for his own safety in the vulnerable-prisoner separation Wing – the Nonce Wing – with the nonces. I later heard that two hours after his release, he was found dead with a bullet in his head. He fucked with the wrong person.

BENT UP

Before I knew it, I'd been in the job for a year. My relationship with Danni was getting strained. I didn't always go home after work, especially if I was on a late shift. You were supposed to finish at nine o'clock but that never fucking happened. Scouse and I had become really close mates. He lived in the staff quarters where there was a spare room. I started staying over quite a lot. It saved me the fifty-five mile drive home and then the drive back in. It was perfect: whatever time it was that we got out, we went and got pissed. We had a lot in common. Scouse loved a beer, too.

I was getting more and more distant from Danni and my whole family. I needed to let go of the stress from work and the Officer's Club was the perfect place. It was full of people who understood what you were saying, plus there was cheap beer and no closing time. They served till you left or fell asleep there.

On this particular day, I went into work with a steaming hangover. Scouse and I hadn't even made it back to the quarters. We'd gone straight to the club after work, without even going to get changed. We were there all night getting pissed. We fell asleep pissed in the early hours. We didn't have much rest; I remember looking at my watch at one point and seeing that it was 05.15 hrs. We didn't even go home for a wash. We woke up (still pissed) stinking (still in the same uniform), and headed straight back to work.

We went to the mess for breakfast and coffee while, at the same time, necking loads of Pro Plus tablets for a caffeine boost.

I went on the Wing and attended the staff briefing. There was this dickhead who had joined the job just before me. There were no two ways about it: the bloke was a complete prick. He had the personality of a goldfish, with the charisma and charm of Hitler. He waltzed around the place thinking he was hard as fuck, when, truth be known, he was a complete coward. I hadn't worked with him many times, thank God. He had been a screw on B Wing. They got the hump with him, so he was moved to D Wing. I didn't give a shit provided he didn't get in my way or act like a cunt.

The briefing finished, I was working on The Ones. That had become my regular landing. The strong staff worked on The Ones. The staff on The Ones pretty much controlled the regime. It was The Ones' staff that called for the other landings to unlock, sent for dinner and meds and were in charge of every other activity. The staff on The Ones had to be the most security aware, knowing when to call for things – and when not to.

I liked it on The Ones. The morning went fine and I headed to the gym with Scouse at lunch time. Work hard, play hard in every respect.

Then we had to unlock for the afternoon activities. I screamed for The Twos to unlock. It wasn't long before I heard the familiar sound of a whistle being blown. I looked up, saw that it was on The Twos and sprinted up the stairs.

Now, when you respond to an alarm, you don't get there and ask what is going on. If you see a con getting bent up, you assist the screws doing it. Remember what I said earlier about finding your own tolerance level? That's what this is all about. You don't determine whether the Officer was right or wrong to drop the con – you weren't even there; but, as far as you are concerned, an Officer has made that call and decided to drop him.

I got up to The Twos in a flash. There was a con fighting with Hitler. He was getting the better of him, as well. I jumped in, grabbing this fella and trying to get him on the floor. He was a bit of a lump and was hard work. I managed to get him to the deck, getting hold of him and applying pain until he complied. Hitler saw this as an opportunity to start bashing the fuck out of him. I told him to ease up, but he took no notice. More staff arrived on the scene, so I quickly got this knob of a screw relieved by another Officer.

When a bastard such as this one decides to start bashing a con up when that con is under restraint, he is putting your career at risk *and* being a cowardly bastard. There you are, trying to do your job and restrain the con, while all he is doing is seriously assaulting him. Then, on top of that, he is expecting you to protect him by saying nothing. I was not in the business of going to Governors and making complaints about staff and getting them sacked. But I still dealt with it – in my own way. It normally worked – I would tell them that this was their chance but, if I ever witnessed it again, then I would go to the Governor.

I knew how to deal with Hitler and teach him the error of his ways. After the incident, we all went down to write out our 'Use of Force' forms. When you have used force, it has to be backed up with paperwork. He was giving it the large, saying how tough he was and how he dropped the con. Did he fuck. He was getting the shit kicked out of him before I turned up – and probably for good reason, the wanker. I thought, 'I will deal with this fucking tosser.' So, there and then I said to him:

'Fancy getting pissed down the club tonight?'

Looking confused and nervous, but equally flattered, he replied, 'Ronnie, that would be top, meet you at the gate at six.'

I could tell by his expression that he actually thought I was impressed by his pathetic actions. What a twat. I met the idiot at the gate at six o'clock, as we agreed. We walked round to the club, which was just behind the nick. Come five past six, it is always full of screws getting pissed up. We got in the club and started drinking. After about six pints, we got on the doubles. It was doing my head in because he is probably the dullest, most annoying person I've ever met. To top that off, he was a bully. This bloke should have lived in a cave on his own – he is no good to anyone. After a few doubles, I thought the time was right to deal with this piece of shit so I followed him to the toilet. He was standing at the urinals, just about to have a piss when he heard me come in. He turned round and said, 'All right, Ron . . . ?'

Before he even finished his sentence, I belted the fucker as hard as I could right in that fat gob of his. For a big lad he went down like a sack of shit. In a bundle of fat mess on the floor, he stuttered:

'A-a-a, w-w-why, Ronnie? P-p-p-please don't hit me again. Th-th-thought we were mates?'

I bent over and grabbed him by his throat, and said, 'Mates!? You fucking horrible fat piece of shit. You are nothing but a gutless bully-boy cunt. You like bashing scroats when they are bent up, do ya? You fucking coward! If I ever see you do anything like that again, I'm going to the Governor. And I will still do ya again! Do you understand me, you cunt?'

'Yes, yes, yes, yes,' he yelled back, with tears rolling down his cheeks, about like a snake in acid, and he'd pissed himself, too, the dirty cunt. When I got out of the toilet, Horrible Scouse was sitting in the bar.

'You just did Hitler in the bog, didn't ya?' Scouse said, grinning from ear to ear.

'Yeah mate!' I answered.

That wanker Hitler only tried to make a complaint about me giving him a clump – when I could have got the useless waste of space suspended! I dealt with him in a better and less underhand way. Some of you will agree with how I handled it; some will think I handled it wrong.

I got called into The Dep's office to explain. The Dep (Deputy Governor) was a gentleman, a real fair man, one of the few left in the Service. He asked me what happened and I told him straight. He asked if I would put in a complaint on paper about what I had witnessed. I said, 'No,' and that I'd dealt with it. He sorted it all out, giving Hitler a compulsory transfer to another jail. He also got the prisoner a transfer to a Cat D.

I later heard that Hitler got dragged into a cell by five cons and had the fuck kicked out of him. His shit interpersonal skills, attitude, manner and bullying tactics eventually caught up with him. He got done properly. He got medically retired after that. Couldn't have happened to a nicer bloke.

Using force to control and restrain a prisoner is something that is always going to happen from time to time. As a Prison Officer, you are entitled to place a prisoner under restraint any time that you feel your personal safety is under threat. Now this is the tricky bit: what I may tolerate could be a lot less than you, or vice versa; however, that does not make it wrong. You might let a con punch you in the face before you attempt to drop him. Not me. I was not paid to be a six-foot punch bag. I'm paid far too little to be that.

I judged every situation at the time. There might be a prisoner swearing his head off at me, saying all kinds of stuff. However, on weighing things up, I might realise that he is blowing hot air. He is frustrated with the system, not me. He is not going to punch me, he just sees the shirt, he sees me as the authority, so he wants to shout at me, but that's it. If you can't handle that, then why the hell choose this as your job? But, on the other hand, there might be a prisoner who would stand close to me, or say something in a particular way, and I would drop him. It could be that he is clucking from smack, or that I've noticed severe irrational behaviour, or maybe I know him and that he loves to bash anything that gets in his way.

People out there who have ever had a fight – in the school playground, in a pub or in the ring – will know, just before it kicks off, that horrible gut feeling that someone is going to try and hurt you. You know it's coming. When I get this gut feeling, that's when I will use force. Don't get me wrong, sometimes I've underestimated someone, or not read the situation correctly and I've received a good clump. I will tell you now that, when this has happened, I have stuck one back on them pretty bloody quickly. I wouldn't let them take liberties with me when I was trying to do a job. On the other hand, bully-boy screws, who take the piss and abuse the use of force, are gutless, cowardly, weak individuals who are scum. When I say 'abuse' it, I mean when other Officers are there helping to restrain a con, and one of them sticks in a cheap punch or whatever – completely unjustified.

When a prisoner gets placed under restraint, this procedure takes three Officers. That might sound excessive or unfair, but it's not. It is the safest and most effective way of using pain compliance, which is essentially what it is. If you have a refractory prisoner who is refusing to comply with a lawful order, he is then controlled and restrained using pain until he complies. When he complies, you ease off on using pain. If he decides to play up again, then the pain is reapplied.

One Officer takes control of the prisoner's head. Once the inmate is under restraint, he will be the one who communicates with him, checking his health, talking to him, trying to de-escalate it to a level where the prisoner can be released from restraint and walk to The Seg. The remaining two Officers are each controlling one arm, using Ikedo-based arm and wrist locks to apply pain when necessary. That is a very basic guide to how it works. It is complex, with a variety of different moves to control a prisoner, but it works very well. It puts the Old Bill to shame. Any Prison Officer – or con, for that matter – will tell you the same. The Old Bill couldn't control and restrain a fucking mouse if it put up resistance. I have no idea what they are taught but, whatever it is, it's shit!

You are also taught to wrap someone up, in the comfort of a dojo, with the prisoner (an Officer acting the part) being relatively compliant. You can act, but it will never be the same as someone truly kicking off. You are also taught the correct techniques of three screws to one inmate – but how often will you be standing there with two other screws ready to assist? Especially when you are on a landing with one hundred cons and two screws. So, nine times out of ten, you will have to start restraining the scroat yourself. That's when you use reasonable force to control the prisoner until other Officers arrive to assist in applying the correct C&R techniques. What that means, one-on-one, is that you do what ever it takes to get hold of the bastard before he gets hold of you. This is sometimes when punches or kicks can be justified because it is one-on-one. But that stops when other Officers attend, because now you have the resources to restrain him properly. That's when it should stop, because the correct way with three does work. One-on-one, it doesn't. But some dirty, lowlife, bullying cowards see it is an opportunity to start punching the prisoner once the other two have turned up and are helping. Scum bags. This is what people think happens all the time, but it doesn't. There are not many of these wankers left, but I would not be being honest if I said there were none.

When you do use force, you have to fill in the 'Use of Force' form to explain why you restrained that prisoner. That, obviously is a reasonable requirement. But let's say you have been involved in a lot of incidents over a period of, say, a month. You might get pulled in and told you are using force too regularly. Now, who are they to say you should get punched first? That's almost calling you a liar, saying that you are bending people up for no reason. I've made it quite clear that I can't stand bullies, but being told you are using force too much is an extra pressure put on you that you don't need. It feels as if your integrity is being put into question. It's bollocks. You do a hard enough job in ridiculously poor conditions. Then, to top it off, you are not sure whether your management is going to support and trust your decision.

There are a few other times when you will wrap someone up, even when your personal safety may not be in question. A popular one is when a prisoner refuses to bang up. He is not necessarily being overaggressive or threatening to you but, no matter what you say to him, he is still refusing to go behind his door. If you are clever with words, you can normally manipulate these people to bang up. But sometimes they just keep refusing. At the end of the day, they can't sleep on the landing.

Another regular incident is when a prisoner refuses to transfer to another prison. The contractors who escort cons to court, and on transfer, won't take any inmate who has refused and been restrained. So, basically, if they refuse, they don't go until the Prison Service provides a Cat A bus for the transfer. This could take a few weeks, which is long enough to keep dealing or whatever else it is they want to stay for. However, they could then still refuse, which would result in them getting bent up and put on the bus.

I was working on The Twos when an Officer from reception turned up with someone for my landing. This fella had transferred to the Well for a court of appeal. When he came on to the landing for the first time, he was quiet but respectful. He was a thickset lad, huge muscles, big stature. I put him in his new cell while I read his file. I always did that, so I could familiarise myself with a new con's behaviour. I would take it into account, but always stay open-minded. I'd had many inmates that appeared to be shitbags, but whom I got on with fine. Once I'd read the file, I would then give them a chat where I told them what I expected of them and what they could expect of me. I would set the ground rules, explaining how it would work. I would always give them a chance.

This fella's prison history was diabolical. Staff assaults, prisoner fights, all sorts. This guy had been down The Block most of the time, a real handful. I got him into the office and gave him the talk. I told him exactly what he could expect from me as his landing screw, his entitlements and regime. I told him that he could start afresh, and I wouldn't judge him. But if I saw him bullying, or assaulting, then I would bounce him all they way down The Block without his feet touching the ground. I told him that I was an easy bloke to get on with; any problems and he could come to me. Just don't cross me. He appreciated my honesty. I didn't give him any bullshit. I told him exactly how it was. He took it well, and seemed like he wanted to keep his head down. He told me the nick he came from was terrible. He said that the staff had it in for him. If I had a penny for every time I'd heard that . . . It was possible though. I wasn't going to get into it. I was interested in his behaviour with me, no one else. We were a similar age. We got on fine. We understood each other.

He settled in nicely, always polite, conforming to the regime. I got him a job on the servery dishing out the food, so he kept himself busy. All the staff found him easy to work with. He understood how things were. He was at the Well for a while; the court case went on and on. He was finally jogged on by his appeal. He had to serve his life sentence. As the case was finished, he had to go back to his original prison. The morning of his transfer had come round. I told him that he needed to pack his kit because he was shipping out. He told me he was happy at the Well (fuck knows why!), that he felt more settled there. His behaviour reflected this. I spoke to the bosses for him; but they said he had to go. But no one *has* to go; they keep who they want. People get stuck at the Well when they shouldn't be, and want to be shipped out, so it's no drama to keep someone there. I pointed out that his prison conduct was one hundred per cent better. I pointed out that he said he was having a hard time at his previous nick. I didn't know the ins and outs, but it was clear for them to see. The staff at the other prison had reported his awful behaviour, but the staff at the Well had nothing but praise for his conduct. For once, prison was working for someone. They didn't give a fuck; sending him back was all they wanted to do. Everything's done the hard, difficult and irritating way with the Prison Service.

I told him that he had to go back. It was out of my hands.

He said, 'Sorry, Guv, you're gonna have a fight on your hands then.'

Calmly, he walked into his cell, and shut the door. He covered the spyhole and was making a lot of noise. I knew he was barricading. I couldn't blame him. I asked him once to come out and, in a controlled manner, he told me he wasn't going to. We had turned a decent con into a barricade situation. Amazing how something so simple gets so fucked up. I informed my SO and Duty Governor who ordered me to get kitted up in protective riot gear.

When you have an incident on the landing where someone kicks off, it happens when you least expect it. On the other hand, there are times when you know that you are going to have to drop someone. Prisoners sometimes decide to barricade themselves inside their cells (or some other confined area). They do this for protests, to take hostages or to be anti-social, rule-breaking cunts.

Yet again, it can be because the Prison Service are one-dimensional wankers, just like they were being in this situation – and it all could have been so easily avoided.

When negotiations have failed, a planned intervention is what comes next. This is when you get a team of Officers to change into full riot kit and enter the area of barricade, using force to take the perpetrator down. The full riot kit is worn for safety reasons as a precaution. If the con or cons have barricaded inside their cell, they would have smashed the place to bits in order to achieve that, which means that they will have chair or table legs, perfect little weapons. You have to devise a tactical advance, how best to get in there and take them down. Since they obviously don't want to talk, negotiations have failed and fighting is all they want to do. Kitting up is the only way. Like anything else, you choose screws who are good at kitting up. You are not going to send in some nine-stone, piss-wet-through wimp. It won't work, never mind how much the 'equality' thing is taking over. Sometimes you would get a bird to go in, a token gesture of diversity. The fact of the matter is, do you send in a lump who can do it well, or someone who hasn't got the ability to restrain a kitten? Being six foot four (and a bit of a lump!), and with the ability to restrain correctly and efficiently, I was selected regularly to kit up if required. It's playing to your strengths. Paperwork wasn't my strong point. Not because I couldn't do it: most of it was a waste of fucking time and effort, preventing you from getting on with the job.

I knew this wasn't a con who wasted words, and he wasn't going to go quietly. They sent the negotiators to the door to try and talk him down. I knew that was a waste of fucking time. The negotiators weren't getting anywhere. He wasn't shouting but he did say that, if they wanted him to go, they would have to go in and get him. I and two others were kitted up, ready to go in. I knew this didn't need to happen, but the Governors wanted him to move. There was no alternative. The three of us moved quietly to the side of the door, charging ourselves up for a fight. The negotiator asked him one last time if he would come out. He didn't want to play ball.

The door was opened. His barricade wasn't hard to get through. He'd broken up his furniture, but not built anything that was too difficult to smash down. But his fucking floor was difficult to walk on; he'd covered it in baby oil and butter. You try walking on that at pace without falling over! He'd greased his arms up the same. He'd been bent up dozens of times, he knew the techniques. He knew exactly how to make it difficult for us. He was strong as an ox as well. When dealing with a barricade, the lead man goes in with the shield. I was lead man and the other screws were tucked in nice and tight behind me. It took us fucking ages to grab hold of him. Restraining him was one thing; getting him out of the cell was a mission in itself. Lots of struggling, lots of fighting. We eventually managed to manoeuvre him out on to the landing. Fuck me, he was strong. Once he was out, we cuffed him and handed him over to three other Officers who were waiting to take over. Normal procedure. Always have a team waiting to assist. The first team could be tired or hurt. If they are hurt, they may lose focus; start getting a little heavy-handed. It's a fine line. The spare team took over and carried him to The Seg. He had a bloodied mouth and was breathing heavily. He'd put up a good scrap.

'It's come to this, Mr Thompson? I stuck to your rules. Why, Guv? Why?' he said, as he was being carried away from me. How could I answer him? How could I justify the reasons for it all? I couldn't, there was no need for it. Red tape; management shit. They ain't got a clue.

Obviously, the waiting contractors would not take him under restraint, since they refused anyone who put up a fight. He was kept down The Block until a Cat A bus was organised to take him away. There was no choice. Ten days later, the bus arrived. He could go on it of his own accord, or under restraint. He walked on to the bus. He knew there was no point in fighting it. He was going no matter what.

Full riot kit can save your life. When you go into a barricade, ninety-nine per cent of the prisoners are tooled up. If they have barricaded, then they are definitely up for a scrap. Every Officer is trained to do a cellular planned intervention – a Control & Restraint entry. You learn that on training in Wakey. At the Well, they always sent in their lumps, so I was always doing the bloody things. Being useful at C&R is a good thing. You get a reputation, round the nick, for being able to handle yourself. It is also good because people trust you and feel safe with you.

Everyone wanted to get trained to Operation Tornado standard. This is a riot response team, which reacts to any concerted indiscipline within any secure unit in the country. That is when the problem can no longer be held at local level; they need more screws, more backup. Be it an HMP establishment, a private establishment or an immigration centre, a Tornado Unit will respond. Some of these incidents appear on the news but many don't. The local police force always receives recognition for anything they accomplish. The Prison Service never gets the recognition they deserve.

I'd been in not much over a year. It normally takes at least a couple of years before you are picked to train for the Tornados. They recognised my strengths. I was told I would be an asset on the team. They knew I was competent; they knew I was good. I was sent on the Tornado course. I was chuffed. I wanted it. I was looked upon with high esteem for being chosen. (Well, by the C&R team, at least; some of the Governors thought I was too hands-on.)

There was an Officer called Si that I got sent on the course with. He was a top bloke; one of my own. We travelled up together. He was full of shit, but harmless. He would tell so many white lies, I didn't know whether he was real or a fragment of my imagination! We turned up to the training centre. It was amazing from day one. We were running around, fighting, shouting, loving it. We got petrol bombed, bricked, punched, kicked, stamped on, the lot!

It is great fun, though, getting to spend a week marching around in full riot kit. The good thing is that, once you have done the training, you are able to go out on riot calls, which are always interesting. On the course, you have Officers from all over the country who've come to train. So yep, you got it; it's like Wakey but for only one week!

There were also Officers from private nicks. What a sorry bunch of useless cunts they were. They hadn't got a fucking clue about bugger all. I feel sorry for the cons banged up there.

Si and I were doing well. We were coming top in every part of the course. It was all practical, no theory. You had to get stuck in and fight. Si and I were fucking good at that! He and I were always jovial, taking the piss, but turning Governor when we needed to. We were Jack the Lads really. Si sensed that these lads from the private nick were annoyed that we kept taking the piss.

They were always fucking things up. When we did an exercise, they would ruin it by being so crap. So, obviously, we got stuck into them, pointing out their errors and how to correct them.

On the Wednesday, everyone went out on the piss. Si and I had been out every night, but on the Wednesday the whole course attended. We crawled from one pub to the next, all of us pissed up. We were in a pub, when one of the private-nick Officers gave Si a bollocking. Si didn't hang about. He didn't want to argue. He banged this fella out. Quick as lightning, I couldn't believe it. One of this fella's mates jumped in so I had no choice, I clumped him and put him on his arse. He jumped up, and I warned him to go and get a drink or he would get another one on his chin. He fucked off. Si was pissing himself with laughter; he thought the whole thing was funny as fuck. I thought, 'Oh shit, we're both going to be kicked off the course and disciplined.' He didn't give a shit, but I was worried that we were in big trouble. Nothing happened, and we got away with it. Full respect to the lads we scrapped with, they said fuck all. One had a black eye and the other had a fat lip. When the instructors asked how they got them, they both said they fell over. The instructors knew exactly what we had done. Good lads, though, they kept their gobs shut. After that week, Si and I were nicknamed Batman and Robin.

You would think that with all the training, people would always be ready to jump in when there is an alarm, right? Wrong. There is a problem at the other end of the spectrum: the shithouses who are scared to react to an alarm and use force. Why the fuck do these people join the Prison Service? What do they really think it will be like? It amazes me. They must think that it is going to be like a school playground. It is obvious that, as a screw, you will have to fight with the cons from time to time. They are criminals, and a lot of them are not afraid to try and cut your face off. But you still get Officers joining the job who are scared of their own shadows. These wankers are just as bad as the bullies. They will see you scrapping and walk the other way. They will see a con getting the hiding of his life and look the other way. They are too scared to do fuck all except save their own arse.

Remember Doubtfire? He had a terrible experience with the shithouse type. He was working on the Fraggle Unit when this incident occurred. Some clucking junkie got into a row with him. All of a sudden, this dirty little bastard jumped at Doubtfire, sinking his teeth into his neck. Blood was pissing out everywhere, but this fucker still had Doubtfire's neck in his mouth. A horrible cunt Officer called Abu was standing next to him when it happened. He walked the other way. To make it worse, he didn't even raise the alarm. So Doubtfire is wrestling with some nutter who is trying to bite his throat out, and Abu walks the other way, without even letting other screws know what is happening. Eventually, a con helped Doubtfire get hold of the junkie. I heard the alarm bell ring, so I ran to attend. When I arrived, there was blood everywhere; Doubtfire was a real mess. We bent that wanker up hard. He didn't respond to pain much, though; he was off his fucking head. The con who helped Doubtfire saved his life. That goes back to what I said about forging good relationships with the prisoners. If Doubtfire had been a bad screw, no con would have given him a second look. Because he was excellent at his job, he had good rapport with the cons and this went on to save his life. The con was well looked after for his help.

An investigation resulted in . . . Nothing. Abu got fuck all for what he did. Doubtfire told me that if he ever became terminally ill, or was going down, he would kill Abu. He is a ginger lunatic, so he probably would. I can understand it, though; this shithouse is watching him get seriously assaulted, which could have killed him, and he walks off. What a horrible cunt. Doubtfire had to have a test for HIV, hepatitis, and every dirty germ a junkie could be carrying. Lucky sod, he had nothing. Abu wasn't watching his back, but someone was, that day, for him to survive all that.

These are the sorts of people you have to work with; it really is a shambles. I hate people who use their race, gender, disability or sexual orientation to manipulate the system. It undermines the serious cases of abuse that really go on. If people are experiencing discrimination for any reason, then I encourage investigation. But people who abuse the system by using these issues are a disgrace.

There are many scenarios you are faced with when force is necessary. You have to be ready to react within a split second because, when you least expect it, you will have to roll around on the floor with some idiot.

As a result of all this use-of-force training and the experience I had built, I was one hundred per cent confident. I knew I would always be able to do the job correctly and professionally. What could possibly go wrong . . . ?

CONS WITH KEYS

The drugs, the weapons, the bullying, the power: that is prison culture. It's all about how much drugs they can deal, how many people they can batter and how many gangs they can lead. I've already said that you get some gear coming through Visits. It's standard; you are always going to get visitors trying to pass contraband to the cons. But you are never going to get the large amounts through Visits that are required to serve up (enough for drug dealing). I'm not talking about a bit of puff, or enough smack to chase the dragon. I am talking about masses and masses of drugs. More than you would get from a dealer on the road. You name it, it can be found in prison. Pills, puff, Special K (ketamine), Charlie, uppers, downers, crack and smack, it is all there. There is only one way that they can get in this large amount of gear and that is from bent screws, or, as I like to call them, 'cons with keys'. These fuckers would bring in an atomic bomb for the right price.

All that these cons with keys are interested in doing is making money for their greedy, bastard selves. They don't have any loyalty to the uniform or to the job that screws are trying to do. They don't even have any loyalty to cons they are dealing to. They will go to whoever pays the most, simple as that. We all have money worries and struggle to make ends meet, but we work hard, we do overtime. I've struggled with money, and pissed all of mine away. But I would not even consider doing that. I would never be a trafficking piece of shit. No matter how low I've got, I have always been proud enough of trying to do my job well and effectively, never to stoop to drug dealing.

Some of these wankers are just too tempted by the money that is offered. Some join the job specifically to traffic. There have been some of these cunts that have been caught out and, once investigated, it turned out they were already part of a firm before they joined the Prison Service. These slags are worse than any con.

You know where you stand with a prisoner. He is a criminal and, if he can, he will get one over you. You expect that, it's all a part of being in prison. You can go back to the goodies and baddies theory. Stick to that, and you can't go far wrong. But bent screws are fucking horrible. Who can you trust? You never know. You don't know who is bent and who isn't. Sometimes you have an idea, but that comes with recognising the signs. You only recognise the signs once you have built up some experience, and your jail craft is good.

You can't teach jail craft, it comes with time. Most of the time you haven't got a fucking clue who is trafficking. They wouldn't be very fucking good if everyone knew what they were up to. It takes all sorts; there is no such thing as a stereotypical bent screw. You would think an over-familiar screw could be at it, but that isn't always the case; sometimes, that's just the screw's way of communicating.

There was an Officer who I had been working with since I had started. He was a good bloke; I had learnt a lot from him. The management hated him. They didn't like his Dagenham accent, his Dagenham ways. He was a geezer.

The Governors thought he was over-familiar. He wasn't; it was his way, his style. It worked for him. He was shit-hot at the job, but if you don't fit into what the Governors want, they will do what they can to fuck you up.

He was a great geezer, had a brilliant way with the cons and the staff. He was straight down the line with all of them. He was never interested in being addressed as Mr or Guv. He would let the inmates call him by his first name and he would address them the same way. Great, it worked for him. He had respect from all the inmates and he got the job done. That way wouldn't work for me, but then we are all different.

The Governors hated his style. You just can't please them cunts! It got him in trouble in a lot of ways. You see, if you suspect someone is at it, or you get some Intel that someone is at it, you report it to the security department. So loads of screws would report him for being too familiar, thinking that he may be at it. He wasn't but, because of this, he had a world of shit from the managers. They were always searching him, telling him that they were 'gonna have him'. He would always tell me what they did to him. They completely victimised the poor sod. They got away with it, too, because they said it was 'work based on

107

intelligence for the interests of the establishment'. Sneaky fuckers. They were acting on Intel but it was still harassment. They knew he wasn't bent, but they wouldn't let it lie.

I was on duty when a Governor called me into his office. A spotty bastard with thick-rimmed glasses, he was. He told me that this Officer had been suspended on suspicion of corruption. He asked me if I'd noticed anything. I told him that, if I had, I would have put it on paper. I told him I thought that he was an outstanding screw, and that the suspension was a load of bollocks. That didn't go down well at all.

I felt sorry for this Officer; he was a good bloke. An excellent screw, fair and firm. You could always count on him, too; he would get stuck in if necessary. Cons felt safe with him and the screws felt safe working with him. His suspension didn't last long, but they still didn't leave him alone when he came back.

If you go to security with some Intel on a bent screw, you have to be very selective as to who you tell. You could get some Intel on a screw, put it on paper and take it to a fella in security; then he runs back and tells that Officer you've put a paper in on him. Great isn't it?! You can't trust anyone. So if the person you've named finds out, they have the right hump. You might think to yourself, 'I would have the hump if someone put a paper in on me.' But that's the business you are in when you put the uniform on. If you have got nothing to hide, then there should be no reason to be worried if a paper goes in about you. I've had a couple of my mates come to me before and say, 'So and so's said that you're at it,' etc etc. I have said every time, 'Put it on paper.' It can protect you as well, you see. Some scroat could be chatting bollocks to loads of screws, spreading loads of shit. Security will get hold of that and deal with him.

It always makes me think twice if someone panics when they find out a paper has gone in about them. That's why I have never felt guilty about-putting in a paper on anyone, friend or otherwise. If you are not doing anything wrong, then you have got nothing to worry about. Bent screws are fucking horrible, and the more that get caught, the better.

There is a lad called Dave that I used to work with. He was a top lad, a real joker. He had about twelve or thirteen years in the Service. He was from the local area, so he knew a lot of the cons. He didn't try to hide this at all. He was always under suspicion for dealing. I'm told that papers went in about him nearly straight away and, thirteen years later, they were still coming in thick and fast. He knew the job inside and out and he was good at it. There wasn't much he couldn't deal with. It would be hard not to be good after that length of time. He could handle, quickly and efficiently, any query thrown his way. If something kicked off, he would get stuck in. So, all round, he was a pretty decent screw.

But there was something that wasn't right about him. I could never put my finger on it. I was obviously aware of all the suspicion of him in the past, and he was open about it, anyway. I'd also made a good contact in the Intel department, so I was also aware of the types of allegations that were made. I would not let any of this sway my judgement. I wanted to make my own mind up about him.

Some screws will hear a bit of Intel, jump on the bandwagon and throw loads of papers towards security. Not lies but, as they watch the suspect so closely, they actually believe they are witnessing corrupt activity. They would be saying things like, 'Oh my God, he just came out of a cell!' Well, of course he did, he's a fucking screw! It's admirable that they want to be a part of the Intel and catch the bent bastards, but they should only tell Intel about what they see, not what they think they see. That's why it's important that sensitive Intel stays in security and doesn't make it back to the Wings.

I worked with Dave closely for a couple of months. He was good but, as I said, something just didn't ring right. Sometimes I would think he was being a bit too close to a con, or that he disappeared too often. I would then tell myself to stop jumping on the bandwagon, but it was happening *too* often. I also heard from a good mate that Dave liked a bit of Charlie at the weekends. But that doesn't make him bent.

Then a lad approached me. He was new on the Wing. He'd never been inside before, so he didn't know how things worked. I showed him some compassion and tried to help him as much as I could. A couple of weeks later, this con told me that Dave was bringing in gear for his cellmate. I put it to paper, and took it to the security PO. I didn't know if it was kosher but I couldn't think why it wouldn't be. The con was new, so he had no reason to lie – except that his cellmate was a little junkie scroat piece of shit. Maybe he told my grass to tell me that, to throw security off the real scent. Or maybe my grass was telling me because he trusted me and hated his little cunt cellmate. I didn't know. I didn't really want to know. I did my bit by telling security. It was up to them what they did with the Intel.

I never noticed Dave doing anything untoward, really. He was, as I said, a fairly decent screw and a good lad. I enjoyed working with him. But since I had that Intel myself, I would be lying if I said I didn't watch him closer. I did. I heard rumours that his taste for coke had got big and he was bang on it every time he went out. I don't know if that was true, but those were the rumours.

Suddenly, Dave was moved off the Wing and put on a job working the gate. He was fuming, to say the least. He was saying he had been victimised, the wankers etc etc. But, I asked myself, was he angry because he was being victimised, or was he angry because he was no longer on the Wing, so he couldn't deal any more? The gate is a cushy number. He wasn't even put on the main gate, either. That can get busy from time to time: visitors, Officers, enquiries, the full works. Even so, the no-prisoner-contact is a stress release. It's a good number. Same money, no stress. Dave was put on the contractors' gate. Easiest fucking job going! I would have begged to be put on there. All you do is let in the contractors, search them and search their vehicles. The rest of the time you can sit there, scratching, itching, sleeping – all for the same money: it is a touch to say the least. How could he be bothered about going there? Why? Something didn't click with him. I didn't know if it was a witch hunt or whether Dave was the most amazing bent screw ever. I shouldn't say 'amazing bent screw'. None of them are amazing; all of them are scum.

I never saw him after that. He went on long-term sick leave. I heard that the police were detailed to spin his house, and all sorts. You never know what's true and what's bullshit. I don't know what happened to him. To this day, I still can't make my mind up about him. I just don't know if he was bent or not. If he was, he was bloody good at not giving the job enough to catch him.

My jail craft was getting better and better. I was noticing more and more. I had networked a nice handful of grasses who were giving me bits and pieces. I was finding weapons, drugs and mobile phones regularly. They were giving me nice finds. Things were going well. I had a good rapport with the security department; I was giving them quality Intel, which was helping the Wing run a little better. I had managed to split up gangs, prevent fights and help the bullied. I'm not stupid; most of my grasses were drug users or dealers themselves. They only grassed to benefit themselves – never for the good of mankind. They would grass on a rival gang or on someone who was bullying them. I couldn't give a fuck about their reasons; I was just interested in the info they gave me. They weren't doing it for an honourable cause but, if it did have an honourable outcome, then great.

I looked after my grasses well. Always made sure they had the best cell, best job, or anything they wanted, within reason. They would normally have a bargaining tool anyway. They would tell me that they had some info. They would then tell me what they wanted in return. If I could arrange it, I would. If I needed higher authority, I would get it. It would normally be a cell move, or a course they wanted to do. Sometimes more tobacco or something like that. If it was really sensitive Intel, they would ask for something bigger, such as a category decrease and a jail transfer. So, if they were a Cat B prisoner, they would ask to be downgraded to a D and transferred to an Open Prison. That is a big ask, but it can still be arranged if the powers that be consider the Intel worth it.

In the Intel I was receiving, Deano's name kept popping up. Nothing specific, just cons suggesting this and that, but I used to write it down, anyway. I was bothered by it, though. Deano was a mate of mine. He seemed like a good lad. I tried to put it to the back of my mind. If he'd done fuck all wrong, he had nothing to worry about.

I went in to work one morning (I'd been at home the night before with Danielle, so I was up at stupid o'clock) and, during my shift that day, one of my grasses approached me and asked for a 'chat'. He was a con who had been in and out of nick all his life. He was a known junkie who normally did runs for the big dealers. He would do a bit of running and they would sort him out with gear to feed his habit. That's what he was like on the road, too; he was always out thieving and robbing. This time inside, though, he had decided to try and sort himself out. He thought that it was time to try and go straight. He was forty fucking five, so you could say it was about time! Shouldn't joke really. It's commendable at any age. He started grassing to me, so it would help him stay off the gear. He saw it as, 'Take away the temptation, you take away the habit.'

In return, I tried my best to help him. I got him on every detox, course and programme available. At the same time, I was managing to find loads of contraband on the Wing. This was great for my reputation and for the Wing. (There are many cons who would disagree with that, though!) It was good to see this geezer had really sorted himself out and got hold of his habit.

On this particular day, when he approached me for a chat, I was surprised because he'd not grassed in a long time. He was clean and keeping his head down, so there was no real motive for him to grass any more. I took him in to the office and said, 'Yes Davis, what can I do for you? You're not back on the gear are you, for fuck's sake?'

'Nah Guv, I'm not touching that shit again. I've got my missus and kid to think about now.'

'What do you want, then?'

'I need me Cat D, Guv. I need to be able to have home leave and stuff, to sort myself out, build me family, you know how it is.'

'I ain't a fucking magician! No chance son,' I said, shattering his dreams.

'It's good stuff, Mr T. I can give you a bent screw, who he's working for, what he's getting paid, the fucking lot!'

'I will have a word, and see what I can do. Tell me who he is first, then I will arrange what I can.'

'You know better than that, Mr T. I ain't a cunt! See what you can do first, and then we will talk.'

With that, he left the office. I wasn't entirely sure if it would be kosher. These people say the sky is purple and that they can walk on water if it gets them what they want. However, Davis did usually come up trumps. It was a big ask, though. He had been in and out of prison dozens of times, always for petty theft and drugs, and that would go a long way to preventing him from getting his Cat D. Plus he'd been a toe-rag on the other sentences he'd served. He wasn't a lifer who had the last part of his sentence to serve, so that was out of the window. So it would be up to the security PO, simple as that.

I went to see them about the chat I'd had with Davis. The security PO was called Mr Leon. He was an ex-Para – straight as a die and hard as nails. There was only one thing he hated more than cons, and that was cons with keys. He despised them. He thought that they should all be lined up and shot. He was five foot ten, stocky and fit as fuck. He would come to work and be in the gym every morning at six. He would run five or six miles. Then at lunchtime he would return to the gym to do weight training. He was a real alpha-male tough bastard. He had the perfect squaddie tache as well. The best thing about him was you could trust him. What you told him, stayed with him.

He wanted to police the prison and do it properly. For that reason, he would have major run-ins with the Governors. He was outspoken, determined and would not let anyone get in his way or stop him from doing his job correctly. Governors included. They didn't like his military way of running things. They always wanted him to ease up. Basically, treat the place like a fucking hotel, and the prisoners as customers. He wouldn't have it. He always did things the Leon way.

He was perfect for the job of security PO. I would always go to him with things. I told him about my chat with Davis. Mr Leon wanted to know whether I thought it would be good Intel. I said that the chances are it would be good, going on his previous for grassing. Mr Leon said that it wouldn't be a problem getting Davis transferred to a Cat D. He has done all of the drugs courses, and offending behaviour courses, so it would appear he had sorted himself out. Mr Leon left it to me to go and get the goods.

The next day that I was on duty, I went to Davis's cell for a chat.

'Hello Mr T, have you got some good news for me?'

'That depends if you are chatting shit or not.'

I had to take him off the Wing for a chat so no cons or Officers would notice we were having lengthy discussions. As he was a grass of mine, it would have been easy for people to notice that we were always talking. If the cons were to get wind of the fact he was a grass, he would be fucked. He wouldn't be safe anywhere.

And if other Officers know you have a grass, they will pester him for info themselves; they will want a piece of the glory. This can break the trust you have with your grass, because he will think that you are telling every fucker in the staff room what he is telling you. That worries him because, as any con or screw will tell you, screws are the worst gossipers in the world. You must keep it quiet for their safety and so that they keep giving you the Intel that you need. Another reason to take them off the Wing is that, if a screw has good jail craft, he or she will notice that you are spending a lot of time with one particular inmate. This would result in him or her communicating with the security dept, suspecting you are bent. This doesn't matter if you aren't doing anything wrong, but dealing with a grass is best kept as low key as possible. You don't even tell your line manager, just deal with the boss of security.

Once I'd taken Davis to a nice quiet spot off the Wing, we began our discussion.

'It's all kosher, Guv. Can I get me Cat D then?' he asked eagerly.

'It's sorted, mate; but this better not be hot air, cos if it is, you ain't going nowhere. So, who is it? Talk to me.'

'Mr Atko (Deano). He's working for Jake's lot. He's bringing in anything for a price,' he whispered to me.

'Fuck off, Davis, you are talking bollocks.'

'Straight up, Guv.'

Jake had the money and he was the main supplier on the Wing. Also, Davis was a cousin of Jake's, so he would be risking a lot sharing that info. I realised he was telling the truth. He wasn't spinning me a load of bollocks. I'd heard Deano's name mentioned before, but nothing direct. I thought he was one of the good guys, though. I'd been out on the piss with this fella a few times. He wasn't one of my good mates, but I did think that he was all right.

Davis went on to tell me that Deano was selling mobile phones for five hundred quid a throw. That's right, five hundred quid for a shitty cheap mobile. Mobiles are a big thing in prison. With them, cons can run crime rackets straight from their cells. They can intimidate witnesses, or just ring their bird. Whatever the reason, mobiles are worth big money and, apparently, Deano was bringing in loads of them. Davis also told me Deano was bringing in drugs by the sack load. Apparently, he was meeting one of Jake's firm on the road to collect the gear and the payment. He would then swap many of his day shifts for nights. When he came in for nights, he would bring in a takeaway pizza. He would then put the gear under his pizza. Once on the Wing, he would hide the gear there somewhere. One of Jake's lot would go and get it once the cells were unlocked in the morning. Davis told me that Deano was earning thousands each week.

I wasn't in the position of making decisions, or even having opinions. I carried out my duty and told Mr Leon. I told him that I was shocked. He wasn't. It turns out there had been a dozen or so Intel leads on Deano. All from good sources as well. Then it all clicked into place. Deano was always skint and then, all of a sudden, he had a brand new Audi and wanted to go out on the piss the whole time. When asked how he got his money, he said that he'd released some equity on his house. We all said that he should be careful not to piss it all against the wall. He didn't seem to give a fuck, so I naturally thought he was just a normal immature male, wasting his money on enjoying himself. Mr Leon thought otherwise. He said it was only a matter of time before he slipped up enough to be caught. How could I have misjudged someone so badly? But it takes all sorts, and there is no typical bent screw.

Once I had received that Intel, I watched him more. I wanted to see if he would let anything slip to me. I wanted to catch him red-handed. The days went by, but I saw nothing. I knew that he wouldn't admit wholeheartedly that he was bent (if he was), but I thought that, with a load of ale and vodka in him, he might just give something up. So, I went out on the piss with him. Not alone; I organised a staff piss up. I made sure that I spent as much of the night with him as possible. What he did give to me was that he loved to swallow pills and go clubbing. He told me that, whenever he went out with his mates, he got bang on it. But he didn't give me anything else at all.

It was down to Mr Leon now. He said that the Intel I had given him was very valuable and thanked me. He was a man of his word and got the move for Davis. So Davis got his move and we got valuable info – it was all good. The only thing, though, was that this bent screw was still at it.

A month went by and then when I turned up for duty as normal, Mr Leon was waiting at the gate for me. He took me up to his office and said, 'Ronnie, this is it, we've got the cunt.'

There were a couple of plain-clothed coppers there, too. Mr Leon told me that Deano was bringing in some gear today. He wanted me and another couple of Officers to meet him at the gate and escort him upstairs.

'What if he refuses to come upstairs, or tries to make a run for it?' I asked.

'Bend the cunt up!' demanded Mr Leon, with the two coppers nodding in agreement.

I went downstairs with the other screws. We were all nervous, thinking about the possible outcome. We all knew what it was about; we had all given some Intel. Mr Leon wanted it that way.

He wanted us to have some of the glory of it. We were all waiting, eager for Deano's arrival – when he turned up, walking through the first security door. That's when he saw the three of us standing there. The colour literally fell out of his face. He looked terrified.

'All right lads, what's up?'

'We gotta go upstairs, mate,' one of the screws said to him.

With that, we escorted him upstairs. He didn't make a fuss at all. But he looked like he was absolutely shitting himself. He did ask us what it was about but we ignored him. The two coppers and Mr Leon were there waiting. Deano looked like he was going to fucking pass out.

'Thanks, gentlemen,' Mr Leon firmly announced, meaning fuck off.

We waited in the other office in case we were needed, and because we were nosey bastards who wanted to know what the fuck was going to happen. After about twenty minutes, they came out of the office. Deano was cuffed with the two coppers and Mr Leon escorting him. That was the last time I ever saw Deano in person.

They escorted him round to his staff quarter, where they had a warrant to search it. On the way round there he was panicking like fuck. When they were asking him which room was his, he was mumbling trying to make out he didn't have a room. But Mr Leon knew otherwise. The cunt wouldn't drive in from the Isle of Man every day would he? Stupid fucking idiot, he didn't know what he was saying.

When they eventually got to his room, Deano was soaked with sweat, and I mean all of his clothes fucking saturated, the dirty bastard. As soon as they got inside, they could see loads of drug paraphernalia on his dressing table. I mean there were fucking bongs, pipes, burnt tinfoil, naked razor blades, wraps, the full works. Apparently, as soon as Deano noticed they saw it, he dived towards it in sheer terror, trying to grab hold of it. So this twat is cuffed, he's got two coppers and the hardest screw in the world with him, and he thought . . . ? ? Well I haven't got a clue what he thought. He was stopped from getting to any of it: I hear it was a firm kick in the bollocks and a clump in the ear. The coppers went on to search the room. They then marched Deano out, along with the shit they found.

I was up in the CCTV room watching as they took Deano round to his quarters, so I saw them go in and I waited patiently until they came out. I wanted to see the look on that wanker's face. It would give me an idea if they found anything. When they marched him out, he was blubbering like a fucking baby. He looked hysterical. I was sitting there with the two other screws who met Deano at the gate. What a prick. What did he think the outcome would be? If you play with fire . . . Old saying, but true. They put him in the back of a car and sped off.

There were all sorts of rumours that he was going down. There were rumours that Deano was a smackhead himself, using it at work etc etc. If he was going down he deserved it. If you are bent, you deserve everything that comes your way.

While the investigation was being carried out, Deano was suspended on full pay. You would think that whatever he had in that room would have been enough to sack him right away. Not for the Prison Service: they do everything arse about face.

Apparently the Old Bill had seized loads of his possessions, including that lovely Audi of his. They spent months building a case against him. Surely this was going to be a good one. Surely he was going to get his comeuppance – after all the excellent work from the screws that got the brilliant Intel and the hard work from the Old Bill.

They decided his fate . . . a caution.

They had Intel of how big his corruption was, they had Intel that he was making shitloads of money, and he got a poxy caution. Pathetic. Apparently, the gear they seized wasn't enough to convict for dealing, and their Intel about his trafficking wasn't good enough to stand up in court. So all he had to do was say that he had a drug problem and the drugs were for personal use. He also got his possessions back because they couldn't prove that they were paid for with dirty money.

I hear that they phoned him up to say that he'd been sacked, and that the letter was to follow. Apparently he laughed down the phone, the piece of shit. OK, he lost his job, but that's it. He then put his uniform on eBay, the cheeky cunt!

The Intel went deeper than even I knew about. On the back of this investigation, they did various night searches. There were unbelievable amounts of gear found. Loads of smack, crack and mobiles. The most worrying thing that they found was half-a-dozen bullets. Yes, real bullets. I heard the Intel suggested that he was going to bring in a gun for fifty grand. For them to find fucking bullets, there must have been some severe shit going down. Imagine that one day you turn up for work and unlock a cell. You get into a row with a con about his canteen which results in him putting a pistol in your boat! It is a disgusting, dangerous possibility. Prison Officers are subjected to shit, but that is a level that should never be reached.

Deano was either extremely clever and one step ahead, or the jammiest cunt alive. I don't know for sure, but I would put my money on the latter. Rumours started to go crazy. There were rumours that Deano was in cahoots with Dave, the lad I mentioned earlier. It was going round that Dave had showed Deano the ropes and they were doing it together. But obviously Deano was taking the most risks. Deano had not been in the job long, and it is unusual for someone to be in that deep so fast, but no one will ever know the exact truth of how they get into it.

The cons were then openly talking about Deano, telling us all sorts of shit. Apparently, Jake's firm had paid Deano an advance for loads of packages that he didn't deliver because he was caught. We heard that he never paid them back and had done a runner. Because of that, there was a contract put out on him. Fuck knows where he is, or what he's doing now, or if he's even alive. I also heard that his mum was an ex-con, something that he never declared when he joined. If that was the case, he only ever joined for one reason, to make money being bent.

He wasn't the only one that I got completely wrong. There was this Officer, in his mid-forties and a northerner, who joined the Prison Service and moved down south to earn a better living than he was getting at the time. Seemed a good bloke; I liked him. He did think he was a super screw; he loved the power. He was very strict, but that was the way he was. The cons knew where they stood with him. He would get into a lot of bend ups, and you could always count on him to back you up. Though he'd not been in the job long, he was a bit of a know-it-all; but, still, he was all right to work with. He seemed fucking good at catching cons out. He would always find them with drugs, mobiles or any contraband that they shouldn't have. OK, we all had our own grasses, little bits of Intel or whatever. If you were lucky, you might find something. If you were good, you would steadily tick over with finds. He was a fucking magician – nearly every fucking day – *and* he'd not been in the job long!

Normally when you have a find, or any incident, the con would point the finger at you. It's a natural instinct to them, so when I heard a couple of times, 'He brought the gear in for me, then nicked me!' I didn't think anything about it. Besides, most of the cons fucking hated him. He fancied himself as a bit of a security guru.

Security had been watching him for a while. Mr Leon had asked me a couple of times what I thought about him. I was told that they were watching him. I said they were wasting their time. They were barking up the wrong tree, as far as I was concerned.

Then I got the phone call. They had spun his staff quarter, found bags and bags of drugs and thousands in cash. He was nicked, bailed, suspended. Yet again, whose dick he was sucking I will never know. He got off, kept his job and got a transfer! I heard that he'd paid off forty per cent of his mortgage in eighteen months. You can get overtime, but that much can't have been paid for by traditional means. Maybe he gave someone up, fuck knows. He kept his job though.

But sometimes there are better results.

There was an OSG that security were watching. They had built up an Intel picture which said he was a dirty bent cunt and, once they had enough info on him, they met this OSG at the gate (as with Deano). I wasn't a part of that one; I had never received Intel on him. Anyway, once he turned up at the gate, he made a run for it. The screws fucking bent him up top class, the lowlife cunt. He was brought to court and received five years. There is a God. When they searched his car, he had forty-two mobile phones and stacks of drugs. He had bagfuls of smack on him when he turned up, too. Forty-two phones at a monkey each; you do the maths. It is a shitload of money.

These fellas are not even the tip of the iceberg. Corruption is a huge problem in prisons. It goes on every day. There are bent scum trying to undo every good bit of work that you do. There is big money to be made and these weak bastards do it every day, not giving a fuck about the safety or well-being of anyone else. They are feeding the habit of the junkies. No one is stable when intoxicated with that filth, so that, in itself, puts the staff and prisoners in danger of being assaulted by the drug addicts. They are not only making money, they are causing violence, injury and, in some cases, death. They are encouraging gang culture. Why can't these cons with keys do the job properly? The temptation of the easy buck. Dirty money is easier to earn. Corruption doesn't stop at dealing contraband: there is much more to it than that. And it doesn't stop at the rank of Officer: it goes a lot higher.

My eyes had been truly opened. It's crazy, really, how you become numb to the dangers of the job. That isn't good, because you become accustomed to the bad conditions instead of fighting to change them. The college teaches you how the bigwigs think the Prison Service operates, but the harsh reality is vastly different. It dawned on me very quickly that, as a screw, you really are a nurse, a copper, a probation officer, a carer, a councillor, a social worker and, of course, an incarcerator all in one. Oh, and a fucking punchbag to the cons and bosses.

POWERS TO SCREW

've told you about the bent screws that exist in the system, but there are many other levels of corruption. You get screws who abuse their authority, and you get screws who don't assist when required in a volatile situation. These cunts are as bad as each other, and should be dealt with accordingly. Do you think that the weak bastards, who walk the other way when a con or a screw is getting bashed, get dealt with? Do they bollocks. The Service doesn't seem to recognise the importance of dealing with these wankers.

D Wing hadn't seemed right for while. It was like something was waiting to happen. I had got to work and started the unlock as usual, but it was quieter than normal. It felt tense, as though something was brewing. A lot of times when there is a big kick off, you can sort of feel it in the air before it happens. The fluffy bastards don't notice fuck-all, but the screw does. It comes back to jail craft. You have it, or you don't.

There were these two cons called Smithy and Jacobs. They were both big cunts who could have a row. They were in rival gangs, but left each other alone. I got on with both of the lads well. I knew who they were, and what they did, but they played the game well and didn't cause staff too many problems. That's how it works: the real hard bastards don't give the screws too much grief. They know that the screws are just doing a job, simple as that. If there is a wanker screw, then they keep out of their way. They are generally the better cons to work with.

That day, though, it didn't feel right. I was standing on The Ones, searching the prisoners as they went out on to the yard for their morning exercise. There were two of us doing that. The rest of the staff were up on the landings, unlocking the inmates. A couple of lads who I got on with told me that something was going to go off. I knew it, but that wasn't enough. There were the best part of four hundred cons on the Wing; I need a fucking name at least! Then Mohammed came down to go on the yard. He was one of my grasses. This little bastard would tell me anything and, if something was going to happen, he would know.

'Morning, mate. You got something to tell me?' I said to Mohammed, with order in my tones.

'Hello, Guv. Nah, nothing at the moment.'

I pulled him to one side, so no one could hear, 'Listen you little cunt, don't ever ask me for fuck-all again. I've done a lot for you, you little shit.'

'Smithy and Jacobs are gonna have it. There is bad blood between them,' he snapped quickly.

'Good lad. Speak to you later.'

Oh shit, two big bastards from rival firms going to fight it out. Like I need that at 08.00 hrs on a Wednesday morning! Before I could even tell the SO about it, I heard shouting. I looked round and saw Smithy and Jacobs fighting. I sprinted over to jump in and try and split them up. I must have been mad, but it is second nature when you are a screw. I dived in with a handful of other Officers and we pulled them apart. I ended up pulling Jacobs off and pushing him away. He had a metal flask in his hand that he was waving around like mad, shouting at Smithy over my shoulder.

'Drop it, and fucking get back!' I barked at Jacobs, while trying to push him away.

He was not listening and was still trying to push me out of the way to get at Smithy.

'Out of my fucking way!' Jacobs screamed at me, while trying to wrestle me and hit me with the flask. With that, I knew I had to take him down. I dug him in the ribs a couple of times, and then managed to get hold of his head. I dropped him, and started to bend him up. One of my pals, Rhys, arrived and helped me wrap him up. At that point I heard loads of shouting: 'Leave him alone, you fucking racists.'

You see, Jacobs was a black fella and Smithy was white. And Smithy hadn't been bent up because, when the other screws got hold of him, he didn't resist and was willing to back off. You always get cons shouting when someone gets bent up. It isn't a pretty sight at all.

I wasn't fazed by the shouting, I'd heard it all before. We had Jacobs under restraint and he was beginning to be compliant. Then Rhys said, 'Look at that cunt,' in his Welsh accent and comical tones. He was indicating for me to look up to The Twos. I couldn't believe my eyes. I shook my head in amazement. There was this shithouse, wanker, disgusting excuse for a human being screaming obscenities at us.

'You bastards, leave him alone. Get off him, you racists,' Wesley screamed.

Wesley was an Officer. A fucking Officer! He was the laziest, most self-centred, useless, scared, awful Officer that I've ever met. I've seen him stand there and watch two cons kick the fuck out of each other. He didn't even raise the alarm so other Officers could run to assist and deal with it. Now, though, he was excelling himself. He was shouting at two Officers in front of four hundred cons. He wasn't just shouting, he was calling us fucking racists.

One thing that you never do is break rank in front of the cons. If you have a problem with the conduct of any Officer, you never raise your issues in front of the prisoners. It encourages riots and sends out a message that screws have lost control, especially when you are shouting about something as sensitive as racism.

So, instead of running down to help with this dangerous situation, Wesley had done his usual and watched; but this time he was inciting a riot. Simple as that, there are no other words for his actions. If he thought 'Racists', then fine, put a complaint in. I have no problems answering investigations.

His vile obscenities caused problems when the other Officers turned up to help get the area under control. His words encouraged other inmates to get involved in an incident that didn't concern them but which resulted in them getting bent up. His actions caused more cons to get wrapped up. Thankfully it didn't cause a riot, but that was only due to the quick reactions of the rest of the screws.

We took Jacobs down The Block. He asked to see Rhys and me for a chat. Neither of us minded, as he was a lad we both got on well with. He told us he heard what Wesley was shouting and said he was prepared to tell any Governor that I bent him up legitimately. Jacobs couldn't believe that Wesley was behaving like that, and he was more than prepared to say that nothing had been racially motivated.

So we had all of that, and other Officers also put in complaints about Wesley. I will add that the Officers were both black and white. You see, Wesley was a black Nigerian fella. But he couldn't say it was a racial witch-hunt. I don't know what he had experienced in the past. I'm sorry if he'd experienced racism. No one should ever have to go through that. But this bastard would claim it about everything. If he was asked to unlock a door, he would play the race card. The Governors had had all sorts of complaints about him from the staff – and now from Jacobs, the inmate who was bent up. Do you think that they took the complaint forward and dealt with this cunt? Did they fuck. And so you see a different breed of corruption: the corruption at the Governor grade.

Governors only seem to move forward the investigations and enquiries that they choose to, instead of those that are presented to them. Why? Because they like to gather their friends around them and protect their buddies. That will happen in every industry in the world; we always look after our own. But in a position with that much power, you should be the most unbiased person going. Don't get me wrong; I will not tarnish every Governor with the same brush. I have met some great Governors in the past. Unfortunately, all too often, there are Governors who surround themselves with an inner circle. If you don't fit into that circle you are fucked.

There are so few, in the Service, who you can actually trust.

When you are lucky enough to find one, you and they both need to watch each other's back. You would think that, as screws, we all stick together. You couldn't be more wrong. There are constant battles between ranks, which is exactly how the job shouldn't be. You should be able to trust any colleague with your life but you just can't. You don't know who is around the corner waiting to stitch you up. I wanted nothing more than corrupt bent cunts to be sacked, through all of the ranks. When the big boys abuse their power, it couldn't be more dangerous. There was a bloke called Anderson – now that wanker was blessed. He was like a cat: the fucker had nine lives. He was an SO when he came to the Well. He was moved from his last prison for being a nasty horrible cunt. He was a fucking bully, full stop. He bullied staff, cons, people on the street, anyone. I felt sorry for his missus, the poor cow. Maybe he had a massive dick or something, because she wasn't with him for his charismatic personality.

He came to the Well because he had to. An Officer had stood up to him and made him look like a twat. Anderson waited for him in the car park. I heard the horrible cunt jumped him from behind, and beat the shit out of him. I mentioned earlier that sometimes things are sorted out in the car park, or round the club. That's one thing. But jumping someone in the dark from behind is not the way to do it. When I said he beat the shit out of him, I mean it. He broke the poor bastard's jaw. The cat that he is, he managed to survive that investigation. Don't ask me how. On the back of all that, he was moved to the Well.

Governor Keenan turns out to be one of his 'buddies'. What a coincidence. Keenan was the Governor that suspended me, remember? So Anderson has to move jails, but he lands a job at the place where one of his cronies is high up. He's been at the

Well for about six months when a post for PO comes up. Guess who gets it? You got it, Anderson. If you are a part of a corrupt inner circle, you can do anything – like break an Officer's jaw and get moved and promoted for it.

There were other people qualified for the post. There was one poor sod who was acting PO in that post for a year. When you 'act up', you are given a temporary promotion for six months until they advertise the job, and you have to seriously fuck it up to not get it. Either that, or some Governor, who doesn't like the look of your face, takes the job away. Well, he applied and didn't get it.

Anderson got the job, and he was smiling from ear to ear on that fat face of his.

Anderson wasn't my direct boss. I'd worked the odd shift under him, and I'd heard the rumours, but I hadn't had the chance to judge him for myself. I did think it was a joke that he got promoted that quickly but it didn't surprise me; I was used to the Governor's shit ways.

There was a fraggle who had to be moved off D Wing. He was a junkie who was clucking like mad. He needed to go to the Fraggle Wing to detox before he killed himself. A couple of screws came over to collect him. The con wasn't exactly refusing, he was just talking incoherent crap. He wouldn't have been able to tell you what planet he was on because he was smacked out of his nut. He didn't need to be bent up, he just needed to be escorted to the other Wing. That is exactly what the screws did. I'd seen bigger-built dwarfs than this fraggle. A cub scout would show more aggression than this fella. He was so off his head he probably didn't even know his own name.

The screws took him off the Wing and to his new location. Within five minutes, I heard a whistle alarm. I ran to the Wing it came from – the Fraggle Wing. It was that little fraggle that had been moved off the Wing a few minutes earlier. He was lying in a pool of his own blood, with Anderson holding him under restraint. It was a sickening sight. That poor little cunt couldn't have assaulted a fucking grasshopper. It was obvious what had happened. The bully had acted exactly how he loved to act.

A couple of my pals who worked on that Wing told me that, when they put that fraggle in his cell, Anderson banged the Wing up and then went up to the Fraggle Wing to pay him a visit. He went in, then the alarm was raised, and there was the fraggle, unconscious on the floor in a puddle of his own blood. The con had severe injuries to his face. Once he came round he made a complaint. He said that Anderson had gone into his cell, said one or two words he can't remember, and started to punch fuck out of him. With that type of injury and complaint, Anderson should have been suspended. But the cat lives again.

His Governor pal was later quick to suspend all of us in order to get Frankie, but not his mate Anderson. It was painful that he didn't suspend him, as it was obvious what had happened.

The inmate was intimidated to try to get him to withdraw his complaint against Anderson. He didn't though, the good lad. They tried to stop him from having visits so his family and friends wouldn't see the injuries that he sustained.

All of us wanted the cunt suspended; he was an animal. He was, and was charged and brought to court. He was looking at going down for five to ten. Fucking bully deserved it. Unfortunately, justice did not prevail. The junkie ODed and the case was thrown out. He came back, kept his rank and I heard he was later promoted to Governor. Unbelievable. These types of cunts are in prisons all over the country.

Sometimes you do get screws who will get one over on the Governors. That is good, but not if it's a bent screw that has that power. That is the worst combination that you can think of, a bent screw having one over a corrupt Governor. They should both be sacked, but instead they both keep their jobs.

Miss Rooks was one of the most notorious bent screws that I'd ever heard of, and I'd not even met her. She was suspended just as I started. From what I learned, she was fucking cons, drug dealing, drug trafficking and everything that she shouldn't be doing. I knew Officers who had also fucked her. Apparently she was a spunk bucket for everybody. There were inmates who admitted fucking her, and admitted that she had been bringing gear in for them. So they suspended her.

I don't know what was true and what was bollocks but there were good friends of mine, people I trusted, who told me that she was definitely bent. Before she even came to the Well, she was an OSG at a nick up north. She was sacked for an improper relationship with a prisoner. Basically she was fucking him at every opportunity. She applied for the position of Officer at a nick down south, and got it. Crazy.

She was suspended for ages. They had enough to do her for trafficking, but she still wasn't sacked. Why? Because she had a Governor in her pocket.

I heard from a good source that there was a Governor called Mr East who loved to fuck Miss Rooks. He didn't give a monkeys that she was always under suspicion. He was a dirty old cunt and thick as fuck. If you asked him a question, you could probably hear his brain tick. He wasn't malicious and didn't try to stitch anyone up, just stupid. I'd seen him out on the piss a few times, and he would always be a mess in the corner, trying to pest up some young bird. His problem was that his wife never put out so he was always thinking with his prick. And if you're a Governor, there is always someone willing to try and shag their way to the top – or a bent female screw who is willing to fuck you to get you in her pocket. Mr East was perfect for that. He held rank, was stupid as they come, and he used to think with his dick. He was easy pickings for Miss Rooks. She saw him as an insurance policy.

Mr East didn't just like to get pissed. He liked a bit of coke as well. It was a match made in heaven. So, they were fucking all the time and getting wasted together. But she was switched on. She took photos of him snorting lines of coke. What a mug, letting that horrible little rat take control of him like that. He was none the wiser, either, the idiot.

When she was suspended, my mate told me she threatened to take the photos of Mr East to the papers so she was not sacked. She was kept on suspension on full pay. They spun her house, but she had nothing. You don't have to be Einstein to work out why.

Governors have the powers to screw over anyone. It's frightening how much authority they actually have. You get a corrupt Governor and, with this power, it is murder. The best way of conducting yourself is be the grey man and not get noticed; keep them at arm's length and stay out of their way. That is something that I could never do (I can be my own worst enemy at times). But in crisis situations, you have to rely on Governors to make life-changing decisions. That is when you pray for a Governor who is on your side. That is when you need a Governor who will back you up.

A true test of danger was only around the corner.

I KNOW IT'S COMING,
THERE'S GONNA BE VIOLENCE

The harsh reality of being a screw is that you lose control from time to time. People who say that the Officers have control of the prison, and that it always works well, are lying. As Rumpole said, *'The cons run the prison, we're just visitors.'* That is the brutal truth of the matter. When there is large-scale concerted indiscipline, you are fucked.

For sporadic incidents, you rely on good screws and good cons; and if you have the Intel that something is going to happen, then you can prepare yourself for it. A concerted indiscipline is when the prisoner or prisoners have planned to break the rules for a particular reason, normally as a protest of some sort. Sometimes the protest has just cause, but there are other ways of dealing with that problem. Sometimes the inmates feel their grievances fall on deaf ears, but you have to keep trying to get what you need through the correct channels.

Then you get the wankers who organise a riot just to be antisocial cunts. These are the types of prisoner who, if you gave them room service and a page-three model, would still find something wrong. They take pleasure in creating misery. These anarchists are fucking idiots. They make a mockery of anyone who has a true problem.

I met one con who didn't do it to cause anarchy, he was just an exhibitionist who craved recognition for his actions. He loved the attention. His nickname was Spiderman. You don't get any prizes for guessing what his party piece was. The little sod could climb up a blade of grass if it was high enough. Anything with height, he would climb it. Every roof, cage, ledge, pole and wall that the Prison Service owns, Spiderman has either climbed or tried to climb to the top.

I was at work when I was told that he was being moved on to D Wing. He hadn't climbed for ages, so they thought it would be all right. The management decided to put him on normal location. Scouse was working on the Fraggle Wing. That is where Spiderman had been located for two months, not causing any drama and keeping his head down. They probably thought that they had rehabilitated his climbing fetish . . .

The night before, Scouse and I got fucking hammered. Now, we had a disciplined lifestyle. We would make sure we were round the club within five minutes of finishing work. We would ensure that we were pissed out of our heads within an hour. Then, we would always go up town, and have it large till no earlier than 02.00 hrs. This would be practised with military precision.

In the morning we would never forget our mouthful of

chewing gum or to put on slightly too much aftershave to blanket the stench of stale ale. Of course, we lined our stomachs with two pints of coffee and, if we were lucky, a bacon sandwich. We had some great times . . .

So, Scouse and I had had a skinful the night before. I remember exactly how I was in the morning – and Scouse was a fucking mess. The booze had hit him hard and he couldn't get his head together. Spiderman needed to be moved from the Fraggle Wing and back to normal location. Scouse, thinking it was a skive, jumped at the chance to walk him to another Wing. Normally it would have been a piece of piss: you walk slowly, get the new cell number from the Movements Officer, locate the con to his cell, have a chat and a brew with a mate on the Wing, go back to your location of work and then disappear for a while and relax. You can even push it out for three-quarters of an hour. So Scouse took the job, thinking he could lie low for a while and sort himself out. Scouse collected Spiderman who was sound about it, didn't cause a fuss. They left the Fraggle Wing, making their way to the centre.

So that you can really visualise the Wing's layout, which is essential to appreciating Spiderman's performance, let me remind you how it works. When you stand on the centre, you can look down all the Wings. On the centre, there is an Officer who sits at a desk and who is responsible for knowing where all prisoners are. The desk is like a reception desk with a wooden roof. It's not very high but it is, all the same, unnecessary. Around the inside of the centre are the landings connecting to the landings on the Wing. So you can look down all the Wings and look up and see all the landings. Unlike the landings on the Wings, at the centre you can't lean over the bars. You can't because there is metal netting for safety reasons. This is to stop some little scroat – or some stressed-out screw for that matter – from trying to jump off. At the top of the fifth landing, the netting creates a little ledge, about four feet wide, with enough room to sit up straight, or crouch on your knees. You could barely get your fingers in the holes of the netting, so you would never think that someone could climb to the top of it. But then, Spiderman is not your average scroat.

Scouse got to the centre, struggling to keep awake. He unlocked the gate and let Spiderman through. He took his eyes off him for a second, while he locked the gate. That was all Scouse needed. The crafty bastard bolted, jumped on to the desk where the centre screw sits, and pulled himself on to the roof. That put him about ten feet up. He then quickly jumped on to the netting and ran up it to the top. You would think it was impossible, but the little cunt went right up it like a squirrel up a tree. Scouse turned round, looking dazed and confused, not knowing where the fuck his con had disappeared to. The centre screw pointed to the top of the netting. Scouse couldn't believe it, his con was staring at him, waving and laughing about thirty feet above him!

He told the Duty Governor who panicked like fuck. Incidents like that don't look good. The people who get thousands of pounds to risk-assess the area should bloody well spot a weakness like that, but I reckon the Well hadn't been risk-assessed since the Dark Ages.

I went to the centre where I saw Scouse with his head in his hands, and ripped the piss out of him. It was funny as fuck! He felt a right mug. He was a blinding screw, but we all fuck up from time to time. And Spiderman should never have been going to a normal location.

The prison was not prepared to deal with a situation like that. They had no safety net for him to land on if he fell. I thought, fuck him if he does. If he wants to be a dick and climb, let him suffer the consequences. However, the Well, being inventive for once, ordered us to get out as many mattresses as we could from the stores. We managed to find enough to cover the floor. These weren't normal mattresses, though: they had the thickness of tracing paper. It was a pointless exercise, really, but I think it made the Governor feel better. He was a good guy and he did think quickly on his feet.

Along with two others, I was deployed to negotiate with Spiderman. I was now a qualified Hostage Negotiator. It was a box that I wanting ticking. It looked good. I thought most of it was a lot of shit, but it was good for my CV. It was a specialist course for which there were several interviews. I don't know how I blagged my way on it, but I did!

Spiderman didn't want to negotiate. There was nothing he wanted. He just loved everyone seeing him up there. It made him notorious. He shouted at all the staff below, 'Get ya sleeping bags, I'm gonna be up here a long fucking time!'

It was about half three when he went up there. It got to half five and it wasn't looking like I was going to be able to leave at six o'clock when my shift was supposed to finish. This berk was not talking to us. He was singing songs and addressing the staff below as his audience.

'Tonigh-e-igh-ight, I'm a rock 'n' roll star! Any requests?' he bellowed out. I must admit it was funny, but I was getting pissed off as my finish time had come and gone. The hours went by. The Governor had called for the National Team to attend and take control of the situation. These boys have the skill and capability to deal with any situation. They are the guys who teach the Tornado course. They are the bollocks and they don't get the credit they deserve. The public know nothing about these guys who are deployed on a daily basis to deal with emergency situations.

They then spoke to him, giving him one last chance to get down of his own accord. He laughed and said he wasn't going anywhere. They filled a huge balloon with air so that if he was to fall or jump he would be OK. Better late than never! They set up their abseiling equipment and worked out the best place from which to climb up and get him. We were all watching, eagerly awaiting the outcome. Just as they got up there, the little shit said, 'OK, I'm ready to come down!'

Two fucking thirty in the morning, all of that time wasted and much money spent. That's what he does time and time again. All he gets is moved from prison to prison. Eleven bloody hours he was up there this time.

Another form of protest is a dirty protest – or shit-up, as we call it. Gorgeous, isn't it? To this day, I have no idea why these creatures cover themselves with their own shit. Agreed, it is absolutely fucking disgusting to open a cell door and see that a grown man has covered his cell, bed and himself in his own shit. But it must be a thousand times worse to live in your own excrement. The risk of disease and germs is incredible. I can't describe the repellent stench that comes out of the cell. However, they take pleasure in making their cells disgusting for the screws.

When they are on a dirty protest, you put on a white suit and surgical mask every time you enter their cell. They are seen daily by the Governor who asks them to come off the protest. When they refuse, they are then left in the cell. At meal times, a couple of you will get into your shit suits and take food to their cell. You also have to collect the plate from the previous meal. If he refuses to hand it over, you have to bend him up. This means having to restrain someone who is covered in their own shit. There is nothing worse.

I have really struggled with cons that shit up. I can't cope with the stink. It literally reduces me to tears, much to the amusement of the con and the other screws.

There was an inmate called Bell. He was a dirty little bastard. He was mad as a box of frogs. He used to be OK one minute, then a real pain in the arse the next. I came into work after a week off and I was told that Bell had been down The Block for three days. The minger had been on dirty protest for the whole three days and, every time he was unlocked for food, he wanted to fight. Each time a dirty protester is restrained, he gets re-located to a clean cell. Good thinking that: he gets the chance to spread his shit all over another cell.

At lunchtime, the Duty Governor put his head around the door. It was Dan Blackwell. A top geezer, if ever there was one. He was the greatest Governor I ever worked for. A funny bloke, he had the wickedest sense of humour. He was brilliant at his job, a great decision maker. He would never stitch anyone up to further himself. He took responsibility for his actions so, if anything did go tits up, he would take the flak for it. If you deserved a bollocking, or if you fucked up, he would rip into you. You were glad to work for him and wouldn't begrudge staying on after your shift had finished if it meant helping him out. All round, a great man-manager, exactly what you wanted and so seldom got.

He had felt the wrath of bullying managers himself when he

was an SO. There was an attempted escape where some con was trying to dig out of his cell. He was one of two SOs on that day. It was down to one of them to make sure that the cell checks were complete. They split the duty up and it was completed and nothing was found. The other SO was a toe-stamping cunt. She didn't give a fuck who she stood on as long as she went through the ranks and looked good. Being female helped her on her way. I know Dan, and he wouldn't miss a thing, but she put the blame on to him. She was also having it away with the Wing Governor, so she could do no wrong. Gentleman that Dan is, he took it on the chin even though he'd done fuck-all wrong. They tried to get him disciplined but, for once, the good guy won. He climbed the ranks to Governor.

I was told that they were short of staff down The Block so I had to go down to help. That meant that I would be feeding Bell. It was common knowledge that I fucking hated dealing with filthy shit-ups. I'm not saying anyone likes it, far from it, but some people can switch off and get it done. I struggled before the door was even opened. I would break out into a sweat and feel sick just thinking about it. So when I was told that I had to go down there to help, I wasn't happy.

Dan popped his head around the door. 'Ronnie, I need ya down The Block, mate.'

'Dan, this is a fucking stitch up! You are having a laugh, ain't ya?' I replied, trying not to smile.

'Nah, get your arse down there now, mate!'

I knew there were bundles of staff down there and they didn't need me. They were going to make me put a shit suit on to feed Bell. I fucking knew it. By this time I was sweating and I had already started to gag at the smell. The Block is under ground, and very small in comparison to a normal landing, and it was also very hot. I had to put my suit on, along with two other screws. You always go in there with three, just in case the con kicks off. Your fluffy fuckers will say this is intimidating, blah blah blah. Well, that is how it has to be – to avoid a possible hostage-take, possible assault and to avoid allegations. Also, if he has to be bent up, it can be done as quickly and safely as possible.

One of the screws I was going in with was my pal Henry. The mate I made during my time in Wakey. He was pissing himself with laughter at the state I was getting myself into. We were all ready, so we made our way to his cell. The mask I was wearing was good for fuck-all: the smell was ripping through it so strongly I could literally taste it. We got to the door. Henry opened it with me behind him and the other screw behind me carrying Bell's grub. Once the door was opened, the smell hit me in the face like a sledgehammer. I started gagging uncontrollably – and then it happened. A piece of shit that he'd wiped all over the ceiling fell on my shoulder. That was it, I started throwing up. My mask filled up within seconds. I retreated from the cell, pulling my mask off, and threw up all over the floor. Bell loved it, laughing his head off. That must be the only pleasure a con gets from shitting up. Henry and the other screw were also laughing their heads off.

Officers get paid extra for dealing with dirty protesters. Wait for it, ten quid a shift. It's an insult rather than a payment.

There is no reason for these filthy bastards to shit up, other than cause misery to the Officers. I think these maggots should be left to wallow in their own scum and rot until they decide to wash. Now charges are brought against them for criminal damage. Good. They are dirty vermin.

When a concerted indiscipline takes the shape of more than one con, you have a host of problems to deal with. That is when people can get seriously hurt – both the inmates and the screws. When these incidents are on a large scale, the cons are aiming for maximum damage and exposure. The roof protesters at Strangeways and the Lincoln rioters, for instance; both made it to the news.

If these types of incident occur, and there has been no indication or intelligence, then you will be fighting for your life and relying on the help of the good cons. Not every con wants there to be a riot. That doesn't make them grasses or screw boys. A lot of cons want to get on with serving their bird and not cause grief. The Wings are their home for the time being, and they want life there to be as comfortable as possible. They don't want a group of cunts smashing the place up and keeping everybody awake all night. You get your big-boy hard nuts who want nothing to do with riots or protests. They will help you – sometimes. I said earlier that cons such as Smithy and Jacobs knew we screws had a job to do. They wouldn't take liberties with us, so we didn't take liberties with them.

Screws can have close relationships with cons, at times. You spend more time with the cons than you do with your wife or family. You want to get on with them because you want an easy life, and for a con it's the same. If you can have a laugh and get on with the prisoners while doing the job, great. People think everyone who goes to prison is a nutter. Not the case at all, although there are some fucking lunatics in prison.

There was a day when I was on duty when I had to rely on the cons. D Wing was worse than ever. It was grossly understaffed, Officers were going sick because of the poor conditions. It was a shit time for cons and screws alike. There were not enough staff to man the Wing safely, so the cons stayed banged up. It was bad enough when we had the correct amount of Officers, let alone when there are only seven or eight Officers for the whole Wing. It was a joke, we could do nothing except basic requirements: exercise, food, a shower and phone call once every three days; and even that was a struggle.

We unlocked them for their medication and exercise in the morning. That was a controlled unlock, only letting a small number of prisoners out at a time. When they had had their meds and exercise, they had to be banged up again. The next time they were unlocked was to collect their lunch. That again was controlled with military precision. Once their meal was collected, it was some more bang up. This took all morning, so we could get no cell checks or searches completed. Security went out of the window.

We broke for lunch after they had theirs. In the afternoon we were supposed to let a couple out at a time for showers and complete all of our other duties. That wasn't done correctly. How could it be with seven screws? No chance at all. When you did let out a couple of lads for showers, they would drag their heels because they were riding twenty-two or twenty-three hours a day of bang up. It was difficult to hurry them along. They weren't interested in knowing that, if they took too long, some other poor cunt wouldn't get out. You try saying to some con, 'I know you have not showered in three days and have not been out of your cell for twenty-three hours, but you've got five minutes to wash and have a phone call.' They were not happy bunnies. Plus it was all double bang up so, if you didn't like your cellmate, you were fucked. I've seen some bloodshed due to that!

All this can turn into a con getting bent up because he kicks off. I could appreciate their frustration, but it wasn't our fault. I hated it as much as they did. Being threatened a hundred times a day isn't nice. I could handle the job, but this was all unnecessary crap that Head Office could have squared away *if only they had recruited more Officers!* But governments don't want to spend money on prisons. Neither do most of the public. I had the same thoughts before I joined the job. I thought, 'Why the fuck should the government spend money on criminals?' But then you have to look at it. If they build more prisons and create more jobs for Officers, more criminals would be banged up, where they should be. At the moment, there are seventy-nine thousand cons. That tells us nothing about the number of criminals there are in a country with over sixty-five million people. We are not even scratching the surface of banging up the criminals that are out there.

Tension on the Wing was at an all-time high; morale for staff and cons at an all-time low. No fucker wanted to go to work. It was unbearable. There was a screw who reckoned he was pushed down the stairs by a con while on duty. We all reckon that he threw himself down there. He fucked his back up and was off for ages. This fella, I'm sorry to say, was found hanging in his flat, a few years later.

There was a huge increase in self-harming among the cons. Self-harming is awful. I feel really sorry for those people; they must have real issues if they want to hurt themselves. There are those who cry wolf about suicidal thoughts, though. They use their status as self-harmers to manipulate the system. Fucking cunts; while they are crying wolf, some poor sod could be swinging in his cell.

I'd never known the atmosphere to be so bad. Everyone was as miserable as fuck. When the cons did get out, it often ended in some of them kicking off and getting wrapped up. At this time, we had the worst possible inmate you could wish for. He was very big, very hard, very young, very fucking dumb and they called him Bear. This lad was six feet seven and twenty-two stone. A giant of a man, only twenty-one, and he was thick as pig shit. On the road, he was a bare-knuckle fighter. This massive, stupid young hard bastard fights for money. You didn't want that dangerous cunt kicking off.

He was a mixed-race fella, shaved head covered in scars – face and arms too. He was solid as a rock, a massive, thick-set strong bastard. He looked like an American wrestler. To top it off, he'd been put on a Wing that was going through the most hostile period in its existence, and it had no staff. You couldn't reason with him, he was too thick. You had to hope that he didn't kick off. There was no way that he was mentally stable enough for normal prison. If he wanted something, he'd punch until he got it.

One day, during this terrible time, the inevitable happened. We turned up to work in the morning to find there were seven screws and one SO instead of ten and an SO. It was a joke with the correct number, let alone with seven. The Duty Governor gave us two more Officers from another Wing to help us unlock. Everyone was fucked off to the max. Officers from other Wings never wanted to come and help. People didn't want to go on to D Wing. They found it intimidating and unnecessarily dangerous. No one openly volunteered to come over to help us. They had to be ordered by the Duty Governor. I knew a screw that refused point blank, even when ordered. He would rather go down the disciplinary route than come on to D Wing. Thankfully, on that day, the two who came over were decent screws.

We had the morning briefing, which was much as usual: unlock for exercise, bang up, bang up, and more bang up. Everyone got into position and began unlocking for exercise. I was on The Ones, which was my usual place. On The Ones, you stand there and wait to receive the cons when they come down to collect their meds and go on to the yard for exercise. It is also your job to rub-down search the cons as they go on to the yard. You search for food, drink and weapons. Food or drink because, if they decided to protest and stay out on the yard, they would have supplies to keep themselves there. Weapons for obvious reasons: maximum damage, skull cracking if approached.

Nine times out of ten, you will get one of the little shits who manage to get it past you. Not enough man power to get things done correctly and efficiently. The unlock was going well, though, nice and controlled. Then I heard a load of shouting and a large bang. A second later, the whistle went. Some fella had kicked off, so he was bent up. They didn't need any more staff, as they had it under control. Movements were then frozen and the cons that were out were locked away. The scroat bent up was taken to The Block.

That incident went as well as it could have. It was dealt with quickly, no injuries were incurred and normal regime was continued with a minimum of fuss. We continued with the unlocking but the Wing was eerily quiet. That place normally sounds like England v Germany but, that day, it sounded like the Pope's funeral. I never could trust it when the Wing was that quiet. It just wasn't right. The atmosphere was really creepy. I preferred it when you couldn't hear yourself think. You knew then that people were having a laugh or even a row at a comfortable level. You knew there was control by the screws, with decent relations with the cons. When it was quiet like that, you knew something was going down, something was being planned: and that wasn't good. That day's silence was deafening.

We managed to get the cons medicated and out on the yard quicker than normal, all of which was worrying as well. We had a hundred and eighty cons on the yard. That was lower than normal. On a day like this there would normally be two hundred and fifty with the other ninety or so banged up. You always get cons who like to do their bird behind the door. Normally, the old lags do this; they pretty much sleep their time through prison. And, of course, you get your lazy bastards who can't get their fat arses out of bed, so they miss exercise and blame it on the screws. Those lazy cunts expect a morning call and breakfast in bed.

It had gone too well. You normally get cons running around the Wing or banging their doors, but not on that day. Three screws went out on the yard to man the inmates, and the two Officers who had come to help went back to their areas of work. That left us with four on the Wing. Everyone left was banged up and we started our duties of answering cell bells and checking the self-harmers. We are also supposed to do cell fabric checks but, with four screws and one hundred and seventy cells to check, do you think it gets done? Not a fucking chance.

I wasn't happy with the atmosphere; I could sense something bad and violent was going to happen. There was no Intel that there was anything planned, though. I had not heard a whisper from any of my grasses, and neither had the other screws working with me.

Rhys was on with me that day. A magnificent, kind, strong and brilliant screw he was. I had a lot of time for him. He was a Welsh fella, with the humour and wit of a razor blade, who took pleasure in taking the piss out of me. I'm always clumsy and disorganised, something that Rhys would pick up on at every opportunity. It was all in good humour. He was so funny. Strange things always happened to him. He told of the time when, aged fifteen, he was at his annual rugby-club dinner. He said things at the club were great for him. His coach had always liked him and gave him extra coaching sessions and stuff.

The night was going really well, everyone was pissed, his coach more than everyone else. Rhys went on to tell me that his coach confessed his undying love for him! I asked Rhys what he did. 'I cried!' he said. The way he told it! The things that happened, always to him. One day, while he was working in his garden, he got talking to his neighbour. When he was asked what he did for a living he said, 'I'm a Prison Officer.' His neighbour went on to tell him that he had spent twenty-seven years in prison, with ten years in Broadmoor! Always happens to Rhys! Top bloke, hard as nails, and a good mate. I had the utmost respect for him.

On the Wing that day, Rhys had not heard anything from his grasses either. He felt the same as I did; he knew that something wasn't right. We got in touch with security to see if they had any info on a possible concerted indiscipline. They hadn't. Jamie and Garry were the other two with Rhys and me that day. We could all trust each other.

Garry was a very good Officer but a bit too militant for my liking. He knew the rules and would stick to them, no matter what. Everyone knew where they stood with him, but you do need to use your discretion as a Prison Officer. Garry had none. He didn't mistreat anyone but he would not give any extras whatsoever. That's why he never handled grasses, because the cons hated him. Don't get me wrong, he didn't bully people: he was just, well, he was just Garry. He was only two years older than me but he had three more years in the job. He went from school to the Army to the Prison Service. Appearances are deceptive, though. He looked nothing like a squaddie or a Prison Officer. He could easily have fitted into a boy band. People would underestimate him and try it on with him. That was a mistake. He was a tough little bastard, scared of no one.

Jamie was a lovely lad. He was from Leeds and a year younger than me. He would always join in and was a decent screw. He would muck in, listen to advice and knew how to work the job well. He'd not been in the Service long, but he looked as though he had been in it for years. He took to it like a fish to water. He had a good head on his shoulders and his jail craft was awesome. He was great at weighing people up.

The four of us were concerned to say the least. We could feel something was going to happen. There were a couple of grasses left on the Wing so we paid them a visit in their cells. We interrogated them as much as we could. They would not give up fuck-all, not even with a bit of encouragement . . . It was nearly time for the cons who were out to come back from the yard and bang up. We went to the Duty Governor to ask for as many Officers from other Wings as we could have. We would normally go through the SO to ask for this. But on that day, we had a right little cunt working for us. We called her the poisoned dwarf. She didn't have a clue about the job, or fuck-all. She was shit. Crap with the cons, crap with the staff and a sickening arse-kisser to the bosses. She didn't fuck her way to SO either. Too much makeup, too fucking short, bad barnet, bad breath, and a cunt to boot! Instead, her old man was drinking buddies with the management, hence the reason why she got to SO and is now a serving Governor. Frightening isn't it? Always the same. Not what you know, but who you know.

Rhys and I went straight to the Duty Governor to ask for as many screws as we could have. The Duty Governor was Governor Wife. He was all right, but a bottler – he was always losing his nerve and backing off. He never made a decision that he believed in. The cunt should have worked in a bakery making fairy cakes, not as a Governor working at the Well! He wasn't a bad bloke, but he was scared of his bosses. He would not commit himself to anything that he had to justify off his own back. He would only do it if the paperwork was there. Sometimes you have to step out of the circle and make a decision, even if that decision is based on gut feeling alone.

He asked us if there was Intel or paperwork to support what we were saying. We told him no, but we could tell that something was going to happen judging by the atmosphere and the behaviour of the inmates. Being the wimp that he was, he refused to give us as many Officers as he could. He was scared in case his boss questioned him. Fucking pansy. He did give us three though, whoopee bloody do!

It was time to call the inmates in, as exercise was finished. We had the three Officers on the yard, one in each corner of the triangle shape. One of them was standing directly by the door of the entrance to D Wing. The other two were at the other corners and left the yard from the rear, entering C Wing. They then walked round to D Wing inside the prison. They couldn't walk across the yard to enter D Wing because that would be a perfect opportunity for the scroats to take them hostage. Once they were on the Wing, the door was opened to the yard. The screw standing on the yard by the door stayed there and called the inmates in, in turn, by the landing that they were located on.

So, we had one screw standing there calling in the inmates, and nine of us on the Wing waiting to receive the inmates from the yard and bang them up. The screw at the door screamed, 'ONES.' The lads started to return, coming up the stairs from the yard and through the door, entering the Wing. They were coming in with no real problems and we got them behind their doors reasonably quickly. Rhys and I looked at each other in recognition that we may have misjudged the situation and were worrying about nothing. We indicated to the screw at the door that we were ready for The Twos.

'TWOS,' he screamed at the top of his voice. Rhys, Garry, Jamie and I were standing just inside the doorway, waiting to receive the inmates. When they came through the door, we ushered them up the stairs, hurrying them to their cells. The other Officers were up on The Twos, banging them up as they returned – but they were coming in at a serious pace.

'Fookin hell, they're returning fooking quick!' Jamie said in his Yorkshire accent. He couldn't have been more right. They were coming in at an alarming rate.

'Just The Twos and no one else,' the screw at the door screamed to the inmates on the yard.

'We have got to stop this right now, we're gonna lose the fucking Wing,' I said.

'Lets shut the fooking door now, or that's it, we've lost it,' Jamie shouted.

The four of us ran to help the screw shut the door. As we arrived, there was a surge of people rushing in and shouting. It was like the gates opening at a concert, but with violence added. The screw at the door got smashed out of the way. That was it, the war had begun. The four of us picked up the screw who had been knocked down and then fought our way to the door. We were punching, kicking, stamping, doing everything we could to stop people from getting in while, at the same time, trying desperately to pull the door shut and lock it. We needed to secure the Wing with the already out-of-control numbers we had on it, and thereby stop the rest of the cons on the yard from getting in.

We had a riot on our hands. These cunts wanted a fight. They had a statement to make and it wasn't a pleasant one. They were rushing in with one thing on their minds: to take control of the Wing. If they could get a hostage that would help them. They didn't want this shit regime of bang up to continue, so they wanted to damage as much as they could in order to force the Governors to deal with it. It was fight-for-your-life time now.

The cons were pushing us out of the way but we were fighting all the same. We knew that we had to get that door shut to give us some sort of chance. If they got in, then that was it, party over. Punching and kicking, we teamed up, using our strength to get hold of the door. With Jamie and Garry on one side and Rhys and I on the other, we finally managed to get the door shut. I pulled it with all of my strength, Jamie and Garry helping me to hold it shut while Rhys locked it.

As I looked round, there was a sea of heads all shouting and fighting. I could hear whistles and alarm bells going off left, right and centre. There were screws fighting with cons, cons fighting with cons. I wished my eyes were kidding me. This was

154

dangerous. It was out of control. We had to act fast, get in there, get stuck in, take back control. The four of us ran in and began fighting. The screws from other Wings rushed in to help us. We needed every pair of hands, feet, anything to help us. The orders over the net was, 'All available staff to Delta Wing, I repeat, all available staff to Delta Wing.' Even with this help, every screw available, the odds were stacked up against us. At this point, there were about twenty Officers to sixty cons. We knew that we couldn't bend them up correctly. We knew we weren't going to be able to drag all of them down The Block. It was a case of 'find any door or gate and lock these fuckers behind it'. It was whatever it takes, just get them locked away – punch, kick, drag, push. Anything goes, just get them secured. Once they were secured away, then we could take it from there and eventually get these inmates into their appropriate cells. But at that early point, we had to worry about coming out of it alive and in one piece. Preservation of life. Contain the incident.

We were all fighting for our lives. We were chucking cons in the showers, cupboards, offices, toilets, anything that had a lock on the door, as well as into the cells on The Ones. The inmates on The Ones were already banged up but we were unlocking their cells and pushing seven or eight cons into each one. There were some Officers running to the centre, retreating, bottling it, leaving us to fucking fight. They didn't give a fuck about the others fighting for their lives, the selfish bastards! They didn't care about us or the inmates or anyone. Just getting their arses safe.

If an area gets really out of control, like D Wing that day, they can chain the gates at all the entrances. It's called containment. This is done when we are outnumbered and prisoners are trying to gain control of the Wing. If they were successful, they would have sets of keys from the screws they were holding hostage and could manoeuvre around the Wing and possibly the jail. So I can see why they do it, but what about the poor cunts in there being held hostage? I didn't see it because I was too busy fighting, but they were getting the chains out, preparing to lock us in.

As I was banging some cunt away, I saw Jamie having the fuck kicked out of him. It was Bear. That crazy cunt was loose. The worst inmate ever, I couldn't believe it. Anyone else but him. He was a fucking handful on his own. We did not need him on the rampage in that situation. I quickly ran to assist; Jamie would not have been able to sustain that sort of beating for long. I could see the pain he was feeling. He was on his knees and Bear was punching and kicking him. He had his hands up, but Bear was smashing through them, hitting him, blow after blow.

I rugby-tackled the big cunt, smashing him straight into the wall. I got him off balance and I had him away from Jamie. I had to get to work in breaking him down. I needed him on the deck. I got stuck into his ribs, punching the fuck out of them, fearing for myself, knowing this cunt could rip my head off my shoulders. It was like trying to chop an oak tree down with a penknife. Bear grabbed me by my shirt and flesh, pulling me towards him, headbutting me. I managed to turn my head down so he caught the top of my head, but it still fucking hurt. It must have hurt him, too, but there was no sign of that. It felt as if he'd split my head like a pineapple. It saved me from having my nose smashed through my face, though. He had me by my shirt and neck, throwing me around like a man-sized rag doll. This geezer made me look tiny and I was anything but that. I was punching the cunt in the side of the temple as hard as I could, trying to get him to let me go.

My punches were just bouncing off him, doing nothing. The man was like a machine. Nothing was working and I knew that if he was to keep hold of me and get me on the floor, I was fucked. If he got me down, it would have been near-on imposs-ible to defend myself. I was strong but he was a lot stronger. So I did the only thing that I could. Punching his face and head did nothing. I couldn't grab his neck tight enough to have any effect. I went for the soft option, the place that would hurt anyone. I stuck my thumb right in his eye, pushing it as hard as I could. I felt it squelching around as I forced it there with as much force as I could manage. I was nearly tickling his brain, trying to stop him from killing me.

Bear screamed out in sheer agony. There was blood pouring out of his eye. He dropped me, but he was still standing, which meant he was still dangerous. I quickly punched him on the nose as hard as I could and then booted him right in the bollocks. As I did that, Rhys and Garry got there to assist. They managed to grab his huge arms and put them into hammer-locks. Jamie was back on his feet and came over to help. We got the fucker to the floor and dragged him into the staff toilets, which happened to be the nearest room we could lock him up in. Once we got the animal in there, we retreated as quickly as we could, locking the door shut.

At this stage, there were fifteen screws left fighting thirty cons. We battled on, doing everything that we could to get on top of the situation. We managed to bang away about half of them. We were actually starting to look like the aggressors, taking back control. It wasn't only due to the screws' guts and determination, it was due to the good cons who wanted nothing to do with the wankers trying to take over the Wing. That's why there were loads of cons fighting as well. The good cons were helping us take back control of the Wing. That's when you can stand side by side with them. Of the thirty or so cons left, about ten of them were helping us, so the ratio had turned in our favour. The cunts were now on the back foot. We were winning.

We carried on fighting, easily banging up ten more. The last ten were shitting it big time. I don't think they could take in that we had regained control. The last seven or eight gave up and were taken down The Block. They only had to say one thing and they were dropped on their way down there. Not one managed to walk all the way. The chains that had been brought to lock us all inside were put away without actually being applied.

Rhys and I walked on to the centre and looked at Governor Wife with disgust. If only he had listened to us. But he was too gutless. I couldn't believe that he had been about to chain us in! We were all battered, some worse than others. Poor old Jamie's jaw had been broken by the Bear, so he went to A&E. Sheer guts and determination got us through it. There were a lot of cuts and bruises, some broken bones as well. There were obviously some who milked it and saw it as an opportunity to have a bit of sick leave. Good on them; you get no other reward for doing what we did – no more than the cowards who ran away. The Service relies on screws to do what we did.

There remained the problem of the hundred or so inmates still out on the yard. I went to look with Rhys and the Duty Governor. As we thought, the inmates were having a sit down. They were huddled together near the centre of the yard, shouting and giving the V sign. They had chair legs, table legs and all sorts of weaponry. They also had bread and water, so it was plain they didn't plan to come in when asked! It was also apparent that they fancied a scrap. They had managed to get the weapons and the food out from the cons who were banged up in the cells. The cells have windows that open just enough for a table leg to fit through. Perfect, hey?! The other side of the window has wire meshing, which is there to prevent anything being thrown out of the window. You don't need to be Lennox Lewis to knock it off. About fifty per cent of it was missing from the windows. The scroats on the yard had supplies to last a long while.

The Governor called an operational emergency. This is when an incident is reported to Head Office and the National Team is called to attend. Anyone working at the Well who is part of the C&R Tornado Unit is called in for duty as part of the National Tornado Team. There aren't enough men from one prison, so they call on every local prison to round up their Tornado screws to attend the Well. If you are at home and are called in for Tornado, then it's the only time a screw will rush in! They turn up for Tornado as they know it is a riot, so there could be some action. Every screw wants to be Tornado trained.

First thing that Governor Wife had to do was deploy a Negotiator, to speak to the inmates, to see whether a resolution could be reached without the Tornado Team going in and dragging them out.

'You're a Negotiator, Ronnie, I need you to get to the door and do your thing.'

'With all due respect, Guv, there is no fucking way I'm negotiating today.'

I'd been pushed too far. I was not in the frame of mind to talk nice things. I wanted to get on the yard and fucking have it. Right or wrong, I wanted it. I was angry.

'Ronnie, don't make me order you.'

'Grow a dick now, why don't you! I will have to tell the Number One all about how Rhys and I told you our concerns today. I will do that on my way home, as I can feel injuries coming on,' I stated, challenging him to order me. I had Wife nicely tucked up. He knew exactly what I was saying. If I didn't get the chance to kit up, I would go sick, so he would lose an experienced screw. On top of that I would put it about that he was a shithouse who couldn't make a decision. He wouldn't have got into trouble as technically he had not done anything wrong, but he didn't have the guts to make a decision. He knew he made the wrong call, and his reputation would be even worse than it already was.

'OK, Mr Thompson, attend The Segregation Unit and put on your riot clothing, and report to the Tornado coordinator,' Governor Wife said, backing down.

'Yes, sir, I will report there right away,' I answered, like an obedient Officer.

You can't be deployed as a Negotiator and as a Tornado Officer in the same incident: it is a conflict of interest. I can understand that; it's good procedure. You can't be standing there talking to the perpetrator for hours on end, only for the negotiations to fail and you then go in and bend them up. It's not right. You either act as a Negotiator or as a Tornado screw. On that day, after what I'd been through, there was no way that I was going to stand there and negotiate for hours, especially with cunts out there trying to get in, take over, and hold me hostage. Liberty-taking wankers. I sympathised with their cause, but you don't do that to people who are doing a job with a family at home. The only way that I was being a part of that incident was in full kit.

I went down the block with Rhys to get kitted up. He was a Tornado screw as well. The Well had mustered quite a few Tornado screws, which was good. Over the next two hours, Officers from all over the area turned up, ready for some action. They are the fellas who plan the intervention and take charge of these situations. They had deployed a team of negotiators to speak to the cons on the yard. The first thing that we had to do was a roll check, to account for every prisoner and make sure the numbers were still correct. Every Wing had to be counted, including the yard. D Wing had to be counted, and the inmates that we'd banged up behind any locked door had to be moved to their correct cells. Bear in mind we had just been fighting with these cunts.

The numbers were correct on the other Wings, so it was time to go on to D Wing to get the numbers correct and the perpetrators dealt with. There was no fucking about at this point. They were given very direct, very clear instructions through the door as to how they were to act and what they were to do. They all had to acknowledge that they understood before we would open the door. They would then come out one at a time. There were fucking loads of screws kitted up, around the cell or area we were unlocking. There would be no chances taken at this point. There were plenty of us ready if they kicked off.

When they came out of the cell, they were told to say nothing, unless asked to. They were told that if they did anything at all they would be restrained. At this stage of an operational emergency, there are no negotiations. If they even speak, they are bent up straight away, no questions. Control has to be taken back. They have to know that, if they don't do only what they are asked, they will be bent up. Seeing that many screws in full kit is very intimidating. They know we mean business. No fucking around.

They came out one at a time and were met by a three-man team who issued the orders. They were taken to the end of the Wing where they gave their name and number to a video camera. They were then taken to the relevant cell. That is, of course, if they hadn't been bent up. If they had, they still stated their name and number to the camera while under restraint. They were then taken to The Block.

The whole procedure is videoed to protect inmates and Officers and to be used in court if necessary, so it was important to do everything properly as Big Brother was watching. One wrong move and you are fucked. But you have to put that out of your mind and do the job. You have to let your training take over.

The first cell that was opened, the fella came out with attitude. He was smashed to the floor, bent up and cuffed before he even knew what had happened. That sent out the correct message to others to play ball. The rest went reasonably smoothly. Around half a dozen were bent up, but the majority realised it was time to call it a day and do as they were told.

Then we got to the staff toilet where we'd locked up Bear. Rhys and I wanted to get this cunt out and so we made sure we were in the team that dealt with him. He was given his orders through the door. He didn't want to know, the big, thick fucking cunt. He was kicking the door, shouting all sorts of shit. We knew then that we were going to have to charge in, drag him out, and get him to The Block.

I was the shield man. The procedure is that the shield man goes in first with two Officers tucked in tight behind him. You advance into the cell as fast as you can while still keeping control. The shield man holds the shield nice and high in order to protect the team. He then smashes the shield into the inmate, forcing him against the wall or the floor. The two screws behind him then come forward; reaching round the shield, they get hold of any weapon and remove it. Once that is done, they secure the prisoner's arms. When they have control, the shield man throws the shield behind him and secures the prisoner's head. The prisoner is then under restraint and removed.

This is how we were planning to deal with Bear. The door was opened. Breathing heavily, sweating buckets, we charged in. Behind me on the shield were Rhys and some other screw I didn't know. We ran in as fast as we could. The Bear ran towards the shield and dived at it. I managed to push him back and hold him off. He had blood coming out of his eye and rolling down his cheek from my treatment earlier. His face and head were covered in lumps, as well, but he didn't seem hurt or threatened at all. He was a machine programmed to create violence.

I smashed him as hard as I could with the shield. Fuck me, he was strong. I pushed with everything that I had. The other two were supporting me nicely. Inch by inch, foot by foot, we were getting him to where we wanted him to be – the back wall. I was trying to contain him while Rhys and the other lad reached round to grab hold of his trunk-sized arms. But he was too strong; every attempt to secure his arms was failing. The shield had served its purpose. I had to get rid of it and help or we were going to be there all day. I threw it behind me. BANG! Bear punched me in the head, quick as lightning. I didn't even see it. I was wearing my riot helmet but the sheer force from his punch nearly knocked me over. He was so powerful, so dangerous.

We were jumping all over this cunt, but we couldn't get him

to the floor. We were bouncing off him, looking like toddlers play-fighting with their dad. He was inhuman: he felt no pain and had the strength of ten men. We wrestled with him for what felt an eternity. After much struggling and fighting, we managed to get him to the ground and hold him in position until he wore himself out. If you just hold them there, let them struggle, they soon tire. They all do in the end.

We got the cuffs on and got him out of the cell. Don't ask me how, but we did. There was another team waiting outside the door, ready to take over. We were fucked. He was hard work. The fresh team got hold of him and took him to The Seg. Not all the way, though; there were a few other team changes on the way down. He was a fucking lunatic. He kicked off even though he was cuffed, so they ended up carrying him.

Once he was down there, he had his health checks, injury reports and whatnot. When they examined him for injuries, he had a broken wrist, three broken fingers, severe bruising to his head – and fuck knows what I did to his eye, but I'm sure he never saw through that properly again. All of that was done in efforts to control him, but he felt none of it. He had also bitten through part of his tongue.

He got evaluated by the mental-health team, as well. They came to the decision that he had mental-health issues and should not be in prison but in a secure hospital. Fucking marvellous: it takes this for them to listen. We said that he wasn't fit for prison from day one. It takes a riot, an Officer to have his jaw broken, and him to have his eye gouged out of his fucking head before they decide to sort it. There are three ways to describe him: mad cunt, mad cunt, and last but not least, mad cunt. They took him to healthcare and jabbed him up to calm him. A few weeks after all of this, I saw him, down on healthcare, while he was waiting for a space at a nut house. I don't know what they gave him, but he couldn't say his own fucking name and was staring into space, not knowing what the fuck was going on around him. He should have never been in prison. Prison couldn't help him.

It took ages to get the Wing counted and the inmates moved to the correct place. It was well into the evening before things were starting to look reasonably normal again. Throughout this whole time, the negotiators were trying to come up with a resolution plan, trying to avoid the use of force. The scroats on the yard were having none of it. They were screaming about how bad the Well is, and how they are treated like animals. There was no argument with that, they were right. The regime was a shambles. I could understand their frustration. But there are ways and means. Well, saying that, there aren't really; the Service is shit!

After our spate of operational duties, the adrenalin was flowing. We wanted to get out on the yard and drag the anti-social cunts down but that wasn't going to happen just yet. Negotiations take a very long time, I appreciate that – they had been going on for over six hours by then – but we all saw that, if they weren't going to come in of their own accord at that point, then they never would.

However, for the human-rights fluffy bollocks, six hours still isn't enough. They never give you a specific time scale, but it always goes on and on and on before they say negotiations are over. Even if they have got a hostage, it makes no difference. Some poor cunt is sitting in there shitting themselves, while the negotiators pussyfoot around for hours. The human-rights bods say it's preservation of life; they say it is damage limitation to the hostage: 'While the perpetrator [the con] is talking, he [the con] is not hurting anyone.' If I was in there as a hostage, I wouldn't give a fuck about keeping the perpetrator talking! I would want them to send in the boys ASAP.

About ten hours had passed now; we were getting well fucked off. The negotiators had been working their bollocks off trying to resolve the issues. There were divisions beginning to show outside with the cons as well. It was apparent who the instigators were. You could tell that some of them wanted to come in. You could hear them saying, 'It's time to give up. We've made our point.' But the instigators were saying, 'No one gives up till we say so!' With that, one of the prisoners bolted towards the gate, screaming, 'Let me in!' The other fellas chased the fucker, dragged him back to the middle of the yard and beat the cunt half to death.

Twelve hours had now gone by and they decided it was time to end negotiations. Big floodlights had been erected so we could see what we were doing. It's like that, no warnings or build-ups. You are sitting there one minute, the next you are in formation, ready to go in. No time to think. The adrenalin was kicking in again by now. Although you were in that kit, ready, you are still scared. You don't know what is going to happen.

Breathing heavily, preparing ourselves, we marched onto the yard in strict military fashion with our shields held high. The commander shouted, 'Halt!' It had been hours; the cons were hungry and tired but they were still up for a fight. They had no plans to walk anywhere. I could have told the bosses that from the start, but the do-it-by-the-book red tape is so thick that no de-escalation process stands much chance of working.

The cons were beginning to throw flak at us, anything that

they could get their hands on. They were getting ready for a fight. You could see a lot of them were scared. It was easy to pick out the nutters, the instigators, the wankers. I would have been fucking scared if I were them. The sight of shedloads of screws in riot kit marching on to the area is an intimidating prospect. We formed a straight line, facing them with our shields up. Same as always, there was a shield man with two screws behind him. There would be no more negotiating.

The commander yelled, 'Advance!' and, in our shielded three-man teams, we moved forward, smashing into the cons hard as we could. We wanted this job done quickly. We had all had enough. We took them out with relative ease. Back-up teams were sent in behind us and so the numbers were huge. We ran forward, bashing into them, doing what was necessary. We broke up their numbers in seconds. They didn't know what fucking hit them. They did fight, but got nowhere. It was like a scene straight out of Belfast in the seventies. People were fighting everywhere. Cons were getting bent up and removed at the speed of lightning. Some of those who were not fighting got de-escalated very quickly and were walked off the yard. The rest were dropped hard and dragged off. The adrenalin was incredible. It was an extremely scary time but we got them all off the yard and banged up. There were eight of them who had organised it and they put up a fight all the way down The Block. The Intel after the incident pointed to thirty-two inmates who were identified as active instigators, working for the eight who organised it. The rest just went along for the ride, or got caught up in it. All of the instigators were transferred to different prisons at 06.00 hrs the next morning.

At the end of the day, we had a de-brief. We were told that

criminal charges were going to be brought against the instigators and that the Service would not let it lie. We all knew that it would probably all fall through because this riot never made the news and people can't be fucked to pursue a case against prisoners, especially if the public knows fuck-all about it.

This whole incident would have cost the Service thousands upon thousands of pounds. And it could have been avoided. If only they would staff the prisons correctly and run a decent regime. But, as usual, things get done the hard way, costing loads of wedge, with people kicking fuck out of each other. This sort of shit goes on all over the country in prisons and the public know nothing about the good, hard work that is done by the screws. They don't know the danger they work in. All they know about is the drug traffickers and the deaths in custody and the fuckups that happen. On TV, Prison Officers are portrayed as meat-heads who stand next to a gate in order to unlock and lock it. If only it was that easy. In so many circumstances, Prison Officers do not get the credit they deserve for doing an extraordinary job.

After a day like that, we deserved a drink even more than usual. Rhys, Garry and I got bang on it, straight round the club. We needed to relax and we did it in the best way we knew how. We were like fucking celebrities. We lapped it up. Garry took full advantage of this, making out that he single-handedly took out every con on his own! Rhys was a good lad, he loved the birds and they loved him, but he was always the flirt and that was it; he had his missus and he loved her.

Instead of sorting out my priorities and getting myself home to Danielle, I stayed there with my prison buddies. The job is weird like that: you want to spend your time with each other even out of work because you know what each other has gone through.

Believe me, you do go through a lot. Being subjected to Britain's worst is going to have repercussions on you in one way or another. Your partners don't really understand what the job can do to you. I found it easier to tip a drink down my neck.

It all happened around the club – fighting, fucking, and drinking. It's where everything got squared away and sorted out, and where people took themselves instead of going home. Many people sacrificed their relationships round there. The place was like a bar in the Wild fucking West! People got sucked into the Service way of life, not just doing it as a job, but doing it as a lifestyle. Was I any different? Was I fuck.

THE SHIRT, THE CHAIN, THE HANDSHAKE

A job? I don't think so. It's a life-changing environment that alters your whole being. Most jobs out there have staff piss-ups, romances, arguments. The Prison Service has all of that times a hundred. It is a way of life. Fact.

Working at a large establishment, such as the Well, there are constant rumours of who is shagging who or who is fighting who. If you've ever worked in a large business or building you will know what I'm talking about. When I worked at the bank, this sort of thing went on. Rumours, a lot of times bollocks, but sometimes true.

In the place of work you make good friends and bad enemies. The old saying, 'Keep your friends close, but your enemies closer,' is one of the truest there is. In the Service, these divides are even stronger. There is always some wanker out to put you down in order to better themselves. Thinking that all screws stick together is the biggest myth going. Of course, all screws should watch each other's backs, but there is always a shirt waiting to stick the knife in. You could say, 'As long as you do nothing wrong, you'll be all right.' Tried that, look what happened to me. 'Survival of the fittest,' Rumpole said. Fucking wrong, but right.

In a job so physically and emotionally charged, these divides can make or break you. If you are in the right clique, then you are safe; if not, then you are lucky if you're flushed only once down the shitter.

You surround yourself with your own, the fellas you can trust. Scouse, Rhys, Jamie, Garry – all my own, trustworthy decent men. Screws understand the job, the pressures, and the lifestyle. Whenever you go out on a work 'do', people normally talk shop for a bit because it's the first common ground that you share with your workmates. Of course, there are other things that you might have in common but, first and foremost, it's the place where you work. On your lunch break, on a works piss-up, on the phone, your first conversation is work and gossip about work. As a screw, the 'shop' conversation never ends. The chat goes on and on. There is always frustration and passion in the chat. Always some important point of view that has to be expressed. Always a complaint about some stitch-up cunt. The thing is, this conversation is only really understood by other screws.

Family members and friends outside the job try to listen and understand, but they haven't got a fucking clue about the pressures. No one has unless they've lived it. Everyone likes to hear the horror stories of prison, the mistreatment of cons, the beatings, the deaths. They don't understand the true effect the Prison Service lifestyle has. The exception, of course, is the partners of a Prison Officer who will be very familiar with the effect of the Service – nine times out of ten they are the first to be neglected or left. But they won't truly understand like another Officer does. Partners tend to think the Service is like a big boys' club. In some ways it is but, trust me, this club has a dangerous and costly membership.

There is a huge Masonic following in the Service. That is an unspoken truth because you are not supposed to be a Mason if you are a Prison Officer (for reasons of preferential treatment, I suppose). I've nothing against that society – I know nothing about them, but I do know quite a few who were open about being a part of it.

Dick had been in the Service for ten or eleven years. He was a screw in the gym, a PEO, and had been for years. He was a slack fucker, always late, lazy and couldn't be arsed. But he seemed to get away with everything. No matter what that cunt did, he would never be disciplined.

He was moved to the Well from an Open Cat D Prison. He was a big fucker who trained hard, but it was obvious he wasn't only eating his greens to grow big. He liked to use steroids. I know a few people who take them, and I think that if they want to end up with nuts the size of peanuts, and the testosterone levels of a ten-year-old girl, then each to their own. Obviously, you are not allowed to use steroids if you are a Prison Officer.

Dick and one of his pals, who was also a screw at the Cat D, were using steroids regularly. They weren't getting them off a dealer at their local gym or anything. They were getting them from a fucking con who was banged up there! Remember how the Open Prison works. The cons pretty much come and go as they please, so it wasn't hard for this con to get the stuff for them. I don't know the full ins and outs of it, just that the con was supplying them.

Somehow they got caught. Don't know how, but Dick got a compulsory transfer and his mate got sacked. Dick knew 'the funny handshake' from his Masonic connections; unfortunately for his mate, he didn't. Dick was at the Well for about six months before being promoted. Sick, isn't it? He was a Governor within two years of his transfer.

Bear in mind that, as a gym screw, you are a basic-grade Officer. He'd been in the job for years, that is true, but the process of going through the ranks should, and does, take years in order to gain the experience to do the job effectively. (The exception is if you have a degree and join under the 'accelerated promotion scheme', which is the biggest lot of bollocks going. Even that takes three or four years to get to the Governor grade, though.) Not Dick: he reached the top at lightning speed, and all 'with a little help from his friends'. As soon as he got to Governor grade, he lived up to his name perfectly, the piece of shit. I didn't particularly like him beforehand: I thought he was a bit of a cunt; but, after his promotions, he would have shat on his mum.

Keeping my mates around me was second nature. I was always cautious about the stitch-up cunts, keeping them at arm's length, with one eye on them at all times.

All of this is spoken about with your close pals. Scouse and I would spend hours and hours putting the world to rights. Rhys, Garry, Jamie and I knew that we had to stick together on the Wing. We knew that there were many who would have loved to stick the knife into us. You could say we were just as bad, but you would be wrong. We did the job well and right, and that's the way it was. We didn't stitch anyone up, cons or screws. Sometimes our methods weren't strictly by the book, but then the book is a bag of bollocks that would not govern a nursery correctly, let alone a fucking nasty bastard place like the Well.

We knew we had a job to do, so we did it. And we needed to relax together. The Officers Club was a place where we could do that and talk about the job . . . and drink about the job . . . and fight about the job. Obviously the screws club was open to all the screws, so you would have your different groups of mates in there. Sometimes over drinks, things could get heated and, from time to time, would end in a scrap. You would have your very close-knit group of pals, but you could still trust the other groups of screws that were decent. It's like when you were at school: you had your group of mates in your year while the lads in the year above were close with each other. You weren't close with them but, if you got into a scrap with the lads from another school, the lads above would fight with you. That's how it was. You knew the ones that were like you, and the ones who weren't.

I had been at work and the shift went OK. A couple of bend ups; nothing to write home about. Rhys, Jamie, Scouse and me went for a beer round the club. A few drinks into the evening, and this silly cunt was pissed-up, making a tit of himself. He got into a row with another screw about something. God only knows what they were saying. I heard a scuffle and saw the silly cunt getting filled in by some bird screw! Apparently he had called the other screw 'a fuckin' nigger'. Obviously the silly cunt was pissed out of his box, not knowing where he was. The black screw was above it, but the bird couldn't let it lie. She split his eye, lip and nose. He deserved it, the piece of shit. Eventually he got thrown out. Don't get the wrong idea, there is no doorman there, or anything; just a bunch of pissed screws who are the police, judge and jury inside them four walls.

The silly cunt went to the Governor the next day to say that he was assaulted round at the club. Fucking mug. After what he said, he was lucky he didn't get put in hospital or, the very least, have a complaint put in for racism. Because he brought the whole thing to the attention of the Governor, there was a full-blown investigation. He ended up being found guilty of what he'd said and was sacked. Fucking right. Good riddance. The cunt brought it up and it backfired, the wanker.

Unfortunately though, racism on the other foot does not get treated the same. There was a group of Nigerian Officers on A Wing who refused to work with white Officers. They refused outright. They wouldn't even communicate with the white Officers. They gave Nigerian prisoners preferential treatment, allowing them to spend hours on the office phone ringing family members and legal teams. They would talk to them in Nigerian, constantly, and when they were asked what they were talking about, they wouldn't answer. As far as I'm concerned, that is a blatant security risk and racism in its purest form. Do you know what was done about this group of Officers? Nothing. Absolutely nothing. Being a white mid-twenties male, what do you think would happen to me if I refused to speak to the Nigerian Officers and gave the white cons preferential treatment? I would be fucked, well and truly, and quite rightly so. Sacked, sued, in the papers, on the news.

It has been drilled into me since the day I was born that it is only acceptable to treat everyone the same, whatever ethnic background or skin colour. Which is right. I constantly hear on the news about people who are not white experiencing extreme levels of racism, which is terrible. But why does it seem acceptable for white people to be treated that way?

Those Nigerian Officers were left alone because they are black. In this politically-correct-gone-mad society, people are scared to be dubbed racist for saying anything confrontational to a black person or anyone who is considered an ethnic minority, even if it has nothing to do with their race or skin colour. People are scared to bollock someone that is not white. Race is brought into play when it has no bearing on the situation.

I've seen Officers wearing a St George cross or a Union Jack tie pin. They were asked to remove them as people could interpret them as being racist. As far as I'm concerned, that is fucking sick. Black Officers within the Prison Service have three unions that they can join: the POA (like me), the Black POA and Respect. Obviously, Respect and the Black POA are unions that I'm not allowed to join. What about the White POA? No such thing; that would be considered racist. There is no need for a White POA, or a Black POA or Respect. There should be one union for all.

The racial argument is all about fair and equal treatment – and integration. Having these separate entities is causing part of the problem. Separation, segregation, separate values and different treatment. How can being proud to be English or British be racist? If there are splinter groups that use English or British emblems for a racist cause, then they should be penalised for it, not the rest who are non-racist and proud of who they are and of their country. I've heard many times, as I'm sure you have, 'I'm black and I'm proud.' That's great to be proud of who you are. I'm white and I'm proud. The patriotic British person should not be considered racist for being proud of who they are. England is my country and I'm proud to be British. I'm proud of the St George's cross, the Union Jack, English rock'n'roll and my country's national football team. Patriotism, not racism.

The Prison Service treats people differently in other ways, too. There was a homosexual Officer who was caught sucking a con's dick. He was suspended and put under a full investigation. He was not sacked, but given a compulsory transfer. I've known a few female Officers in my time who have had sexual relations with a prisoner and who were sacked for their gross misconduct. This treatment is not consistent.

They go on and fucking on about diversity, and how everyone should be treated the same, regardless of gender, race or sexual orientation. That clearly doesn't happen. They can't find any balance, and it fucks me off to say the least.

Another split in the staff ranks is between uniform grades and civvy staff. The civvy staff are your teachers, psychologists, drug workers etc – anyone who doesn't wear a uniform. They generally don't like Officers, they think that we are bullies, and I think most of them are do-good cunts. They have no idea of security whatsoever. They walk on to the Wing, unannounced, and drift around demanding to be let in to a cell to speak to some lad. Or they will be wandering about, talking to prisoners who are out on association. You have to try and picture it. Any Wing is so fucking big, with loads of cons walking around and with minimal staff. It's a fucking nightmare trying to keep control of the place – knowing your numbers and where all the cons are. All the time you are looking around, ready for an incident or potential incident that you may have to intervene with. It's hard for the screws to watch each other's backs and monitor the activities of the cons. That's why it is impossible to stop bullying, fights, assaults and every other dirty trick that goes on. We only have two eyes each.

So, these non-security-aware, useless fuckwits bowl on to the Wing, without telling as much as the landing screw that they are there, and they walk around with their heads stuck up their arses, thinking that they are in a playground with no danger. Most of them honestly forget that they are dealing with criminals who include rapists, murderers, nonces, sickos and every other violent lowlife you can think of. Every time that I caught an unannounced civvy on my landing, I would go fucking mental at them. In the most diplomatic way I knew how, of course . . . !

I would always get bollocked for talking to them without respect. But they come on to my landing, demanding that I drop everything to assist them, and talking to me like a cunt. The way some of them speak to Officers is unbelievable. They give the cons more respect than any of the staff. OK, they have a job to do like everyone else, but you should respect the people you are dealing with. They make the screws feel like they are the criminals. I put in endless complaints about these idiots walking on the Wing, alone, for which I always got, 'Yeah, yeah, they have been told not to.' But they never were.

As bad as it already is, I honestly think that it will take someone being taken hostage, raped, violated or whatever, before these stupid bastards are stopped. Like everything in the fucking Prison Service, risk-assessment comes afterwards and too late, instead of preventative measures being taken beforehand. If and when someone does get hurt, who do you think will get the blame? The landing screw. As far as the powers that be would see it, 'You should know who is on your landing and where all your prisoners are. You should have been there to stop it.'

The female civvies walk around with their noses in the air, looking down on the 'brutal screw'. Get them round the club with half a bottle of Chardonnay down their neck, though, and their opinion soon changes.

One of them was especially like that. A cunt at work, hated the uniform, love the con. She even got moved from inside the nick to outside because, rumour had it, she liked a bit of con cock. She used to turn her nose up at all the uniformed staff. She liked the Governor grade though. She'd had it slung up her by a couple of them apparently.

She didn't go round the club very often but when she did, two drinks later – what a slag! All over every fucker. Right old tart. She was obviously a suppressed lover of the uniform. Garry got into it and was having it away with her, left, right and centre. The dangerous fucker used to do her at lunchtimes in one of the landing offices! Never got caught, though. She had a fucking fella as well, poor cunt. He used to pick her up sometimes. Little did he know she was having cock with her tuna salad.

She wasn't the only one who was a cunt at work and a slag after. There was this female Governor who was a stitch-up bitch at work. Couldn't ask her for fuck-all, she would jog you on. She didn't go on staff 'dos' or to the club very often. Even though she was a twat, I was still surprised she didn't show her face from time to time. They normally do, you see, the wankers as well as the good ones.

I was having a fucking shit day at work. I was working with a right tit, so I was doing everything. I'd had to do two planned interventions: a pair of cunts who were refusing to transfer, and then I had this other nut nut who was trying to tell me he was Jesus and I must obey him. I ended up dropping him as he wouldn't get out of my face. He tried to stop me from walking past him. That was enough.

I had that particular weirdo bent up, so we took him down The Block. I bumped into Doubtfire down there.

'Fancy a pint tonight, lad?' he said in his squeaky voice.

'Not half, mate, I've had a fucking shit day.'

I finished work and rang Danielle to say I wouldn't be home. She wasn't best pleased.

Scouse joined us as usual. Over a few beers, I said that I found it strange that a female Governor never came to staff parties and shit. Doubtfire laughed in a sinister way, looking at me like, 'I know something that you don't know!' He went on to tell me about a Christmas party, a few years before I'd joined. It was a time where there wasn't such a divide between Governors and Officers – a time when you could trust each other, and you always relied on your workmates. I do love hearing the old boys talk about the good old days.

Anyway, the Christmas party was in full swing, the beer was flowing and everyone was enjoying themselves. No scraps, some people making nobheads of themselves, some snogging and getting hold of each other – a bog-standard Christmas party. It was like a school disco: kids having fun, without a care in the world. That sums up a lot of the shenanigans that go on in the Prison Service. Some Officers go to work, leaving their family personality at home. They get their screw head on, which goes further than just being inside the gate. They forget about their families, husbands, wives. When the shift and the party are finished, the screw head is left there, and the family personality is picked up on the way home. It's like a separate life.

Everything was going well at the party, and this Governor was pissed. She was proper pissed, searching for some pork sword and even though Dave was always under suspicion for being bent, that didn't stop her from wanting him. She would do anything to stitch someone up in the nick; outside, she would do anything to have someone stick one in her.

It was near the end of the night, so the crowd was thinning out. The club was split into two rooms: one, a fair-sized hall; the other, the main bar with pools tables and stuff. The Hall was only open for functions, like the Christmas party. Both rooms were now open, with most people in the Hall. Dave was getting hold of her, and it was getting pretty heavy! Dave kept looking over her shoulder to Doubtfire and the rest, laughing and inviting someone else to join them while she was trying to get his cock out there in front of everyone. One of the other fellas went over and got stuck in with them both, much to the cheers and amusement of the audience.

They went into the bar, where there was no one else. She got fucked senseless by both of them. Spit roasted, the lot. As Doubtfire was telling me all this, he had the biggest grin slapped on his ginger face. Everyone round the nick knew about it at the time.

A spouse sometimes gets the hump with the Service way of life, and it's not always the spouse of an Officer. There was a barmaid at the club, who was a nice bird, friendly and that. She enjoyed her job and was as good as gold. She loved her fella. God knows why, he was a fucking prick. Spoke to her like a cunt, treated her like shit. He would sit at the end of the bar most nights, getting pissed up, looking moody, thinking everyone wanted to fuck his missus. He was a tough-looking geezer. He was a ground worker with a thick neck and huge forearms like fucking Popeye. He was allowed in the club because his missus worked there. He didn't even try to socialise or be civil – attitude all wrong from the start. I don't know who the fuck he thought he was.

Scouse and I were sitting at the bar. We were still in uniform. We'd been on a late turn, so it was about half nine or so. We'd had a couple of chasers to relax us before settling into a nice pint.

'You're a fucking dirty whore!'

It was wanker boyfriend in the corner, screaming at his missus. She was standing behind the bar, sheepishly mouthing the words 'I'm sorry' to us. We were embarrassed for her. It was her relationship to deal with as she saw fit. That's what Scouse and I said to each other. It wasn't our place to get involved. This geezer was such a jealous fucker, he thought that his missus was getting poled by everyone in a uniform. She wasn't; she was a nice lady.

His barrage of abuse continued until Scouse could take no more. It was embarrassing for everyone.

'Leave it out lad,' warned Scouse.

'What's it got to do with you, shitbag?'

'Outside ya fat cunt!' Scouse shouted as he marched over to the door. Looking stunned, the boyfriend watched Scouse walk past.

'Come on, fuckface!' Scouse screamed again, bouncing up and down, clearly pumped up for a row. I rose to my feet, knowing that it was going to kick off. I had no intention of stopping it. Scouse had made the decision and, as far as I was concerned, it was a good one. But this fella was a tasty-looking cunt. Looked like he could have a row, plus he had balls of steel. He sat in a screws club, giving everyone attitude, being the only non-screw in there. Either brave or fucking stupid.

'Who you fucking talking to?' he bellowed back to Scouse, walking towards him with his huge hands wide open, looking like a grizzly about to feed. Scouse was by the door, stepping back just as his target got close to him. Scouse was out of my sight, with the back of the other fella in view. I saw the geezer's head move backwards. Scouse had belted him – fucking hard by the look of it. I went over quickly, seeing the big cunt knocked out on the floor. Scouse was standing there laughing, 'Faggot! One punch, useless cunt!' Scouse then told him in no uncertain terms that if he caught him there again, he would get it.

The club, the camaraderie was as much a part of being an Officer as working on the Wing.

HMP HOTEL

I was on The Ones, when a 'new' con was brought on to the Wing.

'Hello Jack.'

'Hello Bill, what you doing here?'

'The cozzers tucked me up so I'm back for a rest!'

The 'regulars' always blame it on the Old Bill! But they are never bothered about being banged up. For them, it's just like being down the pub: they have plenty of drugs, plenty of hooch that the cons like to brew and they have plenty of scraps.

If it's a first timer with a bit of savvy and bollocks, then they'll soon get the hang of things. As they settle in, you can literally see their bollocks grow. They are timid little lambs when they first get banged up but, once they are used to it, they think they are tough prisoners serving hard time. Yeah, really tough and hard –

when they complain that they have not been unlocked to play pool!

It used to be *real* hard time – as tough for them as when we were mega-short-staffed, only then they had a load of screws working the landings. That was the regime back then: bang up, food and more bang up. If they got lippy, they got a good clump. It was a lot stricter in those days – well, brutal in some cases. But they did have more control then. If you speak to the old villains who are banged up now, they will tell you that they preferred prison the way it used to be. They say that they knew where they stood. But in today's prison, there is no consistency. They hate the fact that there is no control, with little plastic gangsters mouthing off, shouting about how tough things are for them. You get cons complaining that they have two slices of beef instead of three! Back in the old days, I'm told you were lucky to get sugar with your shit!

A local Cat B has the worst facilities out of all the prisons. This is because they get shit funding as they are only supposed to be holding prisons. As soon as prisoners are sentenced and categorised, they should be shipped out. But it never happens like that, because the Prison Service is bursting at the seams with very few beds left. The Well is a lot like you would imagine a prison to be: dirty, large and loud. However, even the Well has pool tables, table tennis and TVs in a lot of the cells. It also has a decent gym and sports activities. I think that this is a good thing: it gives them a structured regime and keeps them busy, sometimes learning new skills. I know a lot of you will think, 'Fuck them, they are in prison.' I can understand that, and I think that there should be a cap on how good the facilities are. Outside of prison, we pay for our gym membership, we pay to play pool and go to the snooker hall. So why should they get it all for nothing? I agree that they do get too much for fuck-all. A lot of them are better off banged up than free.

Now Cat A prisons are great! They have single bang up, Xboxes and PlayStation2 in their cells, and some of them have full-size snooker tables and Sky TV! Their gyms are state-of-the-art with plasma TVs, the fucking lot. I pay sixty fucking quid a month for my gym and forty-odd quid for my cable channels. Unbelievable, when you look at it in money terms. The real mental cunts have even more.

I don't believe in brutalising these people but, on the other hand, I think getting all of this for free helps no one. The poor victims get fuck-all. A lot of them think that justice has been done and the criminals are paying for their crimes. Although I hate to shatter that belief, in a lot of cases it's bullshit. The 'condemned' abuse the system and get little or fuck-all punishment.

Every con has a history sheet on which their conduct is entered. So, from reading a history sheet, you should be able to build a picture of what the con is like. This is really important. Do you think it gets done regularly? No. It's the time thing again. Let's say you are on a landing with fifty cells and twenty of them 'abuse' their cell bells, i.e. use them to make what they know are ridiculous or no-hoper requests. That then means there are twenty history sheets in which you have to make entries. It's fucking impossible to get it done, along with the other duties, so you don't bother doing it for all – or even any – of them because there are more important things to deal with.

To add to the insult of this waiter service, the Governors were in the process of installing a system to time how long it took a screw to answer the cell bell. I'm not sure what the time scale was planned to be but, if you didn't meet that requirement, then you were marked as 'poor performed' and disciplined! Another little tool to add pressure to the Officer who is trying to do his real job of policing these bastards. Myself, I think this was one of the things Governors dream up to make sure they keep their four-star rating . . .

When cons achieve three negative entries on their history sheets, they are put in front of the SO. The SO will give them a first-stage warning. This means that, if they have another negative entry within twenty-eight days, they will be downgraded to Basic Regime. Basic Regime is exactly that. No gym, no association, no fuck-all. They are entitled to a shower every three days and thirty minutes' exercise per day. They have to put an application in for a phone call, which they are allowed every three days.

Those are the rules, but the SOs and Governors never allow the Prison Officers to stick to them. Those on Basic Regime should not really be allowed to mix with the rest of the Wing. They should have showers and exercise when the other inmates are banged up. If the regime is stuck to, then it is strict and it acts as a deterrent. Basic Regime shouldn't be easy; if it is, then there is no point in putting anyone on it. However, if an inmate is struggling on Basic and gets bent up a couple of times, the SOs and Wing Governor normally decide to let him have exercise with the others. Or maybe they let him have 'association' time – which is time for phone calls, showers, visiting others in their cells etc – and so the inmates get rewarded for being cunts! They may have tried to punch a screw and have, as a result, been bent up; but the Governor feels that the con is finding Basic Regime too difficult and needs to be given an easier time. Therefore, instead of being punished, they get some fucking benefits! It undermines everything that the regime is trying to do.

If they are put in front of the SO about abusing their cell bell, the SO would normally only give them a ticking off. The con would be all apologetic to the SO who would allow them to be let off. The little scroat wanker would come out of the office laughing at you. It makes a mockery of the whole system. All this fluffy-shit human-rights stuff means the prison is too scared to do anything that will upset the inmate – who is not scared to fuck about, so you have no control.

The Governors are only interested in doors being unlocked and the prisoners being out of their cells. This looks, on the audits, as if the prison is running a good and successful regime. The Governors don't give a fuck about the bullying or the drug dealing or the lack of security. They are only interested in 'time out of the cell'. Come hell or high water, they want those cells unlocked, even if that means the prison is unsafe. They rely on staff breaching security every day, just so prisoners get out of their cells and the audit looks good.

All of the duties that need to be done correctly and well are hurried or skipped. The rub-downs of the cons going on the yard are rushed so things are overlooked. You receive Intel, so you spin the cell, but that has to be speeded up because of other things that need to be done. Spinning a cell should be done slowly and thoroughly. These sneaky bastards could hide a tank in their cells! Like everything else, this gets rushed and therefore things can get missed: weapons, drugs, the lot. The cons laugh at it.

Even if a con is caught and nicked for some offence, the Governors give them fuck-all punishment. I used to find mobile phones all the time when I spun cells. I would nick the owners and they would have to face the Governor. They would normally get fourteen days' loss of 'canteen' – which is when they get the opportunity to buy anything in the way of tobacco, crisps, toiletries and other creature comforts. You might think a mobile phone isn't hurting anyone, so why is the punishment so bad? You have to look at the bigger picture. If he's got a phone, then the likelihood is he has a screw in his pocket. If he hasn't, then he will be linked to someone that has. If he has a phone, then he has money, so he will probably be drug dealing. Also, the phone isn't just to ring his bird or his wife: it will be to run his crime racket direct from his cell, or else he may be using it to intimidate a witness. The punishment should be harsh, as the possibilities of phone abuse are endless; it doesn't end at simply having a phone.

As often as not, the powers that be in the prison system dole out either laughably feeble punishments or no punishment at all. One con said to a female screw, 'Miss, you are well fit, come to my cell and I will fuck your brains out.' So she nicked him, quite rightly. The Governor said that she should be flattered and that, although his suggestion was inappropriate, she didn't need to nick him! Cheeky fucking cunt! He said that in front of the con, I kid you not. Like a fool, she didn't complain. She was too scared to cause trouble. It's like that in the Prison Service; a lot of the screws put up and shut up. They let the Governors bully them into nearly anything. If you have a voice, then you make enemies, simple as that. Unfortunately, I have a very loud voice, so I was always going to have enemies.

You don't get any support at all. Many a time I've made a decision only to have the Governor undermine me, making me look a right cunt. The con wins, and your authority has been taken away.

One day I was on the Wing, carrying out my fabric checks. That's right, fabric checks for once! I had this pikey called McCarthy who was a real nasty bastard and a druggy. He was a pain in the arse. He wanted a cell move, to be with his mate. His mate was a piece-of-shit bully who was always up to no good. I gave McCarthy the chance to change his ways, but he never took it. He was about my age, average build and height. I used to give him a way out every time he was being a knob, but he never took it. I don't know if he was too thick, or just loved to be a cunt.

'Oi Thompson, I'm moving cell,' McCarthy stated to me.

'First, it's Mr Thompson or Guv to you. Second, you have more chance of breaking out than having a cell move, you rude cunt.'

No way was he moving cell to be with his bullying mate. They would be a right pair of wankers together. Also, I won't have anyone tell me what they are going to do. It's about manners. I was brought up to have them and so, if people are rude to me, they get fuck-all. Politeness costs nothing. I demand it of everyone and I'm rude to nobody without good reason.

McCarthy disappeared to his cell. About five minutes later, he emerged from his cell with all of his kit packed.

'What do you think you are doing, McCarthy? Didn't you understand me?'

'Fuck you, ya fat cunt, I told you before, I'm fucking moving.' He wasn't scared of fuck-all, and there was no reasoning with him.

'Put your kit back into your cell, go have a shower and make a phone call. That is what association is for. I won't tell you again, you are not moving, and it's not up for discussion.'

With that he dropped his kit bag and squared up to me shouting, 'Try and stop me, you cunt, go on!'

Standing nose to nose, I said calmly, 'Why do you do it?'

Confused, but aggressive, he shouted, 'Do what . . . ?'

Before he even had a chance to wait for an answer, I grabbed him by the back of his head and dropped him to the floor. I had him bent up before he knew what hit him.

'Arrghh! What are you doing, let go of me,' he screamed.

I told him that he wasn't allowed to move. I'd given him a way out, but he was too stupid to take it and there was no way that I was going to risk taking one on the chin from him; that's not my job. So the minute he was in my personal space, I dropped him. OK, I'm not always the most diplomatic person and I use terrible language, but I won't apologise for being me. I'm still fair, but this twat took liberties with everyone. I'm not just talking about Officers, either; he was a horrible cunt to everyone.

Once I'd wrapped him up, we took him to The Block. He was then seen by the healthcare team, and the Duty Governor. The Duty Governor, on that day, happened to be my Wing Governor; he was a cunt who thought he was great at everything but he was nothing more than a bully to staff.

He went down to speak to McCarthy and asked him what his problem was. He gave the Governor a sob story of how he wanted a cell move and how big bad wolf Mr Thompson wouldn't let him.

My reasons were clear: in short, he was a troublemaker. The Governor then made a typical Governor move and gave him the cell move he wanted! After being told 'No!' by me for valid reasons, he then kicked off and got bent up. And after all that, he still got what he wanted. Amazing, isn't it?! It sends out all the wrong messages. If you don't get what you want, then kick off because, if you do, then you will get what you want in the end. It also made me look a cunt and put my integrity into question.

A fucking mug that Governor is. He would never stand by his staff. The cheeky fucker said, 'Ronnie, you have to give and take sometimes, you can't be too hard on them.' He knew what McCarthy was like, but he didn't give a fuck that one of his screws had made a decision and needed to stand by it. He never stood by the staff.

I was so accustomed to this shit management that it didn't shock me. It should have, but you can't fight the system the whole time. It's draining. It shouldn't have to happen. As far as I'm concerned, you make sure of the safety of all the staff first. Then you make sure of the safety of the inmates. After that, you can try to stop the drugs and bent screws from operating, and finally you make sure every fucker is banged up and has not escaped. That is the basis of pounding the landings in my eyes; everything else is secondary and a bonus.

You do get other screws who are idiot enough to pick up on every little lapse and misdemeanour because they love the authority. But trying to discipline inmates over everything wastes time that could be spent better – and trivialises everything. These Officers are earning no respect whatsoever from the cons and they usually end up getting the fucking shit kicked out of them. Once that happens, they either change and become good screws, or they fraggle out and leave, probably dosed up to the eyeballs on Prozac, and then sit at home rocking in a chair, too frightened to leave the house.

I had this scroat move on to my landing who was always mouthing off, complaining about everything. He was disrespectful to staff, especially the women. The dirty little bastard was filthy. He would drop sexual remarks at every opportunity and whenever a woman unlocked his cell door, he would expose his little worm and start wanking. Bloomfield was his name. He was a twenty-one-year-old white fella who thought he was black. He was one of those geezers who talks in a Jamaican accent, but he was born and raised in Devon by his Catholic parents! He was your typical fucking good-for-nothing. He didn't want to better himself, he was too busy being angry at the whole world. He was just bad, simple as that.

He'd come through one Young Offenders Institution after another, so he'd been in and out of nick from the age of fifteen. When he got to the Well, he had just turned twenty-one. That's the age they leave the YO establishments and join big-man prison. He was a fucking dick from day one. Always fighting with other cons, always being abusive to everyone. Bloomfield was on my landing, so he was my problem to deal with. I tried everything with him. I tried to relate to him on his level, but he wouldn't have it one bit. He had had to be bent up loads of times, but that didn't work either.

I went into work: bacon sandwich, pint of coffee. In the morning briefing, I was told I would be working with a female Officer called Marge. She was in her early fifties and had been in the job for years and years. You couldn't wish for a better lady. As you can imagine, my methods of being a screw were quite different from hers but, all the same, she was good and could do the job. Of course she didn't get into bend ups; she didn't need to. As she had been at the Well for her whole career, all the cons knew her. Most of them had respect for her and would not give her grief. They knew that she knew her shit. Also, they knew she was a lady who was getting on a bit, so you have respect.

Bloomfield respected no one at all. He had been nicked loads of times and been put on Basic. Nothing worked because the punishments were pathetic. He used to laugh at them but the powers that be reasoned that, 'He's only twenty-one, we have to work with him.' For fuck's sake! Only twenty-one? He's a grown man! He didn't give a fuck when he robbed his own parents, the wrong bastard. How many chances do they want to give someone?

It was time for this prisoner to realise he was in prison. It was lunchtime. My landing was The Threes on that day. The Ones' screw called up to indicate that he was ready to receive my inmates to go and collect their food.

It's none of this 'dining together' bollocks at the Well. How it works is, The Ones' screw shouts up to one of the landings, telling the screws to send down their cons. They acknowledge, and send their prisoners down to collect their food. There are two sets of stairs on D Wing, so the cons go down one set to The Ones, go into the servery and collect their food. They then go up the other set of stairs back to their landing and return to their cells. It's a nice and simple – one-way traffic down to the servery and back up again. That is how it is supposed to work.

The cons use this as an excuse to run around the Wing. They go to other cells on other landings, and get burn passed to them under the doors. Of course, this is a perfect time to drug run. During feeding, it's fucking chaos. We always tried to control it, but it was hard with the sheer numbers.

Bloomfield had been down to the servery to collect his lunch. I heard him shouting at the servery Officer, so he obviously had the hump about something yet again. He came up the stairs and was walking towards his cell shouting about some bollocks. Marge was closest to him so she was going to bang him up. I thought that I'd better walk over because you never knew what he was going to do. As I got near, Bloomfield threw his tray at the floor and walked off leaving the mess everywhere.

By this point, Marge had unlocked his door. As he got there Marge said, 'What's the matter, dear? Can I help you? Let's go back and tidy that mess up, and talk about it.' That is her way you see; she is lovely and has this calming and motherly way of dealing with everything.

'Fuck you, you old slag. You clean it up, you fucking whore.'

I had just got there so I heard it all. As he saw me he walked into the cell. Marge shut the door, looking flustered. She didn't even work on D Wing any more; she was only helping out because we were short.

'Don't worry Marge, love, I am going to sort him.'

I walked over the mess that he had created. It was stew, or something, and mash. I picked up his plate and scooped up as much of the mess as I could. I walked calmly back to his cell.

'Marge can you unlock his cell, love, I think he forgot his dinner,' I asked politely.

She unlocked the door for me.

With that Bloomfield jumped up from his bed and snapped, 'What the fuck do you want?'

Walking towards him I said calmly, 'You forgot something.'

With that, I whacked the plate full on in his face, covering him in the food that I'd scooped up. I grabbed the little bastard by his throat and began throwing him around the cell.

'You have pushed your luck!' I screamed in his ear almost deafening him, while pinning him to the wall, with my forearm to his throat. He was struggling and trying to hit me, but I was stronger. As he was struggling and shouting at me, I shouted, 'Play nice,' at which I then gave him two sharp digs to his ribs. I then dragged him to his toilet and shoved his head down it. He was a dirty creature, who lived in absolute filth, so you can imagine what his toilet was like.

'Ahh, ahh, all right, all right, I'm sorry!' he shouted, begging to be released.

'This what it takes, for me to shove your head down a shitter for you to play ball?'

'No Guv, no Guv, I promise!'

Still having him pinned to the toilet, I told him, 'You have been nothing but a cunt since you have been here. I've been patient with you, I've tried to be nice to you, but you don't get it; you continue to be a wanker to fucking everyone. So help me God, I will come to this fucking cell every fucking day, and shove your nut down the bog until you learn, you little cunt. You have had ya fun, now play the game and wind your neck in. Do you understand me?'

'Yes, Mr Thompson, I will behave now,' he answered, child-like.

Releasing him and letting him stand up, I said calmly, 'Now, clean yourself up, get yourself out on that landing and apologise to Miss Cowan. You beg her not to nick you and you tell her that you are turning over a new leaf. When you've done that, clean up the rest of the mess you made. Do it quickly, and then get yourself downstairs and get another plate of dinner.'

Standing there covered in food and shit, he answered, 'Yes, Mr Thompson. I'm sorry about the way I've been.'

Shaking my head I said, 'You haven't just got to say sorry to me. You have pissed off a lot of people on this Wing. You've got a lot of bridges to build.'

'Yes, Guv.'

Marge came up to me about ten minutes later and told me that he was really apologetic. I told her that we had a chat and he'd agreed with me that his behaviour was unacceptable.

Bloomfield did change has attitude completely. He started having more respect for people and, more importantly, for himself. I eventually got him a job cleaning the landings and I introduced him to education. He wasn't fucking perfect, by any means, and occasionally he would spit his dummy out, but he could be spoken to and would normally see reason.

Some will think that these methods are brutal, and maybe they are. Unconventional, but they worked, and I went on to have a fairly decent relationship with Bloomfield. I am disgusted at how the disciplinary procedures are so pathetic that cons continually get away with everything. I would deal with it exactly the same if I were in that situation again. If the punishment were severe enough, or acted as a deterrent, then maybe these sods wouldn't play up so much.

That's what good screws do, they find a method of dealing with someone to get him to get his head down and serve his bird. It doesn't always result in a con getting his head stuffed down a toilet. A lot of the time matters can be dealt with by a personal chat. It didn't always need to be something physical. I could talk and level with these people. I would tell them how it was. If the cons fucked about, I would fuck them about. I would not sneak to others about them or stitch them up on the quiet. I would tell them honestly that I would make life as difficult for them as they made it for me. I kept it nice and simple, and always stood by my word.

We had this lad on the Wing called Stav, who was a nasty bit of work. He was in for kidnap and torture. He was a Spanish fella who was absolutely minted. He had properties all over the world, top motors and everything. Of course, he didn't come by all of this legitimately. He was a drug baron. When he was on D Wing at the Well, he controlled the place. Jake had finally been transferred to a Cat A nick. You lose one boss, you always gain another.

Stav had bent screws in his pocket; he was the main dealer on the Wing. He had every fucker under his thumb because of his wealth. He was about forty years old, six feet tall and average build. He wasn't tough, but he had his henchmen who would look after him because he paid them to, so he wasn't shy of throwing threats at people (although he didn't usually aim them at the screws). You would never see him fighting, but you always knew when he was behind someone getting done over. He would never admit it outright, but he would always let you know. He was arrogant and rude. He wouldn't be abusive, just rude. Never said please or thank you. Instead of 'Can I have', he would say 'Give me'.

I was detailed as the Servery Officer in the morning briefing. The Ones was my regular landing, but one of the jobs was servery. Garry usually did it, with Rhys and I as the landing screws. Together, we three were a tight ship on The Ones. But Garry was on a rest day so I was on servery.

The servery looks like the canteen where you got your school dinners as a kid, only dirtier – and the dinner ladies are hairy-arsed prisoners! As the servery screw, I would stand there and make sure they got what they had put down for, and the right amount. They pre-ordered their meals for the coming week. Of course, you would get the odd mistake, but some of the cons would take the piss and say it was wrong all the time. For that reason, you need a strong character to be the Servery Officer, someone who can say no to a con and move them on.

When you work as the servery screw, you recognise the usual suspects, those most likely to say their meal is wrong. You have to use your discretion. For example, if you have a con of a particular religious denomination, who has stipulated that they can't eat a particular dish – and that's what they've been given, you go and get them something else because you know it's a mistake. But there are others who will say their food is wrong just to cause trouble.

It was a roasting summer's day, so you can imagine what the heat was like in the servery. I was hung over and tired, plus I'd had a blazing row with Danielle the night before. I had been out on the piss with Scouse and then stayed in the staff quarters again. I was soaked with sweat and wearing my itchy, old-fashioned uniform was adding to my misery. The servery workers were knackered and moody, but they were digging in and getting the job done. During the hot weather, tempers do rise and there are a lot more fights and bend ups.

We were halfway through serving lunch. It had run relatively smoothly. I had a couple of lads call me a cunt when I said 'No', but that was it. That is just water off a duck's back. Then Stav came in and I wasn't in the mood for his shit one bit. The person he had kidnapped and tortured had all his fingers cut off, his kneecaps drilled and had been battered half to death. This wanker was proud of it, which is the sort of lowlife that he was. I could picture it, his big fucking henchman holding that person down while that sadistic cunt tortured him. It made my skin crawl.

Anyway, Stav came into the servery in his normal arrogant manner. He always complained that he didn't get the meal he'd ordered. Cheeky cunt used to say he was victimised! He rolled up to the servery and gave his plate to the workers to serve his meal. Every con was scared of him, they knew the sort of power he had. The servery workers gave him chicken, just like he'd ordered.

'Give me something else NOW. That is not mine.'

'You get what you are given. Take it and fuck off,' I snapped at him, before he even tried to hand back his plate. I was already losing my cool and acting unprofessionally. I wasn't in the mood to humour him and be tactful.

'You will regret talking to me like that,' he said, trying to be menacing.

'Really? Great. Get your fucking chicken and fuck off out of my servery!' I was shouting, showing my frustration, something I never liked doing.

Laughing at me, he said, 'How about I cut your wife's face?' Now he was quite capable of that, but he was just trying to scare me. In my moody hung-over state, I saw red. It was quiet in there by now; all the cons were listening to us. For a split second, I pictured Danielle being hurt by someone. You get threats, but you can't respond to them; you are supposed to inform security and that's it.

I smacked the cunt right in his mouth, dragged him out on the landing and bent him up. The Officers on the landing saw me drop him, so they ran over to assist. Stav was crying his eyes out. I couldn't believe it! The fucking wimp. He can hurt and kill people but he couldn't take a punch in the mouth. Once I had him bent up on the floor, he was crying saying, 'Mr Thompson punched me! He punched me!'

We took him down The Block. He made a complaint to the Governor about me, so I was under investigation. It so happened that the Governor wasn't one of my fans, so he would have loved to sack me.

They investigated it by questioning the other cons in the servery. Not one of them said that I punched him. What a good bunch of lads. They heard what he said to me and most of them got on really well with me, so they said that Stav was being aggressive and tried to hit me. I was chuffed that they helped me out.

I acted like a cunt that day. I let my feelings come into play, which is something you should never do. But I am only human. It could have been avoided if I'd spoken to him diplomatically in the first place. When he was threatening me, he was five or six feet away so I didn't need to walk over and belt him. He wasn't an immediate threat to me. Stav got categorised to Cat A. He was shipped out to Whitmoor the next day. I'm not proud of how I acted: it wasn't right.

Six months later, I was to face an investigation that was a lot, lot worse.

CRIMES INSIDE AND THE BASHING OF JONO

There is a code of discipline within prisons. If a con does anything that warrants being placed on report – or nicked, as it's better known – then they face the Duty Governor the next day for the adjudication. They would be nicked for such things as possession of drugs, fighting and having to be restrained. For the less severe things, like misuse of cell bell or being where they shouldn't be, they don't get nicked – they'd just get a negative entry in their history sheet. As I've already explained, three negative entries result in a first-stage warning. If they get another negative entry within twenty-eight days, they are down-graded to Basic Regime.

Sometimes they do something that can't be dealt with in house. If it is severe enough, it is handed over to the police.

You might think that if a con fucks about, they will get days added to their sentence, but Governors have lost that power and all they can now do is give cell confinement or loss of canteen or something along those lines. This is kids' stuff, which most cons don't give a fuck about. It works with some (being banged up all day isn't nice) but, for the real cunt, it's nothing. The only punishment they don't want is extra days on their sentence. So, now that the European Court of Human Rights has taken this power away, nicking someone is a waste of time.

It does stipulate, however, that, every twenty-eight days, an outside adjudicator – a magistrate of some sort – will visit establishments with the power to add extra days to sentences. However, if the con gets nicked for something that warrants extra days but is released before the adjudicator is due, then that crime goes unpunished; it just disappears.

That said, if the powers that be want someone out of a Prison Service job (as they did with my suspension over Frankie) they hand over the investigation to the police as quickly as they can. The police don't really want to go into a prison to investigate crimes; as far as they are concerned, these should be dealt with by the prison. And, all too often, things that ought to be handed over to the police never reach them; while those that are handed over just seem to fall by the wayside.

Meantime, the cons get up to all sorts of shit inside for which, if they did the same on the outside, they would receive severe punishments. A typical example was a prisoner called Cooper. He was a crackhead in his late thirties who had been in and out of nick since he was a teenager. He knew how to manipulate the system and he could be a handful at times. I would get on with him fine one minute, then the next I'd be rolling on the floor fighting with him. The next day he would be fine again. That's how Cooper was with everyone. All the staff knew him, all the cons knew him, and he was local so, when he was out, you would see him walking around fucked out of his head. He was part of the furniture at the Well. Because he was a massive crackhead, he was always on the rob. He was linked with different firms, as a runner or whatever, but his habit was big and he couldn't afford to support it, inside or out.

I was working on The Ones with Rhys. We had him banged up on our landing for a couple of weeks. He knew us, we knew him. We could normally handle him a lot better than others did. At that time, Cooper was bang on the gear. He was out of control, always getting bent up and scrapping with other cons.

Rhys and I were having a lively morning. We'd spun a few cells, found some smack and a couple of phones. The morning had gone well. Cooper was looking more shifty than usual. It was obvious he was in debt, and worried about a kicking.

'He's gonna do something today. Bet we have to bend him today,' Rhys said.

'Lets try not to play into his hands,' I suggested.

Shortly after that, Cooper went into his cell and smashed it to pieces. I mean completely fucking trashed it. He ripped the sink off the wall and kicked the toilet from the ground. There was water pissing out everywhere. The cell was filling up. The water was pouring out from under the door. He had completely smashed his bed up and cupboards. Due to the rapid rate the water was coming out, we didn't have the time to kit up before going in. He would have probably drowned. Rhys and I ran to his cell to get him out. I was the one who undid his door. As I did so, torrents of water came flooding out. I was faced with Cooper, soaked to the bone, bouncing up and down like Rocky.

'Come on then you screw cunts, lets have it!' he screamed.

Knowing what he's like, I took no chances and dropped him.

The cell was like a fucking sauna – when he smashed the sink off the wall, he smashed a pipe which carried hot water. The room was full of steam and the water on the floor covered my boots. On top of all that, I had some dickhead wanting to fight. I grabbed hold of Cooper who barely resisted at all. Apart from getting soaking wet, no one received any injuries.

The other Officers on the Wing were banging up the cons who were out on association. Standard procedure. When an incident like that happens, the Officers bang the Wing up as quickly as possible, with support from Officers on other Wings who would have arrived to help when the alarm was raised. Inevitably, though, some cons see who has got bent up. In this case, they knew it was Cooper because of the flood the prick had caused. Besides, everyone knew what a cunt he was.

We took him to The Seg, but he didn't fight and was compliant throughout. It was obvious he had planned to get bent up for the show.

'In debt are we Cooper?' I whispered in his ear, as we were walking him under restraint to The Block.

Laughing he replied, 'Who me? Never, Mr Thompson!'

He had no shame at all. It turns out, he smashed his cell to bits so we would run in there and get him out. He knew exactly how far to push it to get bent up. He must have thought it was Christmas when I walked in because he knew how I worked. He knew that, during such an incident, I would drop him if he did anything other than what he was directed to do. That is exactly what he wanted. He knew it was association, so everyone would see him get bent up. He also knew that he would then be taken off the Wing, which is exactly what he wanted. He owed loads of money for the crack he'd already smoked, but had nothing with which to pay for it; so they had begun to threaten him.

When he was down The Seg, he refused to go back to D Wing, so the soft bastards let him go to B Wing. No doubt the lads he was in debt to would catch up with him eventually. Cons move around all the Wings at the Well for one reason or another, plus most have friends on other Wings and it is easy enough to get a message across. Cooper wasn't stupid, and he knew this, but he knew it would also buy him some time before they caught up with him. At which point he might well have the money or some scam that they would be interested enough in to let what he owed go. Getting bent up was his way of getting off the Wing without grassing. He would say that he had the money but some bully-boy screw picked on him. He was the slipperiest cunt in the world. He had lived his life like that, always just getting away with it. It was a dangerous game that he played, though, and I've no doubt he is probably dead by now. If he isn't, it won't be long before he is.

Perhaps I shouldn't have dropped him and then his little plan wouldn't have worked. But, Cooper was a nasty cunt and would have done what it took to get bent up. He wouldn't have walked out of that cell. If that meant him wrapping a table leg around my head, he would have done it.

So he was nicked for threatening and abusive behaviour, and damaging prison property. He stayed down The Seg for the night pending adjudication. First thing in the morning, he was in front of the Governor to answer the charges, and we were called down to give evidence.

The Governor should have recommended investigation by the

police because he hadn't got the jurisdiction to punish appropriately for the damage caused. Did the Governor do that? Did he fuck. He decided to give Cooper three days' cell confinement suspended for three months. What that means is he would have to spend three days down The Block *if* he got nicked and found guilty of something else within three months. Cooper laughed his tits off. Criminal damage to the degree that Cooper caused would probably get you six months in prison if you were to do it on the road. In prison, you don't even have to stay down The Block! So these cunts are not bothered about doing anything because they know they will get fuck-all punishment. That's rehabilitation for you.

I do think it is a waste of police time, but they need to deal with these things to stop them happening. They have the power to sort the problem, the Prison Service doesn't. The Governors don't want to hand over trivial things like that, though, so the con gets away with it, which is wrong.

And when a screw gets assaulted, the punishment is pathetic. Of course, there are different levels of assault. Touching someone can be perceived as assault but, when the assault is more serious, the punishment is still crap: seven days' CC (cell confinement) or some shit like that. On the road, they would be nicked for ABH and go down. Assaulting a Prison Officer should be dealt with in the same way as assaulting a policeman. As a Prison Officer, you have the powers of a constable while acting as one, so assault should be treated the same. But it's not. It seems to be more acceptable for a screw to get done over than a copper. The Governors never offer to refer the matter to the police if you've been assaulted; you have to insist. I have known cons to be dealt with through the courts for assaulting a screw, but very seldom.

I got into work that morning and I was told in the briefing I was being cross-deployed to B Wing. They were short-staffed, and it was my turn to cross-deploy. I wasn't bothered; it was something different. I finished my brew and headed over there. I reported to the SO. He told me I would be working with Jono. I was pleased. He was a good lad. I got on with him well. He was six or seven years older than me and ex-army. He was quieter than your average squaddie or screw but, if he had to get stuck in, he would. He was laid back, good at his job and I enjoyed working with him.

B Wing was always a lively place. It was the Remand Wing, so it was full of 'innocent' people. It was a large Wing as well, with a few more staff working on it than D Wing.

Jono was pleased when I turned up. The morning went fine and we got everything done that we needed to. You never knew everyone on B Wing; because it was remand, they were in and out of court, and new inmates were coming in on a daily basis.

Everything went well until we got to lunch. Things normally go wrong at lunch, association and exercise. That is because the screws are at their most vulnerable during those periods. You have more cons out than is comfortable.

We were working The Fours when we heard the call to send down our inmates for their grub. Jono took one side of the landing and I took the other. We began to unlock the doors and Jono and I were talking as we were doing it. There was about thirty feet (ten metres) between us and the suicide netting, so we were shouting more than talking. As we got further down the landing, Jono undid a door . . .

'Arrghh!' Jono screamed.

I quickly looked over and saw that an inmate had smashed

Jono in the face with a metal flask. I blew my whistle and yelled, 'Fours!' to raise the alarm and let the staff know where it happened. I gate-vaulted the barrier, landing on the suicide netting, scrambled across it and jumped over the other barrier to aid Jono. This was quicker than running around to him. Jono was still standing, but he was all but knocked out on his feet. He was slumped over the inmate trying to keep hold of him, but the cunt still had hold of his metal flask and was repeatedly whacking him.

Great, isn't it. The Well gives its inmates flasks to collect hot water when they get their dinner. But they don't give them any old flask, they give them a fucking metal one – a beautiful little weapon, which can cause some decent damage.

I quickly pulled Jono away, while kicking the inmate in the stomach. I couldn't believe the amount of blood all over the floor. I didn't have time to take it in properly. I booted the fucker while grabbing the hand with the flask and trying to disarm him. That is when I first got a good look at Jono's face. The poor bastard's nose looked like it had exploded across his face. His top lip was split up to his nose, and blood was pissing out everywhere. He didn't know where he was. By now there were other Officers turning up to assist.

I still had hold of this cunt's arm as we stood in the doorway of his cell. He was strong. I was struggling to take the flask from his right hand while he was punching me in the kidneys with his left. I was aware of it, but his blows just seemed to bounce off me as I concentrated on getting his fucking flask. Then the mad cunt bit me under the arm by my ribs. That did fucking hurt.

I had to think quickly. Because we were in the doorway of the cell, no one could get behind to pull him off. So I stamped my size tens down on his toes as hard as I could. This made him loosen his teeth from my side. As he did that, I slightly loosened my grip on his arm, allowing me to elbow the fucker in the face. I did that two or three times, driving my left elbow into his face as hard as I could.

There was a screw facing me who managed to rip the flask from his clutches. I completely let go of that arm, so I would be able to drop him to the floor and get him bent up. He was dazed from where I'd elbowed him in the head. I rugby tackled him, smashing his furniture out of the way and taking him to the ground.

This allowed the other screws to get into the cell and help me restrain him properly. I had him on the floor and he was now disarmed. Two other screws helped me from there. It was bog-standard stuff. We got him cuffed as quickly as we could.

The con wouldn't respond to anything that was being said to him. I didn't know if he didn't speak English or if he was just being non-compliant. At that point, I realised that he had not said anything throughout the incident. That was unusual, as cons would normally be shouting obscenities. He didn't even wince at the pain I had to apply to him, and I nearly knocked his fucking head clean off his shoulders when I was elbowing him. He looked dazed, but didn't show any form of pain: fucking weird.

Once we had him cuffed and under control, I was relieved by another Officer who took over from me to take him to The Block. As I came out of the cell, it was apparent to me then how much blood was on the floor. It was fucking everywhere. It was a disturbing sight, knowing it was all Jono's.

'Where's Jono? Is he all right?' I asked nervously.

'He's down healthcare, mate. He ain't good, they're gonna blue light him to the hospital.'

I quickly went down to see him before he left. He was a right fucking mess. He was still bleeding. His top lip had swollen and looked like a lamb chop split down the middle. One of his teeth had been knocked out and his eyes were turning black. He seemed confused – it was obvious he had concussion or something. He could talk fine, but he was just taking a little longer to get things out and in the right order.

'What happened, mate?' I asked him, still confused.

'Ron, I undid his door as normal. He was standing there, right behind it. I didn't even have the chance to say hello, and the cunt cracked me in the face for no reason.'

I believed Jono. He wasn't the argumentative type. Besides, I didn't hear any commotion just before it happened. The first thing that I heard was Jono screaming.

I was checked by healthcare. Thankfully, the dirty little cunt didn't manage to break skin when he bit me. I just had a large bite mark and bruising from where he was punching me.

It turned out the fella who did it was waiting to be sectioned. He was a complete fucking nut nut with a history of violent and unprovoked attacks. The medical analysis stated that he wasn't fit for prison and that he should be in a secure hospital. Obviously there aren't always the spaces, so they have to wait. But if they do have to wait, then it should be on the Fraggle Wing, which can cater for them a good bit better than a normal residential Wing. If there are no spaces there, then he should have been transferred to an establishment that has spaces on their healthcare Wing. If there were still no spaces to be had, he should be in The Block, where he would pose a lot less risk.

This didn't happen because, like everything else, the Prison Service systems are rubbish. The cunts didn't even tell the staff that this con was waiting to be sectioned. If we had known, then at least we could have taken extra precautions.

But they don't tell the staff because they know that Officers would – quite rightly – kick off about having to deal with a fraggle. You can't cater for someone with mental problems on a normal Wing in a local Cat B nick. It's not fair on the staff or the con.

The assault was handed over to the police to investigate. Jono and I were interviewed, as were the other screws who attended the scene. The minute they knew the con was a nut nut, the police, as usual, didn't want to pursue it.

Jono, the poor cunt, was on the sick – not only for his horrific injuries, but the poor sod was suffering severe depression and anxiety. He developed a phobia about opening doors. That's the last thing you want when you are a Prison Officer. Understandable after the ordeal he went through, though. He was on medication to help him but he didn't receive the support that he'd hoped for. They didn't offer him counselling or fuck-all. What they did was put him on half pay, after a period, because he had gone over the threshold of full pay for sick leave. That kind of decision is discretionary to the Governor of the Well. The cunt didn't think Jono's illness was severe enough to be off, so he ordered the half pay.

The police investigation dragged on for ages and finally fell apart; they said that due to the prisoner's mental issues, there was no case to put forward. I bet if that happened to a copper there would have been a case. In the end, Jono got one of the solicitors on the case to sue the Well for their incompetence: the inmate should never have been there at all.

Eventually Jono came back to work. He is a very brave man in my eyes. I don't know how he did it, really, especially going back to the same prison. But he wanted to give the Well the chance to discriminate against him and make things worse for themselves, which would have helped his case.

Things like this happen in prisons all over the country. I've seen nutters on normal Wings dozens of time since the Jono episode. The Well doesn't learn. They try to live on luck. If something does go tits up, then they hope the screw will roll over.

NONCE

The crime that we know is not sentenced correctly is paedophilia. The punishments are pathetic. They are treated so differently inside too . . . This is a painful subject: the unspoken crime. People don't want to talk about dirty filthy nonces. But you have a right to know how they are treated in prison and the disgracefully puny punishments they get for their sickening crimes.

Of course, high-profile scum appear in the papers: Gary Glitter, Ian Huntley. But that is not even the tip of the iceberg.

I have no sympathy for these people. Some believe that it is an illness that needs to be treated. I can't sympathise with someone who has raped and murdered a child. Even saying those horrible words, that 'A child has been raped', brings the majority of us to tears. I am struggling even to write these words. It upsets me so much. But I need to try and explain to you how difficult it was to be near those horrible bastards.

Nonces are considered VPs (vulnerable prisoners) so they are segregated from the rest of the inmates. The official name is the VP Wing but we call it the 'dirty nonce Wing'. They are kept away from the other prisoners for their own safety. The VP Wing is full of sex offenders. You also get the odd con put there as a result of threats that have been made to them. Sometimes famous people (usually considered vulnerable) would go there, but normally they refuse.

Sometimes for security reasons a con will be ordered to go on the VP Wing so as to prevent a fight or riot. They then most probably kick off with someone and get taken instead to The Block. I think that most of us would do that. I would rather live in The Seg than with these lowife cunts. They are hated by everyone in prison.

They don't serve hard time at all. The Governors are very hot on how they are treated. If one of them is bent up, they investigate it straight away to make sure they haven't been dropped for being a nonce. So they actually get treated better than other inmates. There are many outside agencies whose job it is to keep an eye on paedophiles and make sure they are not mistreated. And all of that is funded by us, the taxpayers.

The dirty buggers know this so they get themselves all nice and comfy in prison. The prison authorities run courses for them which are supposed to give them the chance to talk about their crimes, to admit that they are wrong, to come to terms with them, and move on. It's not that at all. It's just a breeding ground for them to get off on each other's filthy crimes.

A good friend of mine was a probation officer and she

believed that these people could be worked with and helped to control their sexual desires. I used to row like fuck with her over that. I don't think that you can change them. All they do is get turned on by each other's stories of how they have abused children. Prison is a place where they can meet more of their own kind. That's how these brutal fuckers work. They all know each other. Nonces are the masters of manipulation. That's how they groom kids (and their parents for that matter) to get their wicked ways. They get inside people's heads, and enjoy the power and control they gain when they do.

The sentences for their atrocious crimes are an insult to the victim – and an insult to other offenders whose crimes are not remotely in the same league. Let me give you an example for comparison. There was a lad called Andy serving five years for ABH. He was a top lad who had not been in trouble with the police before. He was the same age as me and could easily have been one of my mates on the road. He was at home when his fourteen-year-old brother came running in with a fat lip and a black eye. He told Andy that he was playing football in the street when he accidentally hit the car of one of their neighbours. He said the neighbour came out of the house and started having a go at him and his friends. They gave him some lip, but nothing too bad. But the geezer had been drinking, lost his rag and beat up Andy's brother. The geezer was in his thirties, for fuck's sake. What teenager doesn't give lip? You don't beat them up.

Andy went round there and he put it all over the bully. The police were called and Andy was arrested for ABH. He was on remand for eighteen months, but he had bail and therefore had to report to his local police station once a week for this period.

He never missed one. He had a good case and he never denied what he did, but when it got to court, they sent him down for five years. Considering it was his first offence, it was a harsh sentence. Prison was not needed for this bloke at all. He was no threat to society. Remember this, if you are pissed up downtown and thinking of banging someone. It's all too easy to end up in the nick. It really is wiser to walk away. In Andy's case, he couldn't walk off, and I think most of us wouldn't.

There was a nonce at the Well who was on his second prison sentence for his vile behaviour. This time he was in for indecently assaulting a young boy. He had also downloaded indecent images to his PC. This cunt had so many images downloaded that, if he was to spend eight hours a day for the rest of his life looking through them, he still wouldn't manage to see them all. That's how many he had.

For downloaded images and indecently assaulting a boy, this piece of shit only got eighteen months; so he need only serve nine, and then he'd be back out in society. How can this happen and be called justice? How can these sentences still be given to sick bastards? How many times does there have to be a public outcry before something is done? Compare that sentence to Andy's – how can that be right? There is one answer – it fucking isn't, simple as that.

One of the most dangerous paedophiles in the country was at the Well at one time. This bastard had been banged up repeatedly for his sick crimes. On each release, he would tell the authorities there was nothing wrong with him or what he had done. On the last occasion, he told the authorities he was going to find a boy to rape and murder – and they still let him out! Why?

So, what did that fucking cunt do? Exactly what he said! If I had my way . . .

I'd stayed at the staff quarters. Scouse and I had both been on a late shift. For once though, we didn't get hammered after work. A couple of cans then bed. It caught up on me from time to time. We both went in to work in the morning with a reasonably clear head. I was fucking tired though.

In the briefing I was told I was being cross-deployed to the Visits Hall. It was an easy touch. I was pleased with that. I'd not been home in days. I'd done loads of shifts back to back. I needed a break from the Wing – indeed a break from the prison.

I rang Scouse up to tell him what my detail was for the day. He said someone was getting cross-deployed to Visits from his group as well, and he sorted it so it was him. We always did that, when the opportunity arose; but as Scouse was on the Fraggle Wing, we didn't get to work together that often.

We reported to the Visits Hall and were both given the post of runner. That is when you have to go and collect the prisoners for their visits. There was one problem: it was nonce day. Like everyone else, I hated them. There are screws I know who can work with them fine. It's something I couldn't do. I had a young child at home and I was a young man.

Scouse could work with them if he had to. He could just switch off. Scouse and I went to get half a dozen of these cunts for their visits. The Nonce Wing was the furthest away from Visits, so it was a long walk there and back. I had collected nonces for visits before. I would say very little to them. The nonces would sense if a screw was one of the real haters, and wouldn't push for conversation.

Scouse and I got to the Nonce Wing to get the six we were detailed to collect. We unlocked them and began walking back to the Visits Hall. I took the lead, followed by the six scumbags, Scouse on the end. The nonce directly behind me tried to engage in conversation. I told him I didn't want to talk to him.

This nonce was a really tall bastard, taller than me. He was in his fifties and was fucking horrible. He stank like a poll cat. He could see I was uncomfortable with him and what he was. He seemed to revel in it. He asked me if I liked children, even though I told him to not speak to me. The more uncomfortable I got, the more he talked. His topic of choice then turned to what he liked to do to young children. I snapped at him, telling him to shut his disgusting mouth. He laughed and continued with his obscenities. Scouse was unaware of what this creature was saying to me as he was at the back of the line. No one could hear except this pervert and me.

He continued, loving every minute of what he was saying. That was it, I couldn't take any more. I punched the cunt so hard. I ripped into him with everything. I was screaming for him to shut his filthy mouth as I was battering him. I have never wanted to hurt anyone as much in my life. Scouse quickly ran towards me and dived on in to stop me.

He raised the alarm as he was running over. He knew he had to bend that nonce up, or I was in serious shit. As Scouse pulled me off, I was still trying to get at the nonce. By this time, a couple of screws had arrived on the scene and Scouse dived on the nonce who was a mess on the floor. He bent him up. He shouted at one of the Officers to get me away and that the nonce had assaulted me. Other Officers turned up on the scene and assisted Scouse. A couple walked with me to The Block and asked if I was

OK. I was in tears. They then took me to an office down The Block and made me a brew. The Duty Governor happened to be the Dep. He was a real gentleman.

'Ronnie, Scouse told me what happened,' the Dep said to me.

'I'm sorry, Guv. He was sayin' . . .'

'Scouse has told me what happened. You have every right to defend yourself if someone attacks you. I think you should get yourself home and have a couple of days off.'

That episode haunted me for a long while. I cried many times with Danielle about it. I struggled with nonces. It was something I wouldn't want anyone to go through. I couldn't handle what he was saying, I admit that. I just couldn't listen to it any more. No way.

I don't know what should be done with the dirty filthy cunts, but what happens to them now is a disgrace. They should have life dished out to them. The poor children they sexually abuse have a life sentence of memories and physical scars. How the law can justify its weakness on these crimes is beyond me. These creeps live the life of Riley inside and out. And they get every funding under the sun to protect their anonymity.

One of my mates, Browny, almost lost his job over a nonce. He had been in the job a lot longer than me and was about seven or eight years older. He was a likeable chap with many friends. Browny had a nonce on his Wing who had asked to be on normal location. Now, not all nonces look like your stereo-typical old bastard. This lad was in his early thirties, and had been in and out of prison for various crimes. He was a normal toe-rag, but he had a little secret: he liked to rape young boys as well.

Browny couldn't take it when he saw all the other cons he

knew talking to him like he was a good lad. The secret was burning inside his stomach, just bursting to get out.

This nonce was found lying on the floor in his cell severely beaten. He had a cracked skull and a punctured lung, among many other injuries. There was a paper that went in to the Governor saying that Browny was the last on the landing when everyone else went to lunch. The paper detailed that everyone was banged up except the landing cleaners – who were out cleaning. The Officer who found the nonce half dead on the floor was the screw on lunch patrol. It never came out who put the paper in.

The finger started to point more and more directly at Browny. It was beginning to look as though he had undone the nonce's cell to allow the cleaners in to bust him up. Browny was suspended while the investigation took place. The nonce couldn't give a time when the door was unlocked and he didn't see the face of the Officer who unlocked it. He knew who the landing cleaners were, but was too scared to identify them.

As far as the investigation was concerned, they had no proof that the assault took place at this time. It could have been earlier. When the screw found the nonce half dead, his door was shut, so he could have been lying there for ages. As the police couldn't identify who did the assault, or who unlocked the door, or even if it was unlocked for that reason, they couldn't take the action any further.

The investigation got to this point after six months, but the Prison Service kept Browny off for another year while they tried to build up a case that was at least enough to sack him. I met up with Browny for beers while he was on suspension. He was a Mancunian lad, very streetwise and knew that, this time, he couldn't trust anyone. He never said whether he did it or not, but only that they'd got nothing on him. When it was all over and he did come back to work, I asked him if he did it, but he would still neither admit it nor deny it. He was as hard as a coffin nail.

I feel guilty being an Officer and dealing with nonces. I feel that by being one of the people who lets them eat, sleep, go to Visits and finally be released to harm a child again, I, just as much as the system, am betraying the victims. It just isn't fair.

THE ROPE AND THE
RAZORBLADE

Rhys and I had been detailed to work on The Threes. It was not our normal landing, but we didn't give a shit. If we were on the same landing, we were pleased. As usual, with us two together, things were going smoothly. We were having a laugh and Rhys was taking the piss out of me. Comical genius that fella, funny as fuck.

It was mid-morning and we'd done our cell spins, fabric checks and all self-harmer and suicide watch checks. The cons had been out on exercise and were now out of their cells on association. Things were running well. We had no trouble. The cons were getting on with their business, leaving us to do the same. We were both good at bluffing the cons with a politician's answer, leaving us to have a brew and them feeling satisfied. The atmosphere was good. We were standing on the landing, showing our presence while relaxing because we'd done our duties, when we heard a scream and a con shouting 'Guv, Guv!' He was pointing to a fella standing on the suicide netting, wearing just his pants. He was standing there, hacking the fuck out of his body with a razor blade. Literally cutting chunks off his body. We looked at each other in complete shock, both shouting 'Fuck!'

A split second later, we were both running towards this crazy cunt, reacting to it all like second nature. You react first and think later. But he was cutting himself to bits, bleeding all over the place and possibly contaminating his surroundings. He could have had HIV, hepatitis or whatever. Your instinct is the preservation of life, and so to disarm the man and get control back. We gate-vaulted the barrier on to the suicide netting. We didn't have time to blow our whistles and raise the alarm. A screw on The Twos saw it, though, and blew the whistle for us.

The alarm raised, other screws came to attend the scene and help bang up the other cons. Whatever's happening, the cons get banged away. They don't need to see what is going on. Emotions run high and that can result in an escalating incident. Bang them away, deal with it, then let them back out.

After landing on the suicide netting, Rhys and I managed to stay on our feet. The netting was fucking old and looked as if it wouldn't be able to handle the weight of a mouse, let alone two fucking great lumps like us! But we didn't have the time or capacity for this to be a concern. We were focused on grabbing the mental bastard. If a con has a weapon, the first thing you are supposed to do is draw your stave. But the stave, for some reason, is always the last thing on your mind. You just want to grab hold of the fucker.

We got to him at exactly the same time. The blood – fuck me

it was everywhere. It was a sickening sight, fucking disgusting. But we couldn't think about it; we had to get hold of the weapon and get him down. He waved the blade in an aggressive manner and I managed to knock that arm out of the way. I grabbed his head as hard as I could, pulling him straight to the ground. At the same time, Rhys grabbed the weapon-holding arm, applying an arm lock and demanding he let go of the blade.

'Blade clear!' Rhys screamed.

By that time, other Officers had arrived on the scene. I knew that the weapon had been secured, so the initial threat was over. He could no longer hurt us or himself. I had control of his head, Rhys was on one arm and some other Officer was on the other. But, fuck me, the blood. We really noticed it then. Rhys and I were soaked through. Our white shirts were completely stained red. All the other faces expressed their shock. And now we had to get him off the netting and back on to the landing. Being on the head, I tried to de-escalate the situation, giving him the opportunity to be compliant. He didn't want to know. He was shouting obscenities, not intending to listen to anything. The loss of blood, or the damage he had done, did nothing to his aggression. Crazy fucking bastard! We had to pass the inmate over, under restraint, to a waiting team of screws. The problem was, no one wanted to take over! Who wants to be covered in some lunatic's blood? At that point Rhys and I were getting the hump.

'Count of three?' I said.

With that we threw him over the barrier on to the landing. He landed on the floor in a heap of mess. We jumped over quickly, restraining him again as he was getting up preparing to fight.

With no one willing to help, and the bosses standing there, taking no control, there was nothing else we could do. That fella could be bleeding to death – we could be bleeding for all they knew – but standing there was all they did.

We got the con down The Seg and were relieved by the staff down there. When the Duty Governor attended, the first thing he said was, 'Is the prisoner OK?'

Rhys grabbed my shirt to stop me going for him. The Governor didn't see it, but a few of the lads did. Fucking lowlife, scumbag cunt. That could have been our blood, our injuries, our assaults. He didn't care about our welfare or our health. Just his hotel guests.

Seeing large amounts of blood never gets any easier. You'd think it would, but it doesn't. Well, it doesn't for me. I could deal with it at an incident, and do what I had to do, but afterwards I would sometimes struggle, feeling sick and uncomfortable with what I'd seen.

Rhys and I both went home. I went back to Danielle: 'I had a lovely day in the office, dear; I had someone trying to slice himself up in front of me!'

Self-harming and suicide is never going to be stopped in prison. People are always going to want to kill themselves whether in prison or on the road. If someone is feeling suicidal, or seems like they are about to hurt themselves, then you open up a document designed to monitor them and you act accordingly, offering the support they need. But how do you know when someone is having those thoughts and feelings? Exactly. You don't. Rhys and I hadn't got a clue that that fella wanted to cut himself. We didn't notice any signs. This is why the screw needs to have his eyes wide open. You need to try and spot a change in behaviour, for instance someone becoming withdrawn, lonely or unusually aggressive. It can be nigh on impossible to spot these things when you have all your other duties to perform and not enough staff. And the problem is made that much worse because, out of the (say) fourteen self-harmers you are monitoring, only one or two of them are genuine; the others are merely time wasters. Because the Prison Service thinks that you should give potential suicides and self-harmers everything they say they need, you get some wanker who will lie about feeling suicidal just to get what he wants. Everyone who says anything about suicide or self-harming has a form opened on which to monitor them because you may not believe it but they may still do it. Basically, it's an arse-covering exercise – all it does, though, is create extra work monitoring idiots who are abusing a weak system. Why don't the powers that be come up with a better process? Or even make the one they do have work correctly? Because it's easier to heap more shit on the landing screw. Even with a better system, people will still slip through the net and hurt or kill themselves. You can't be there twenty-four hours a day, watching their every move. Impossible. It only takes a few minutes to kill yourself so, if you really want to, then you will do it. And, in my experience, people who kill themselves say fuck-all about it. They are truly depressed and have lost the will to live. They don't want to discuss it with some screw, and they certainly don't want to be monitored. They want to die.

The next day I was back in. I was on The Ones again, on alarm response. When you hear an alarm or whistle, wherever it is, you run to it. Early on in the shift, I heard the familiar whistle sound. I reacted, shouting for direction.

'Bravo Wing . . . Twos!' the centre Officer screamed.

I sprinted as fast as I could, as always, I didn't have a Scooby what I was heading into. You never know. It could be violence, it could be death, it could be anything.

As I approached the gates of B Wing, they had already been unlocked for easy access. This is the only time you can go through a gate and not secure it behind you. The centre screw does that for efficiency. The last thing you need is to be fumbling with a bunch of keys, shaking as you try to get one into the lock, while some poor bastard is getting kicked half to death.

I was about second or third through the gate, rushing up to The Twos. We had piled through the gates and were now on the stairs. The only noise I could hear were size tens stamping on each other, trying to get up to the next landing. As I got to the top, there were no cons out, just a screw standing outside a cell, gesturing for us to go over. I thought that, if there had been any trouble, it had been controlled and the alarm raised for back up. As I arrived at the cell, I was horrified by what was before me. An Officer was inside the cell, with his hand over the con's neck.

'Fucking doctor, now!' he screamed.

He had the con half sitting on the cell table and half standing, pressed against the wall. The blood, fuck me, the blood. The con had cut his own throat. He had done it so brutally, his Adam's apple was hanging out of his fucking neck. The Officer was holding it, trying to put pressure on the open wound to stop the bleeding. But blood was pissing out everywhere. The con's face was pale, his mouth wide open, making no noise or expression. He was breathing, though; he wasn't dead. His cellmate was bawling his eyes out, poor fucker.

It had been patrol state on B Wing. That's when the cons are banged up, the whole Wing is locked down and the screw answers cell bells. The throat-cutter's cellmate was having a nap (a day in the life of a con, hey?) when he was woken by the noise of banging. He looked round, thinking that he would see the other cell occupant smashing up for some reason. He was ready to give the wanker a slap for disturbing his nap, but he wasn't smashing up at all. He was falling all over the fucking place, unable to control himself, having just cut his throat. The inmate couldn't believe what he was seeing. He'd done a lot of bird over the years and seen pretty much everything. Self-harmers, the whole fucking lot. But never had he seen someone so savagely brutalise their own throat. He jumped to his feet and starting banging the door, screaming for help. He was hysterical. He felt a whole lifetime pass before help arrived.

Once an Officer got there and opened the door, he was greeted with a sight that will never leave him. A hardened prisoner screaming in terror, with the other one slumped against the wall in a puddle of his own blood. Dying. The alarm was raised and we attended. The doctor arrived a few seconds after us. The trauma of seeing that was hard for me, but fuck knows what his cellmate was feeling after waking up to that. Or the poor fucking Officer, running in to be faced with an Adam's apple on the wrong side of a neck. Oh yeah, we only bully, unlock and lock doors as Prison Officers.

Surprisingly, the con survived. For a week or so, that is, until he cut his throat again in hospital. Someone should have told him that you swallow on the inside and that he would be best to leave his Adam's apple where it was. Could he have been saved? Don't know, I'm not an expert on mental health. But that is what that fella was – mental. He shouldn't have been in prison. So, could he have been saved? If he was where he should have been, with professionals capable of treating him and who had the facilities to deal with his condition, perhaps. But not in prison. It's funny that, now the prisons in this country are bursting at the seams, they have decided to use police cells in a temporary measure to help the crisis. The Old Bill, bless them, have said that they will not take any prisoners of severe crimes, or prisoners with mental illness. It is OK for them to stipulate, but the Prison Service has to take all sorts that they can't handle. Typical.

That same morning, Rhys and I were called to The Seg to kit up – some wanker had barricaded himself in his cell and was refusing to come out. I didn't know why, I didn't need to know. We had a job to do. One way or another, I would be leaving that cell with the con.

He'd smashed his cell to bits and covered his spy flap so you couldn't see fuck-all. We got kitted up, Rhys, an Officer called Nat and me. Nat was a good lad, a block screw. He kept himself to himself, which was rare for the Prison Service. He knew his shit, though; you could trust him. I was happy with the team. I was confident that we could get in there and get it done.

Rhys and I were used a lot in cell take-outs. Even in the most dangerous conditions, Rhys would still be witty and funny. The guy would have me pissing myself just before we were about to go in and restrain a fucking monster. Don't get me wrong; he was good, fucking good – but a comic to the end. I think that he used to do it on purpose to try and relieve the pressure of the situation; to take away the fear. I was on the shield, Rhys and Nat tucked in nice and tight behind me. The adrenaline was pumping. We were ready. The cell door was opened. The barricade was fairly good, so I had to work hard to break through it. We were getting hot and sweaty and I'd not even seen the scroat yet!

When we finally got through, the con was standing at the back wall with a table leg in his hand. He looked passive, but he still had the weapon. I smashed into him with the shield.

'Drop the fucking weapon now!' I barked at him. He didn't know what fucking hit him. I think I might have knocked the table leg out of his hand, with the force that I cracked him.

We quickly got him under control, without much resistance at all. We got him out of the cell, walking him under restraint. I tried to de-escalate it, so he would walk, but he wouldn't talk to me. We took him all the way to The Seg under restraint. Once we got him into the strip cell, I told him that we would be performing a strip search and that, if he didn't comply, he'd be dropped. We released the locks and stood him up. He complied with my orders, not saying much. I noticed that his eyes were shut. I looked a little closer. Fucking dick had sewn them shut! I told the nurse at the cell door, but said I would finish the strip search before he came in. The last part of the search is inside the mouth, ears and hair. I told him to open his mouth, which he did, but not very much. I told him to do it again, but he only did it a little bit again.

'Open your fucking mouth. Don't make me drop you,' I ordered, while placing my index fingers and thumbs on his chin.

The con winced in pain. Fucking nut nut had sewn his mouth shut as well! I hadn't noticed and I was getting pissed off with him for ignoring me. So there I was, trying to force open a mouth that had be sewn shut; what a silly cunt I was! Rhys obviously was pissing himself laughing at this point!

If I ever fuck up or do something stupid, Rhys would always see it, guaranteed. Gives him more ammunition to revel in my stupidity. I'm my worst enemy at times! I will admit it. I can be a dumb fucking blonde! I always lose my keys and wallet. That's right, I was a Prison Officer who always lost his keys and wallet! It was like a switch: security aware, careful, on the ball at work; leave the nick, become a doughnut.

In my defence, the material he'd used to sew his mouth shut was skin coloured. Besides, I'd never met some weirdo who liked to stitch their body parts closed. It's not something that I thought I had to look out for. It turns out the nobhead had done this sewing as a form of protest. Crazy, fucking crazy! If you feel like things are not going your way, or you are upset about the rules and regulations that you are facing, don't complain, no, no, no. Get a needle and thread and sew your eyes shut so you can't see and, for good measure, do your mouth so you can't talk or tell anyone your problems. I can't put into words how fucking ridiculously stupid and idiotic I find it. As far as I'm concerned, put them in a fucking great hall together, with a huge amount of thread and needles, and let them sew each other to the curtains! It's like shitting up. 'I know, I will cover myself in shit to protest!' Where is the bloody logic of these people?

It turned out needle-and-thread boy was getting released that day. He was bailed, as he was an illegal immigrant waiting for his trial to find out if he would get asylum. He had nowhere to go, so he wanted to stay in prison.

Night shifts have a different set of responsibilities. When you work a night shift, your last duty is to count the number of cons you are handing over to the day staff. Make no mistake, you aren't counting to check for escapes, you are making sure that there are no swingers. You have to do this. If you don't then you are fucked. You are the night man and the Wing is your responsibility.

Of course, you get the lazy cunts that can't be arsed. Silly, that is: it's leaving yourself wide open. It's an arse-covering exercise, but it has to be done. The day staff are also supposed to check the numbers, before the night man goes. That doesn't happen. It should, but it doesn't. You trust the night man. You trust that he has done it.

The morning regime went fine that day, no incidents, no bothers. The workers went to work, the lazy cunts stayed in bed, the junkies got on their gear. A normal quiet and pleasant morning at the Well. Lunchtime came round and feeding went fine. No problems. The staff signed for their numbers and went to lunch. They had their lunch-time pint, or workout, and returned to the Wing. The staff briefing was fine: the SOs applauded the good work of the morning and requested the same for the afternoon. All the screws returned to their landings and unlocked them for the afternoon's regime. That's when the alarm was raised. There was a con that was dead as a fucking doornail!

The lazy, silly-old-cunt night man hadn't checked his numbers before he knocked off. He was pillow hungry. But then, as usual, the day staff taking over hadn't checked, either. After that – once the cons have gone to work, exercise or whatever – the landing screws should check all the cells in their control so that, if there were a stand-fast roll check (usually an emergency checking of prisoner numbers), they could account for all their cons. The morning consists of meds, exercise, gym, work and courses, so you should be checking your numbers all morning. Even if that gets missed, you make sure you count once your cons are banged up with their lunch. On this day, even that hadn't been done, the lazy bastards!

The con had been dead since the middle of the night, and wasn't discovered until two in the afternoon! Some fellas got disciplined over that, I can tell you. Fucking right, though. They wouldn't have been able to save his life, because he wasn't on suicide watch. They'd had no hints or clues because he wanted to die. However, if you declare your numbers when you haven't, in fact, checked them, and someone's been dead for fucking hours, that ain't gonna wash!

Seeing dead bodies is something else that all Prison Officers experience during their career. It's a strange feeling, seeing a body there like a slab of meat, decaying. At the end of the day, though, that's what we are. It's not nice when you find a dead body swinging either. Nine times out of ten there is piss and shit everywhere. The body loses control of its bodily functions when you kick the bucket. And, on top of that, some bloke is hanging there, dead. The trauma of it all. It could be a con that you got on well with, someone who was a decent lad. One minute they seemed OK, the next they're bright blue. Then you ask yourself the question, 'Could I have done more, or noticed something?' All things considered, the answer's 'No'. You do what you can do. You are a Prison Officer, not a miracle worker. Self-harming, suicides, assaults will always go on in prison; it's a group of problems that's impossible to stop.

Dealing with these situations makes you see things differently. You become numb to a lot of shocking things. I remember the first time I saw a dead body at work. People had come to collect it. Talk about lack of respect for the dead. They were banging its head off the railings, dropping it and all sorts, laughing and joking through the process. I don't know what I was expecting, really. A coroner does it every day for a living. It's a job, pays the bills. I suppose if they were quiet and depressed every time they dealt with death, they would go fucking mad. And as a Prison Officer, it's your job, too. It was my job. And it was a rollercoaster ride that was getting closer to being out of control.

CELEBRITY CIRCUIT
(HER MAJESTY'S PLEASURE)

'd had a boring morning at work. D Wing was quiet. No alarms, no drugs – nothing found, anyway. As much as it had been a slightly safer place to work in for a while, I was bored. I went into The Ones office to give Danielle a ring. Danni told me that she'd been watching the news and that a well-known rock star was being remanded in custody for various alleged crimes.

I was a huge fan of this fella, and his band. I'd been to see them play live a couple of times. After I got off the phone, I rang my pal in reception who told me it was true, and he was coming in later. I was curious to meet him.

There was a buzz around the nick that night as everyone heard the news. I was detailed to go to reception and assist with receiving new prisoners and banging them away. My duties included taking their property and giving them instructions about what would be happening to them that night. After that, they would be strip-searched to check that they didn't have any weapons and drugs, and then they would see the doctor before being given a microwaved dinner and taken to their cells.

I was in the process of strip-searching and locating them to their cells. It was a conveyor-belt process – the escorting staff would bring them into the nick from the sweatbox (prison van) and the con would then be met by the Property Officer whose desk was just behind where the strip-searching took place.

'Name?'

I heard the con answer: it was him.

I looked round and clapped eyes on him. I was kind of nervous and thinking to myself, 'Get a grip, you soppy cunt!' He looked every bit the rock star, with a striking resemblance to Sid Vicious of the Sex Pistols. He handed over his prop, looking a little confused.

He walked towards me and the other searchers. As he got closer, I saw he looked fucked out of his head. I knew his style and I'd seen him perform, but I hadn't been as close to him as this. He was an awful lot taller than I imagined. People look small on stage and you can never tell in the papers. He looked well over six feet, easily looking at me straight on.

He wasn't fazed by his surroundings at all. He had been in prison before. Getting nicked and banged up was something he took in his stride. I was shocked to see this bloke, someone who made music that I liked, looking so bad. It was a surreal moment to say the least. There I was, about to strip-search a geezer that I'd paid to watch on stage. Here he was, standing in front of me, waiting to be strip-searched and located to his cell. Talk about a fallen star.

I cracked on with the strip search as quickly as I could. I don't know who was more nervous, him or me. He had no idea I was a fan – I was just a screw in a prison to him. He was very polite, doing what was asked of him. He would always address an Officer as 'mate'. Some screws hate it when cons do that and are quick to let them know. I didn't mind, provided I got on OK with the con.

I said, 'Bet ya had different plans for Friday night!' trying to relax him, and show that I would be civil. He laughed and chatted freely. I took him to see the doctor and waited outside, allowing them the privacy to discuss issues. He then came out, so we went to collect his meal for the evening. I took him through to the first-night Wing and put him into his cell. I chatted with him on the way there, but not telling him I was a fan of his. I didn't want to start talking to him about music and gigs when he had just been banged up.

I finished the rest of my duties and went round to the quarters, got changed and went out on the piss with Scouse. It being Friday night, we lived it up. I was staying all weekend because I was working all weekend; I couldn't be arsed to go home.

I got to work first thing on Saturday morning with my head splitting from the booze I'd polished off the night before. All I wanted was an easy day of it. Garry came in and said, 'Come on, Ronnie, we got to go over to the first-night centre and spin the rock star's cell.'

Garry no longer worked on D Wing, He had moved to security and dealt with all the Intel that was received. He'd heard that our new celebrity guest had been passed drugs under his door. Garry was pleased with himself – he thought he was going to get the opportunity to get in there and nick a celebrity.

He got me to assist, as security was short of searchers. We

reached his cell and went in. Garry is very militant and strict. He sticks to the rules, but could be a real cunt with it. He would be unnecessarily harsh. We walked in and Garry told the rock star and his cellmate that we were there to search them and their cell. Garry and I searched the cellmate first, and got the rock star to wait outside with a third Officer. Garry blasted through the orders to his cellmate and we found fuck-all. His cellmate had received searches dozens of times. He was then told to go outside the cell with the other Officer, who locked him in an empty cell further down the landing and then sent the rock star into the cell to be strip-searched.

'Mr Thompson and I have come into this cell to perform a strip search on you, and to search this cell. Is there anything on you, or in this cell, that you shouldn't have?'

Looking dazed and confused, not understanding what the fuck was going on, he gestured that he hadn't.

Garry was being so fucking abrupt, I wanted to punch him. The rock star didn't recognise me from the night before – the state he was in, he wouldn't have recognised Prince fucking Charles if he'd walked into that cell.

He was facing Garry and I was behind him. Garry was giving all the instructions, and I was searching an item of clothing that was given to me upon Garry's request. Once I'd done that, I passed the item back and then Garry would tell him to pass me another item. When there is Intel on possible possession of drugs, they must do only what they are ordered to do; if they move or do anything when they are not supposed to, then they will be dropped because they could possibly be concealing the item(s) that the Officers are searching for.

Garry seemed to enjoy being a cunt to our famous inmate.

Celebrities who get banged up can get it worse than other cons from some screws. Our rock star was confused as fuck: he was coming down from all sorts, and he would be the first to tell you that. He was struggling to do what Garry was asking. He was fidgeting, looking around and was obviously clucking.

I felt really sorry for him. The geezer is one of Great Britain's finest songwriters with adoring fans. He was going out with one of the fittest birds in the world, but that still wasn't enough for him to stop ramming that poison inside of him. The lad needed help. One time I had been singing the words to his songs, screaming 'come on!' while jumping up and down at one of his gigs, watching him thrash his guitar playing an awesome set with the rest of the band. I was having a top night watching a top band. But now, I had this same genius standing in a cell while another screw and I strip-searched him. It was a fucking weird moment to say the least. Plus I had Garry, the arrogant cunt, who wouldn't give him an inch.

'I've told you once, don't put your hands near your groin area again and stop moving. If you do it again I will place you under restraint,' Garry ordered him in military fashion.

He was moving around a little and struggling to concentrate. It was obvious he was just coming down and he didn't really know what was going on. It was highly unlikely he'd been passed anything at all, but Garry was as abrupt as ever. I knew Garry would drop him if he didn't stand to attention.

There was no need to be this military; we were acting on Intel, not a pass that had been seen. When you act on Intel to spin a cell, you do have to be careful, but there is no need to go over the top because the likelihood is that the inmate will have got rid of whatever it was, anyway. You have to be strict, but not over strict, which you'd have to be in Visits when they might try to plug it, or whatever.

Garry was outdoing himself when we were searching the rock star. He was dying to catch him out, because of who he was.

'I've told you . . .' Garry threatened, stepping towards him, getting in a position from which he could restrain him.

Quickly interrupting him from behind, I touched him on the arm and said, 'Thanks mate, all over, let's go. I will put you in the other cell while we search in here.'

With that, I walked him out of the cell, with Garry giving me a confused but dirty look. I banged him away in the empty cell with his cellmate. They had both been searched so that was fine. I returned to the cell where Garry was, and helped him search it.

'What the fuck did you do that for?'

'He had nothing on him. You were being a prick, mate.'

He didn't like it and would normally argue, but I gave him a look to say, 'I'm not in the mood, you cunt, so don't even try it.'

We finished the search and put the rock star and his cellmate back into their cell. Just as I thought, nothing was found. I don't think he realised quite how close he was to being dropped; a little bit different to playing in front of an audience! I only just got through the day, as I was so hung over, but it was now Saturday night and it would have been rude to stay in, so Scouse and I went uptown and got minging all over again. That's how Scouse and I spent our weekends on duty. We never minded working weekends because we would always have a giggle on the piss in the evening.

I got back to work on Sunday and I wanted to have a chat with rock star before I left that day. It was near the end of the day and it was quiet. Rock star wasn't on my Wing, so I had to walk over.

His landing screw was a pal of mine who was sound when I said that I was going to have a chat with him, and came with me. I unlocked his cell and went in. There were bunk beds, and rock star was on the top one.

The Rock star glanced up, looking knackered to say the least.

'Hello, mate, how you doing?'

'Hello, mate, I'm fine,' he answered, yawning.

'I thought I'd come and have a chat with you, as I'm a fan of your old band. I've been to see you a few times.'

He perked up and was really friendly. That's one thing; he seems to be good to his fans.

We went on to talk about the gigs that I'd been to and the times I'd seen him. He was concentrating hard on the conversation. I noticed his really badly done tattoo of a bird's name on his arm.

'How's it going with her?' I said, nodding towards the name on his arm.

He went on to tell me how much he loved her and that she was his soul mate. He said things were going really well. I felt really sorry for him at that moment. This bloke was going out with a gorgeous bird and he had the world at his feet, but he was still just another a junkie; that will wreck everything if he doesn't get clean.

He has a child, which we spoke about. He sounded really proud. He told me he had been on the gear for two years non-stop. I told him he needed to get off it for his kid, bird and band, blah, blah, blah. He agreed, probably as he does with everyone. He said that he would sign my CD the next time I was in, but when I came back he had been bailed.

He was a nice bloke, really friendly; but, fuck me, has he pushed himself too far. Since then, the lad has been nicked and banged up loads of times. I just hope the geezer doesn't go the same way as Sid Vicious.

Sometimes when a celebrity is sent down, they have to be told that they are no longer in their five-star hotel and that they are now a prisoner who has to fall into line like everyone else. But that isn't to say that they are treated like any other prisoner, because they are not. Screws can be harder on these inmates because they want to be the one who drops a famous con, or nicks him or whatever. They also get a lot of attention from the other inmates. Again, this can be good attention, but sometimes it's unwanted – and can be bullying. This is unfair but, then again, they are celebrities who have done enough to be banged up and, if that's the case, then they just have to deal with it.

Sometimes the famous con will have a hissy fit because they are not getting the treatment that they are used to. There was a legendary rumour that went around the Well about a certain professional footballer who got annoyed during his sentence because he wanted to keep his fitness up so he could resume his career when he was released. This, he claimed, he couldn't without being able to visit the gym more often. He applied to the Governor to have extra gym sessions and the Governor agreed.

At that time, cons weren't allowed to wear their own trainers. It was in the days that the dress code was very strict, long before my time. The footballer asked if it was possible to have his own trainers to train in, as that would prevent him from injury. In those days, prisoners were issued with shoes, and that was it.

The Governor said no. It wasn't much he was asking for, just a pair of trainers. But the Governor didn't want to look like he was being soft, so he fucked him off and said no.

The footballer kicked off and got bent up and was taken to The Block. He then covered himself in his own shit as a protest and stayed like that for four days! Once I was told that story, I used to laugh every time I saw this footballer on TV! I would giggle as he gave his interviews after the games he'd played. It's a funny old world. He got the trainers in the end, apparently.

You also get prisoners who are famous for committing high-profile crimes, or maybe just famous for being in prison. These types are the likes of Maxine Carr, Myra Hindley and Ian Brady. There was one, a few years ago, who was in the papers for his crime, but for a different reason.

Tony Martin lived on a farm in Norfolk where he had been burgled a number of times. The fourth time he was burgled, two lads broke into his house while he was asleep. Being a farmer, he had a shotgun and so he shot at the perpetrators because they had intruded into his house and he was looking out for his own safety. One of them died. Tony was charged and convicted of murder. There was public outcry, he appealed and his sentence was reduced to manslaughter. There is still an ongoing argument about how much force you are entitled to use when someone breaks in your house; many believe that he shouldn't have been banged up at all.

Anyway, during his stay with Her Majesty's Prison Service, I came across him once. He was treated well by the screws who all sympathised with him and his crime. I don't think there was a homeowner in the country who didn't sympathise with him. The cons never gave him any shit at all either. He kept himself to himself.

Sometimes you might come across a famous prisoner, or well-known gangster, and not even know it. Back in the days when the

Prison Service still had control of the transportation for the inmates to court, my mate Paul got to work one day and read on the detail that he was on court duty. He was pissed off as sometimes you got back late and he was going out that night. He asked all of the other screws if they would swap with him, but none of them would. Always the way, when you need it, no cunt will help you! So, Paul went to the holding room to collect his con who was a bloke on trial for murder. He called out his name, 'McLean?'

This mountain of a man got up and walked over to Paul not saying anything. Paul cuffed him and they went and got in the car. Paul said that the con didn't say a word to him on the way to court. As they arrived, his brief was standing there waiting for him.

'Good morning, Lenny, how are you?' he said to the prisoner as they got out of the car.

They began to engage in conversation about the trial, which meant they were standing on the pavement for a couple of minutes. This annoyed Paul. He wanted to get inside the building where it was secure, and, above all else, fucking warm!

Paul interrupted, 'McLean?'

There was no answer.

Getting angry, he said again, 'McLean? McLean!?'

'Listen cunt, you ever call me McLean again and I will rip your head off and stuff it up your fucking arse!'

He was only dealing with Lenny 'The Guv'nor' McLean! The hardest bare-knuckle fighter in Britain! Paul, the dozy cunt, hadn't recognised him.

HORRIBLE SCOUSE AND THE PRESENTS FROM PRISONERS

'd been in the job just over two years and I'd made some good relationships with cons. They can become mates, to a degree. Obviously you have to keep that professional distance, or try to, but it can be hard. If the con is banged up on your Wing for six months or a year, and you spend forty-odd hours a week with them, it is human nature that you will build up a friendship if you get along. There were a few inmates I got along with well over the years. Cons will always ask screws to bring things in for them. When you are banged up, you don't get the things that you are used to having so, if you have got the money and a screw willing to bring in the stuff, then why not? What have you got to lose? I always set my boundaries early on, though. I made it quite clear that I would not traffic anything and that I thought that bent screws were cunts. From the start, they knew that if they were decent and played the game, then Officers wouldn't come fairer than me. They knew where they stood with me. I never wanted to have to pull anyone in line; my perfect day was doing fuck-all while having a laugh, with no one causing problems. But days like that were few and far between. I always tried to stay professional, not getting too close and keeping that distance. But I'm a human being, so sometimes I would give them the odd touch here and there that maybe I shouldn't have.

There was a lad called Olivant who was banged up on The Ones. At that time, he'd been on my landing for about eight months. He was a nice lad and this sentence was his first time in trouble with the Old Bill. He was doing a five-year stretch for ABH. He admitted that he'd been a pissed-up idiot, but five years was a little harsh for a first-time offender, especially since the geezer he did over was one of his mates who used to come and visit him! How fucked-up is that? His mate didn't even want to press charges, but the Old Bill did and the CPS (Crown Prosecution Service) thought there was a case, so it went to court. It was at a time where there was a massive crackdown on drunken violence, so he felt the backlash of that.

Anyway, he got his head down and made the best of it. He didn't receive any bullying because he had a bit of savvy and would stand his ground. He wouldn't let anyone intimidate him. He was a chubby little bastard who would clench his chubby little fists if he needed to – which only happened once or twice when he first arrived. After that, he was left alone. He was a likeable lad; he got on with the cons and the Officers. The cons knew he wasn't a junkie and that he wasn't interested in getting involved with the gang culture. He just wanted to get his head down and serve his bird.

I took a liking to him. He would always do as he was asked and he was always doing things with a big grin slapped across that chubby face of his. He was a character who would try to make a laugh out of everything he was doing. He was banged up, but he joked about and got through his time as best he could. I respected him for that. I got him a job on my landing as a cleaner. He deserved a job: he was willing to do anything to kill the time and he was a good worker.

As I got to know him better, I realised I had a lot in common with him. He liked the same music as me; he had the same interests and was just a normal lad. It turned out that two of my mates, Jim and Craig, were facing charges similar to Olivant's. I would tell him about their case and he would give me advice to give to them. Not that it would do much good, but he still took interest and gave advice. (Jim and Craig didn't go down; they got community service – but that is a whole other story!)

Olivant was due to be transferred out of the Well, as he'd been categorised. He didn't want to go because his girlfriend lived locally and it would be hard for her to visit him at another nick. I squared it away for him to stay. I wasn't supposed to, but I helped him out. He shouldn't have stayed because the Well is a holding prison but, fuck it, he was all right so I helped him.

As his sentence went on, the poor little fat bastard was starting to look malnourished. Being prison-slim and healthy didn't suit him; he'd lost his chubby grin! I would bring him a bacon-and-sausage sandwich from the Officer's Mess every weekend when I was working, as a little treat.

If he had started to fuck about I would have dealt with him, but he didn't. So I didn't mind doing that small thing for him. He never asked me to; I did it because I wanted to.

My mate Garry knew about the sandwiches and said, 'It's the same as trafficking.'

The fucking twat! I think buying someone a sandwich is decent and a little bit different to being paid five grand a week to bring in smack. Besides, I paid for the fucking sandwich out of my own pocket! That was Garry, though, always the knob. Sometimes, I didn't know why I was friends with him.

The Well could be an OK place to work when you had good relationships with the cons. Scouse used to work much like me but, being a crazy little cunt, he would take presents from cons no matter how risky! He was obnoxious, but in a really funny way. He was liked and had many friends, was brilliant at his job and did it well, and he had the respect of all the cons and the screws. And he hated bent screws, but . . . he was still an idiot in what he took.

He had one con on his Wing that he got on with really well. He never used to give Scouse any shit and always did as he was asked. This con used to make Scouse brews all day, when he was hung over from the night before, and Scouse used to sort him out as much as he could.

It turned out that this con's brother was head doorman at a certain posh club, so Scouse grabbed that with both fucking hands! He had that con ring his brother and get him on the guest list of this club. Fucking lunatic! If he had got caught, he would have got the sack for sure. I warned him of this, but he wasn't worried at all,

'He's sound, mate, I'll be fine!' he said to me in his thick Scouse accent.

I was fearful for him, but he didn't give a shit. As I was really good mates with him, though, it wasn't long before I went along for a drink! This nutcase was on first-name terms with everyone, getting free champagne and being treated like royalty.

'Fuck me, Scouse, how have you managed this?!' I shouted in his ear, over the thumping music,

'It's fookin' mega, Ronnie. Lets have it!' he shouted with a bottle of champagne in one hand and a fag in the other.

I couldn't believe it! We had a top night! He didn't tell me which doorman was the con's brother, and I didn't want to know. By this time, Scouse knew all of them, anyway, the cheeky bastard. He was lucky because this lad never told anyone that he was doing that for Scouse. The con got nothing out of it at all. He just really liked Scouse

The next day, Scouse and I were on a bed watch for overtime. A bed watch comes up when a con has to go out to a civilian hospital. You have to put your name down on the list for one. It is a twelve-hour shift, but it's normally easy money; the two of you sit there, while one is cuffed to the con; and you can usually have a nap, if the con is all right. Billy, an old villain I had on my landing, was going out to hospital. He was sound as fuck. I knew it would be an easy one, so I got Scouse and I on it straight away.

Billy had been in and out of prison for years, long before I was born. He was in his mid-fifties and a proper cockney lad. His cockney slang was so fluent, it was like another language. He was a real character. I loved his old-villain stories; I would get him to tell them to me every day. He was a brilliant storyteller; he would keep you interested, sitting on the edge of your seat, waiting for the usual comical conclusion. He knew all the old lags and famous villains.

He hadn't been in prison for over fifteen years. He had made millions in properties, doing them up and selling them. He claimed he had gone straight, something that I didn't believe as he couldn't help himself. Nonetheless, he was now a millionaire and was no longer out thieving like he used to be. His sentence was for drink driving, so maybe there was a little bit of truth in him being straight.

He never gave the Officers any grief at all, and he knew a lot of cons in there as well. He wasn't fond of the new breed of con, though. It used to rattle his cage when you would get a twenty-one-year-old who would complain about how hard prison life was. He would quickly slap them into line and tell them how it used to be. He hated crackheads, smackheads and the new junkie dealers. He was from the generation of armed robbers and hard men.

I got on with him really well. He was almost fatherly to me. 'Watch yourself, son, a lot of these bastards don't care that you are a decent lad, or that you have a family. Be careful, always watch your back,' he once said to me. He was a real, old-school gentleman.

He knew I loved his stories of all the well-known villains I had read about. He knew a lot of these gangsters personally, and he got one of them to send in a signed copy of his autobiography. Billy called me to his cell and gave it to me, and I was proper made up about it: very happy indeed. If he liked you, he would do anything for you. I didn't ask for it and I shouldn't have taken it but, fuck it, I did.

While Billy was serving this sentence, he was in a lot of pain and needed a hip replacement. He couldn't be fucked with the NHS, and he was worth a few quid, so he went private. The date came through for his operation. He was going to be in hospital for a couple of days at least.

Scouse and I turned up at the prison at eight in the morning to collect him. We went into the jail as normal and collected Billy from his cell. We then took him to reception, where we performed the mandatory strip search. I knew Billy didn't have anything, but we had to do it all the same. Next, I cuffed Scouse to Billy and had the Duty Governor check them and the paperwork. It was all in order, so we made our way to the taxi waiting in the yard.

Scouse and I were chuffed to fuck; we knew bed-watching Billy would be an easy job. The last thing that you wanted was to do a bed watch with some cunt who was a real problem.

'You will love this place, Ronnie, you will want to do as much overtime as you can!' Billy said to me, grinning from ear to ear.

We went out through the gate where the screws checked the vehicle and paperwork once more. Everything was OK, so we were on our way to the hospital.

Scouse said very little on the way there; he was a moody bugger in the morning. We pulled into the driveway of the hospital – and I couldn't believe my eyes. It was a large, Victorian-style building that looked like a fucking stately manor.

'Fuck me, Bill, is this the Queen Mother's gaff or what!'

'Wait till you get inside, Ron!'

Billy wasn't wrong. It had marble flooring that you could see your face in. The place was immaculately clean with the kind of reception that you would expect in a five-star hotel. The receptionist was a fit dolly bird that was all tits, make-up and perfume.

'Good morning, Mr Manning, you are in room twenty-two on the ground floor,' she said. The huge smile that spread across her pretty face revealed her pristine pearly whites.

'Cheers, treacle. Can you send Jack to my room?' Billy answered in his gravelly cockney accent.

'He is consulting another patient at the moment but will be around to see you in twenty minutes or so. Shall I get some menus sent to your room?'

Scouse and I were fucking gobsmacked! This was supposed to be a bloody hospital! I'd not received treatment as good as this in hotels I'd stayed in. Scouse loved it; he now looked much more cheerful than he had in the car on the way over. He couldn't take his eyes off the receptionist, the dirty little bastard.

'Send them down, love. Whenever Jack is ready, I ain't going anywhere!' Billy showed her the cuffs locked on his wrists.

We made our way to the room, with Scouse grudgingly leaving the reception.

'Ronnie, ya bastard, I was *in* there!' he insisted happily.

The place was amazing. The staff who walked past were all quick to say, 'Good morning,' with welcoming smiles on their faces. Billy's was a fucking great room, with a king-size bed sitting in the middle. It had a nice wide-screen TV, at least 28 inches, that had the sentence 'Welcome Mr Manning' projected across the screen.

'Fookin' hell, Billy man, this place must cost a fookin' packet!?' Scouse said. He had completely forgotten that it was still morning and that he should be moody!

'Money talks, son, and this place is far from free!' Billy answered.

Billy showed us the bathroom. Marble floors and tiles everywhere, with a separate shower and bathtub. The place was amazing. Billy flopped on the bed, and I quickly took the cuffs off. You were supposed to keep the prisoner cuffed, but I trusted

Billy, he was sound. Billy grabbed the remote for the telly.

'What do ya fancy watching?' he asked, while flicking through the menu page of the TV. He had Sky TV with all the channels, plus a selection of films that weren't out on DVD.

'Fookin' overtime, don't you just love it!' Scouse laughed. He grabbed the remote and switched on Sky Sports. I looked down, a little embarrassed at the way Scouse had done that, but Billy just laughed, acknowledging me with a look that said, 'Don't worry about it.' A bird then walked in. I couldn't make out if the uniform was that of a nurse, doctor, housemaid or stripper.

'Good morning, sir, I've got the menus that you wanted.'

Scouse was jumping up and down on his seat, struggling to contain his excitement. This was proving to be a hospital full of beautiful people!

'Fancy any grub, lads?'

'Fookin' right, Bill.'

'Hang on a minute, Scouse. Cheers, Billy, that's nice of you, but we can't, mate.'

'Listen, Ronnie, you have what you want, it don't bother me either way. But feel free, I really don't mind, you lads are the better ones. I ain't some scroat that will blab. I've no reason to.'

Thinking about it for all of two seconds, I said, 'Pass the menu then, Bill!'

We all had steak and chips with onion rings and garlic bread! As we were tucking into the grub, with Spanish football on the TV, it suddenly occurred to me that maybe Billy shouldn't be eating as he was having an operation. But I figured since it was the nurses who had brought up all the food it wasn't a problem. It was turning into the best overtime that I'd ever done.

'Hello, Billy, I see you are watching your diet like I said.'

'Jack, good to see you, mate. How's ya missus? And don't worry, these two lads are good.'

Jack was the doctor dealing with Billy. It was obvious they were mates on the road. He looked a similar age to Billy, only in better shape and with a strong tan.

'OK. When do you want me to operate?'

'I wanna have a few days in here, I'm sick of the Well.'

'Understood. I'll push it for as long as I can, mate, but I can't do that for ever.'

I was only half listening to the conversation as I was too busy shovelling the ketchup-smothered steak and chips into my gob. Scouse wasn't listening either. But I realised why Billy wasn't sticking to the nil-by-mouth order set for before an operation. Jack, being his mate, would square it away for Billy to have a little stay. We didn't give a fuck – Billy was all right and a load of Officers would be able to earn a bit of extra cash. Everyone was a winner.

After I'd loosened my belt from the huge meal I'd eaten, I remembered I needed to write up the occurrence log, where you fill in everything that happens. Well, not entirely everything in this case! I also had to ring the Well – you have to call in every four hours to let them know that the con is still alive and has not escaped. When I did that, they told me they had some bad news. They hadn't organised a night shift to come and relieve us, so they asked me very politely whether Scouse and I would stay on and get more overtime. I didn't need to check with Scouse, and they certainly didn't need to ask me twice!

Even though working twenty-four hours straight was completely illegal, the Well did it all the time. They were shit at organising things. I figured they would probably get around it somehow by saying it was an operational emergency. When they needed you in this situation, you had them by the balls and so you could get them to agree to loads. At the end of the day, if Scouse and I didn't want to, then they would have been fucked. But that's the Prison Service through and through – relying on the staff to get them out of the shit.

I swiftly negotiated twelve hours' overtime and twelve hours' toil (time off in lieu) for the night shift. When I told Scouse, I thought he was going to shove his tongue down my throat, he was so happy.

As everyone had their own room, the hospital wasn't too bothered about sticking to visiting times. And when a prisoner was out on a bed watch, it was down to the discretion of the Officer to allow visits. There is no reason for bed-watch patients not to have visits, providing it's not a security risk, and Billy was sound, so we were happy for him to have some. He asked me if his wife could come and see him. I couldn't see why not, so I agreed. She turned up with loads of decent grub from Marks and Sparks. It was proper good tucker; I'd not eaten so well in ages! She was a motherly type, but a proper Boycey's wife – fake tan, loads of gold, leopard-skin clothing and perfume that was so strong it tickled the back of your throat. She was in her fifties, from what I could see, and had a Pat Butcher look about her.

She quickly began to fuss, telling Billy that he needed to look after himself better. She addressed Scouse and me as 'love' and rustled up some sandwiches for all of us to tuck into. She was a nice lady and I could tell that Billy relied on her. The visit was good but she was too much, going on at Billy and buzzing around the room. It was getting on all of our nerves – especially Billy; he was getting the right hump with her.

'Fuck off now, love, ya givin' me a blindin' headache,' Billy snapped, throwing her a look that said enough was enough.

'Well, I'd better go; the traffic around here is murder and I wanna get home tonight. Nice to meet you boys. You take care of yourselves and my Billy,' she said politely to me and Scouse, pretending Billy hadn't told her to fuck off. She was the perfect little housewife. She would run around Billy like there was no tomorrow, but she knew when he had had enough. It was obvious Billy wore the trousers in that relationship.

Once she'd gone he said, 'Sorry about her, lads, she gets on my tits half the time, but her heart is in the right place.'

'Bill, she seems a lovely lady; you ain't got anything to say sorry for.'

While Billy and I nattered, Scouse was prowling around the room. He found a menu on a side table, which he clutched in his sweaty little palms like it was the World Cup while he grinned at Billy and me.

'You found the wine list son?'

'Sure have!'

'Fill ya boots, lads!'

With that, Scouse set about looking through the list.

'No fucking way, Scouse,' I quickly said in protest.

There was no way I was going to let him order booze – that meant our jobs for sure if we were caught. No way could I let that happen . . .

Two hours later, the three of us were singing along to 'Going Underground' by The Jam as it blasted out of VH2 channel, pissed out of our fucking heads! We had necked pink champagne, vodka, After Shock liqueurs and more Guinness than there is in Dublin. Scouse has this way of talking me into anything. He was a persuasive little shit. I tried to stay strong and keep a small amount of professionalism, but Scouse got the better of me. It didn't take him long to persuade me, if I'm honest.

It was late into the evening, when Billy said, 'Ronnie, do ya mind if my missus and her mate come and visit me?'

Answering loudly, over Scouse singing along to "Twentieth Century Boy', I said, 'She only left a couple of hours ago. Can't she come tomorrow?'

'I'm not talking about me wife, I'm talking about me bit on the side!'

'Ha ha! No dramas, Bill; but only those two, mate. Tell them to hurry up and get here, it's fucking well late.'

'They are already here, son. When reception called a minute ago they told me they had arrived.'

'You cheeky old cunt!'

Billy laughed and phoned reception to tell them to send his guests down. There was a knock on the door.

'Come in,' Billy shouted.

Scouse had gradually turned the TV up louder and louder, so now I grabbed the remote and turned it down to a more reasonable level. Even though Scouse and I were acting dangerously, I still had a bit of responsibility about me, even if it was small.

These two birds walked in. 'Hi ya, Billy!' they said together, as if it were a lyric to a song. They were both trashy-looking birds. They were late twenties to early thirties, fit bodies with lumps in all the right places. They had legs up to their armpits, with skirts that barely covered their arses, and tits that were the size of

259

medicine balls and obviously fake. They were both wearing so much make-up that it looked as if they had applied it with a paint brush. Their hair was dead-straight bleached-blonde and seemed in good condition. And their suntan – fucking hell! It was so dark it looked ridiculous. They both looked every bit the page-three model. Scouse's jaw hit the floor; he loved anything trashy!

Both birds went over to the bed and sat next to Billy where they hung on every word he said. They laughed over the top at Billy's jokes, which I found embarrassing. But Billy didn't give a fuck, he was lapping it up. He was quickly snogging both of them and rubbing his dirty old hands all over their firm bodies. They obviously weren't with Billy for his youth or his good looks.

Scouse and I carried on drinking and watching VH2 on the box. Scouse's tongue was hanging out of his mouth, watching the two birds with Billy. I was beginning to get uncomfortable and I was sobering up quicker than I could drink. I kept picturing the Duty Governor turning up to check on us. We would be right in the shit if he did.

From time to time, the Duty Governor would make a trip to a bed watch to make sure everything was going OK and check that the Officers on duty were doing their job properly. He would have a fucking heart attack if he walked in to Billy's room! It was seldom that they did come, but it had been known . . .

'Treat these two lads nice, girls. They are the best screws at the Well.' They both came and sat next to Scouse and me. They were flicking their hair and flirting with us outrageously. Scouse loved it and quickly moved in closer to one of them. It was obvious that Billy was treating them to such a good lifestyle that they would do anything he wanted them to do. Scouse was getting sucked into the mood the birds were trying to set. Meanwhile, Billy was lying on the bed, giving Scouse and I approving nods as he gulped down some more Guinness.

One of them began to focus her attention on me. She was talking and moving provocatively. I backed away, to suggest I was uncomfortable with her being like that. That didn't stop her and she was being as suggestive as she could, doing what Billy had asked her to do and 'treat us nice'. Enough was enough and I wanted them out. I had to get a grip of the situation and myself.

'Visit's over.'

Scouse looked up at me, giving me a disapproving look that only lasted a second before he, too, came back down to earth, realising where he was.

'We gotta go, Bill?' asked one of the girls.

'Ya fookin' heard Mr Thompson, out ya go,' Scouse answered her, before Billy could.

They got their stuff and fucked off.

Scouse and I had a harsh attack of reality and we quickly rallied around to clear up the empties.

'Ronnie, don't worry. I told you earlier, I ain't gonna say fuck-all,' Billy said, trying to reassure me.

We cleared up the mess and sorted ourselves out. We all had a chat to say, 'This stays in the hospital and no one needs to know about it.' I told Billy to not do this with anyone else. He agreed, saying that he wouldn't want to anyway. He only gave out treats like that to people he liked.

When the morning relief came to the hospital, we were able to leave while Billy was asleep. Scouse told the screws that Manning had been well behaved and had not caused any problems. On our way back to the staff quarters, Scouse and I did have a giggle about it. I told Scouse how important it was that we didn't tell a soul about us getting pissed with a prisoner on a bed watch. He agreed, but didn't seem to register the severity of the situation if we were caught.

The doctor told the prison that Billy wasn't well enough to go under anaesthetic, and that's why the operation wasn't performed on the first day. The prison agreed to let him stay in hospital since he would be ready in a day or two and it would be impractical to take him back to prison and then return him to hospital again.

I had a couple of rest days due, so I went home to Danielle. Scouse was off for a few days, too, so I thought he would go back to Liverpool, like he normally did. Not this time, though. He wanted to earn more money on that bed watch and obviously had plans to enjoy Billy's hospitality. He didn't tell me he was going to do another shift; he knew that I wouldn't have liked it. I just wanted to keep away. We had behaved badly and I didn't want to get caught. Scouse booked himself in for the following night. He was on it with a screw called Victor.

Victor was a typical 'Mr No': an old dinosaur. He had been in the job for donkey's years. He was a nice old geezer, but he spent most of his time blind drunk. Everyone knew him, the staff and the cons. No one asked him for anything because he was the laziest old bastard that God ever put breath into. He wasn't a bully or anything, just plain lazy. He was a comic who would have people in stitches, but his drink problem was well known. He was someone the managers wanted to be rid of. He was a liability. He turned up to work pissed more often than not. A couple of times he was so minging that the bosses had no choice but to send him home and discipline him. He had been given his final written warning, so one more strike and he was out. And when he was pissed, he would speak before he thought – which was his downfall.

Scouse met Victor at the club where they had a quick pint before going round to the front of the nick to be collected for their bed watch. They went to the hotel – I mean, hospital – to relieve the day staff . . .

I turned up to work three days later and was greeted by loads of people coming up to me and saying, 'Have you heard about Scouse and Victor?'

I had a sinking feeling in my stomach. Right away, I guessed what they had got up to. I went straight to the mess where I knew I would find Scouse tucking into his bacon sarnie and mug of coffee.

'What the fuck has happened, you prick?'

'Fookin' Victor and fookin' me got fookin' pissed on that bed watch.'

'You got caught?'

'Nah, lad. Victor gobbed off about it round the club. The stupid cunt was pissed up, telling everyone how we had free booze all night long and how we cleared it up five minutes before the day staff came in.'

'*You* stupid cunt, I told you to go home to Liverpool. You know Victor is a drunken mess and you can't trust him.'

'That ain't all mate. There was a Governor in there that heard everything. I'm fooked.'

'You need to speak to Rumpole, quick.'

'Already on it, lad. See ya after.'

With that he walked off to his Wing. It looked like he was in for it, big time. Drinking on duty is gross misconduct and could mean instant dismissal. I thought he should play ignorant and say fuck-all. Rumpole thought differently. He said that, because their antics had been heard first hand, they were screwed. Rumpole advised them both to admit that they had had one beer each, and that all Victor's boasting was drunken exaggeration. They had to admit to some misdemeanour or they would be sacked, for sure. If they offered something, they might be able to keep their jobs.

They had their disciplinary hearings. Victor had been given so many chances that they had no choice but to sack him. He was fifty-two at the time and had been in the job since he was twenty. He didn't know anything else. He was single and living in the staff quarters, so he lost his job and his home. He only had a few more years until retirement. And all because he couldn't keep his gob shut.

I was with Scouse just before he went for his hearing. For the first time ever, he looked uneasy. He realised all of this could have been avoided. He had been stupid and complacent. Together, we'd acted like idiots. Once was stupid, but twice was mental.

I waited outside the nick for Scouse to see what fate had dealt him. He came out of the gate wearing his cheeky grin, so I knew he hadn't been sacked.

'Final written warning, mate!'

'You've had a touch, mate. Fucking think about things in the future, you mug.'

I put my arm around him and we went straight round to the club to celebrate and to give Victor a send off. Victor was already there, looking suicidal. The job was everything to him. Scouse had no sympathy at all; he saw it as Victor's fault. Getting caught may have been, but Scouse should never have done it again. Or even done it the first time.

Scouse and I had acted like nobheads that day at the hospital. I look back on it with a sigh of relief. I was so fucking lucky – and stupid for risking everything. But it was a good laugh.

A few weeks later, I wasn't so lucky. Detailed to Visits, bend up – suspension. Just like that.

I have done some stupid things, but I never expected to end up suspended for doing my job. I knew that Frankie, AJ, Bob and I were all innocent of any wrongdoing, but that meant nothing. We didn't know what was going to happen. We could lose our jobs or even go to prison. Our fate was out of our hands, and there was nothing that we could do about it.

PISSING IT ALL AWAY

The morning was unbearable. The rumours flying around. Then it happened; I was suspended. Saying goodbye to Mike at the gate was like a bad dream. I sat in my car, staring into space not knowing what to do. I had been suspended; really suspended.

Bob arguing with a con and calling for assistance. Running over as quickly as I could. 'He's got drugs, get him out of here!' Frankie, Bob and I escorting this con to the strip-search room. The con gobbing off like fuck on the way down. Me telling him to calm down. Him punching Bob. Me dropping the piece of shit. It was so fucking quick. AJ running down the stairs and jumping in to help us bend him up. The alarm being raised, the cavalry arriving. Frankie getting relieved by Neil.

Think, did Frankie punch him? Did he?

Perhaps . . . No. What the fuck was I thinking?

Over and over again, the incident was played in my mind. I started to question my judgement and, at times, my own sanity. I had everyone telling me to point the finger at Frankie. Some were saying to drop him in it even if he didn't punch the con. But no way was I going to do that. No fucking way. I had loads of people telling me that this was typical of him and no one would think any less of me if I didn't cover up for him. I started to fucking imagine Frankie punching him. But I knew he didn't, and there was no way that I was going to say any different.

Bob was on the floor, knocked out, not having a clue what the fuck was going on. AJ, who got to the room at around the same time as Neil, maybe a split second after, said he saw fuck-all. He told me to be honest, that it was the only way. And that was something that I wanted to do – I wanted to be honest. As far as the Governors were concerned, though, Frankie was guilty and they didn't want me standing in their way of getting rid of him. If I did, there could be serious repercussions for me. All they would say was that I needed to think and to do the right thing.

Sitting in my car, dazed and confused, I decided to call my brief straight away. He was a nice old man, bundles of experience and straight talking. He went on to tell me that I was required to go to the station to be interviewed under caution, and reluctantly told me the worse-case scenario. How was I going to explain all this to my family? How was I going to tell Danielle? I'd spent the weekend getting pissed out of my head, ignoring her. The last thing I said was, 'I'll sort it.' And I had sorted fuck-all. I thought my family would think that I'd let them down, even though I'd done bugger-all wrong. The last thing that I wanted to do was let anyone down. Once I'd called my brief, I sat there in shock, crying my eyes out. Trying to gather myself, I eventually decided that I had to go home. Face the music; face my family.

The journey seemed to last for an age. The drive was too much. I needed a fucking drink. I still hadn't decided how to tell my family. I could have had all the time in the world but I still wouldn't have found the right words. I got two phone calls on my way home, one from Bob and one from AJ. They had both suffered the same fate as me. They were suspended for conspiring to assault a prisoner.

Although Governors said that Frankie was their man and we needn't worry, they were still quick to suspend us all on conspiracy charges – in other words, they were willing to accuse us of planning to do over the inmate. Any way you looked at it, that was a serious allegation and one that we couldn't take lightly. Fucking cunts. We didn't know the con and we didn't really know each other that well. It was bollocks, and they knew it.

I got home and Danielle was there. I broke out in a cold sweat. I thought that I would have a few hours before I'd see her. At least that would have given me time to think a little. And to have a drink – fuck me, I needed one. Walking to the door, I was shaking with apprehension; my nerves were getting the better of me. The thought of upsetting her was destroying me. I pulled the key out of my pocket and put it to the door as slowly as I could, trying to squeeze a few more seconds out before facing her. Breathing heavily, I unlocked the door. Once I got inside the house, she looked at me, smiling but confused because I was home so early.

I didn't know where to start, or how to say it, so I blurted it all out, without even catching my breath in the middle. Her smile began to drop as my words exploded out of my mouth. The smile turned into a wobbly bottom lip, which turned into tears. She couldn't hide her anguish. She was devastated by the situation. She knew that none of it was my fault. She knew that I wouldn't protect a bully and risk everything. She tried to tell me that everything would be all right, but she couldn't hide the fear in her eyes. I left it for her to tell the rest of my family. I just couldn't face it. I didn't have the strength to go over it again. It was hard enough for me to understand what had happened, let alone explain it to them all.

The last thing Mike told me to do was to keep a low profile but I went against all advice. I got on the piss five minutes after I'd told Danielle. She begged me not to go, she wanted me to stay in and open up to her; she wanted to take care of me. I didn't. I went straight out. Same old story with me: drink when I'm happy, drink even more when I'm sad.

I belled my mates. They realised – after the weekend we'd just had – that some shit had gone down at work. They knew that I was in a bad way. I got to the pub, my mouth was watering at the prospect of my first drink. Beer, no chance; whisky, neat and large. One after the other. My mates were looking at me with worried eyes.

'Slow down, Ron, take it easy,' Dow whispered to me. Always the pacifier, always looking out for others.

'If I wanted to be told what to do, I would drink with my fucking mother. Get them in, ya cunt.'

I was half pissed within twenty minutes or so. The spinning had begun, but my pain was still rich. More, I needed more. No one would have slowed me down that night. I got minging.

My attitude was all wrong from the start. I think everyone knows whisky is fighting juice as well. Mix my attitude with gallons of Jack Daniels and it was obvious something was going to happen . . .

This twat gave it to me at the bar, which normally I would have laughed at. I wasn't a kid any more; getting into scraps downtown was not the sort of thing I did. I got enough confrontation at work, so it was the last thing I wanted in my own time. On that night, though, I was in no mood to laugh. I had no tolerance inside me. He had picked on the wrong bloke. A nudge and a V sign. A dirty look. Fuck-all really, but enough to send me over the edge. So I belted the prick right on the chin and, before he'd hit the ground, I smacked his mouthy mate. All of his mates stepped in and they also got a clump from me. The bouncers came running over and tried to grab me. They wanted the carnage to stop. I was having none of it. I was a loose cannon. I started fighting with them as well. My mates got involved, sticking up for me. It was one big fight. My mates were scrapping with his mates, I was scrapping with the bouncers. Punches, kicks flying everywhere. It spilled out on to the street. It was getting messy. It wasn't long until the Old Bill turned up. It was a mess. My mates grabbed me and shouted, 'RUN!' I ran off without getting nicked, thank fuck. I could see the headlines, 'SUSPENDED SCREW BATTERS PUBLIC'.

I was lucky; that would have been the nail in the coffin.

'Keep a low profile,' Mike had said.

I had royally fucked that up.

A couple of weeks went by. Drinking, gym, sleep, that's all I did. I got a phone call from my brief asking me to come and meet with him. All of us who were suspended were asked to go. It was time to learn what was going to happen and how long the shit would last. I was already struggling to cope. With much trepidation, I made my way to see him. I met the rest of them there. Bob and I were both fairly jittery, but the other two were as cool as ice. I think that they were nervous inside, but they had both got bags of experience; sitting in a solicitor's office, discussing their prospects, was not new to either of them. We went in and sat down, looking at each other, waiting for the damage to be pointed out.

The brief told us that he thought that at least one of us would be charged with ABH, suggesting that it would most likely be Frankie. The rest of us had the possibility of being charged with conspiring to cause ABH. This was not set in stone, just his opinion. He didn't pull any punches: he put his cards on the table straight away. He was honest; he said that this was definitely not a good situation to be in. There was a lot said in that office, with all of us firing questions at him. He answered the best he could, but it was all hearsay. I respected him for not painting a rosy picture, not pretending that it was all going to be OK because it was clear that it wasn't.

He did set out a worse-case scenario: he told us that, as we were Prison Officers, we would be dealt with very severely if we were found guilty. It was abuse of authority, which is seen in a very dim light. If found guilty, they would almost certainly make an example of us. He also told us he had no idea of the time scale of all this. He didn't know how long it would be until the police interviewed us, let alone if or when it would go to court. These things have a nasty habit of taking ages. It was all 'ifs and buts'. He couldn't really tell us anything. We had to wait for the law to do its thing. And as well as the criminal investigation, the internal one still loomed.

Not being charged, not being convicted, not being sent down, that was the immediate priority. Keeping our jobs was the last thing on our minds. As far as we were concerned, being sacked wasn't a matter of if, but when. I left the office in total turmoil; I didn't know what to do with myself.

The weeks went by and my drinking and behaviour got completely out of control. I got pissed at night and became introverted during the day when I had no energy to do anything apart from sleep till mid afternoon, then get up and go to the gym. By the time I'd finished, Danielle was returning from work. I had done nothing for the family, none of the housework nor anything else she had asked me to do. The poor cow had been at work all day, had picked up our son from nursery and had come home to a tip of a house with a boyfriend who did nothing. I didn't speak to her or anyone, for that matter. I just got on with doing fuck-all, sinking deeper and deeper into depression. If anyone asked me about it and what was happening, I tensed up and snapped at them. I didn't want to talk about it. I just wanted to sleep, drink . . . anything other than think or discuss my situation.

Within an hour of Danielle getting home, I would piss off down the pub. She would tell me that I couldn't carry on like this, that I needed to talk to someone. I would tell her to piss off and leave me alone. I would tell her I was fine, I was coping. But I wasn't. I was pressing the self-destruct button with both hands. I was spending more than I earned, drinking far too much and not talking to Danielle about the way that I was feeling. I withdrew completely, only interested in getting pissed and staying out all night. It was the wrong way to deal with things, but I didn't know what else to do. Instead of turning to my only true stability and rock, I was pushing her away. I was wrecking everything in my life. I was letting the Prison Service ruin me.

Then, one day, it all got too much. I was barely talking to Danielle at all. I wouldn't even say hello to her when she walked into the room. I was finding it difficult to live with me so I can only imagine how bad it was for Danielle. I was destroying myself in front of her very eyes. She did everything to try and help me, but she couldn't. I was in my own shattered world and I didn't want to face my problems. Danielle told me that she could not take my behaviour any more. She said that she deserved better. She told me she couldn't help me if I wasn't prepared to try and help myself. She told me she was leaving.

I never thought that she would leave me, but she did, and quite rightly so. It broke my heart. I probably could have stopped her if I'd changed my ways. But I didn't.

My mate Scott moved in and rented a room. I could always count on him. If I fucked things up with a bird, he would move in. And then I began to party hard. Losing Danielle destroyed me. Instead of fighting for my family and begging her to give me another chance, I got out of control. I was living like a playboy. I was acting like a teenager. I was drinking so heavily, it was dangerous. The drink only masked the problems – I would break down when I was on my own. And I couldn't help thinking that the managers back at the Well couldn't give a fuck. I could have cut my wrists and they wouldn't have known. I didn't even receive so much as a phone call, the fucking bastards. That's Prison Service support for you; they don't give a fuck who they ruin, as long as they get the result they want

It was a Saturday. Scott, Jim, Fox, Khany, Sam and me decided to go out early doors so that we could be in the pub soon after lunch. We were drinking all day, having a laugh, round after round, from pub to pub, sinking them for fun. We ended up in a nightclub, by which time we were hammered. That's when Sam told us that some bird he'd met the week before was coming to meet him. Even in the state I was in, I remember thinking that it wasn't an ideal date. Turning up to meet a guy who had been drinking all day, fucked out of his head with five mates. Not what I would call romance!

I was standing next to the dance floor, drinking my pint, watching Jim and Khany cut shapes to the shit music. Then I noticed this big skinhead giving it to Khany. Jim appeared to tell this geezer to fuck off. He wouldn't, so Jim punched him. Khany started rolling around on the floor with one of the skinhead's mates. Scott, Fox and I were pissing ourselves laughing. As that happened, I felt a tap on my shoulder. It was Sam with his new bird. Sam was trying to introduce her to us, not really managing to string a sentence together as he, too, was so pissed. She looked stone cold sober.

'That's Jim, the one punching the skinhead,' explained Sam. 'He's just come off tag for fighting. Khany is the fella rolling around on the floor fighting that bloke. This is Fox, he thinks he's Liam Gallagher. That's Scott, the one cheering on Jim and Khany. This is Ronnie. He's a suspended Prison Officer, but don't worry, he's not had any criminal charges brought against him yet!'

I had no relationship with Danielle. I stopped talking to her or visiting my son. I was in no condition to see my boy and I didn't want Danielle to see the state I was getting into. I was in a bad place. I couldn't get any lower. Days were turning into weeks. There was still no news of when I had to attend the police interview. There was no noise from the Well. I was alone, in the dark, knowing fuck-all. My fate was scaring me. The tension, the pressure, I was losing control. I didn't know if I was coming or going.

Frankie took things in his stride, but it was affecting him. We spoke on the phone, every week or two, to see if either of us had heard anything and to keep each other's spirits up. Frankie wasn't stupid; he had his theories about what was going to happen but, like me, he was pissing in the wind.

Bob was fucked up to say the least. Every time I spoke to him, he ended up in tears, which rattled my emotions. I would tell a funny joke and get off the phone as quick as I could, trying to hold back the tears myself. He knew I'd split up with Danielle, so he tried to get me to open up to him when we spoke. He knew that I wasn't right, no matter how hard I tried to fool him.

I had become everything that I didn't want to be. I couldn't believe what I'd turned into. I had been a Prison Officer who wanted to do his job. But I'd come to this.

One day when Scott was out, I found myself swigging from a vodka bottle, sitting in my boxer shorts, crying my eyes out. It was one o'clock on a Tuesday afternoon. He came home to find me pissed out of my head and sobbing. He came and sat with me. I was embarrassed that he was seeing me like that, but I finally broke down and opened up to someone. Scott was there when I needed him. He put his arms around me and I just blubbered on his shoulders. We sat there like that for hours.

I needed a resolution. I wanted my life back.

SERVICED

The worse-case scenario was playing over and over in my mind. I kept seeing a vision of the four of us in the dock together. I was dreaming the same dream – us in court, being given the verdict: guilty. I would wake up covered in sweat. When I say covered, I mean the bed was saturated, as if I'd got out of a swimming pool and dived straight in. It was fucking horrible! All of this stress was doing my fucking head in. My family were constantly asking, 'When is the case? When are you seeing the police? When are you going back to work? Why is it taking so long?' I had no fucking idea and all those questions only put more pressure on me. They weren't doing it intentionally; they were concerned. I could see the anxiety on their faces, especially my mum's.

Mum would get angry with me; she thought that I was hiding

something from her. She couldn't understand how the Prison Service could do this to me. She was frustrated with it all; she couldn't believe it was happening. But her worries were pressing down on me. It was the last thing that I wanted, or needed. My dad knew that some shit was going down, but that's as far as it went with him. My sister was lovely as always. She didn't say much about it, but I knew she was there if I needed her. My brother came out on the piss with me quite a bit, even though he didn't really understand what I was going through. But that's what happens with family or friends who are not in the Service – they can't understand. And that's when the company of fellow Officers is so comforting. They do understand; they know the Prison Service madness.

Even though Danielle and I had split up, she was still concerned. I used to get text messages asking if I was OK, if there was anything that she could do. Looking back, it was obvious she still loved me. I loved her, too, but I was in no place to be the man she wanted. I was in a dark, dark place. She would encourage me to see my boy, but I often couldn't manage it. It was too painful. I was a mess, I was ashamed. No son of mine was going to see his dad like that.

I would get up at lunchtime, hung-over, feeling like shit. I would force a bowl of porridge, two Ibuprofen and a pint of orange down my neck. Normally the Ibuprofen wasn't enough, and paracetamol would soon follow. Then I would head to the gym at 14.00 hrs. That was my routine. I would beast myself: circuit training, running, weight training, the full works. I would sweat it out. I needed the bellyache, the rough feeling, to disappear. If I felt really bad, I would put on a black bin liner under my gym kit. That would really make me sweat it out. I would follow that with a sauna just for good measure. Then home, change of clothes, down the pub.

It was a day when I had worked really hard in the gym that I went back to the changing room, out of breath, soaked. Breathing heavily, I undid my locker. My phone was ringing. 'Who the fuck is that?' I thought. The lads and my family knew my routine. But it was my brief. I'd become so used to living in limbo, I never expected to get 'the call'. Trying to compose myself, I answered. It was quick; my day had come. I had to report to the police station. Standing there, sweaty and out of breath, I didn't know what to feel. I was glad that it had finally come but I would be lying if I said I wasn't scared. I phoned Rumpole to let him know. He answered the phone saying, 'I know.' That old fucker knew everything! I spoke to Mike, he said that he would come to the police station with me, if I wanted. I wanted.

On the day, I met Mike at the Well. Not inside – I was suspended. I wasn't allowed inside. It felt weird and painful being there. I saw some of the screws walking in and out. Most of them said 'Good luck'. It was good to see Mike. He was a great union rep. He tried to relax me, telling me that I would be fine.

But I couldn't relax at all, I was as fidgety as fuck. As much as I wanted this to be over with, now that it was finally upon me, I was scared about the outcome. What if I was charged?

The journey didn't take long. We were only going to the local police station, which was where they were handling the investigation. As we arrived, I was thinking, 'This is it, just keep a hold of yourself.' Getting out of the car, I took a deep breath, Mike gave me a reassuring nod. We walked up to the reception desk and Mike told them who I was and what we were there for. There were loads of scroats in the reception area for one reason or another, staring at us, mainly at Mike because he was in his screw's uniform. I was paranoid as fuck, thinking they would know what I was in for. I felt everyone's eyes burning into me. I began to sweat and fidget; and all I wanted to do was get out. My brief was already there. He ran through how the interview would work etc. I was trying to listen, but it was hard to concentrate.

I waited for what seemed a lifetime and then two plain-clothed coppers came down to meet me. They greeted me in a firm but fair manner. They took me to an interview room. We walked through many gates, down many corridors – just as I used to lead the cons at the Well. Only this time, I was the con and they were the screws. They sat me down and asked me if I wanted a drink. I asked for water: my shirt was soaked with sweat and I needed something to cool me down.

I sipped the water, taking deep breaths to try and compose myself. They told me the interview would be under caution, which is when the police read you your rights to say that the evidence you give may be used in court. So, they read me my rights, which made me even more apprehensive. I kept telling myself that all I had to do was tell them how it was, not hide anything and just be honest. Fuck the Governors! Those bastards were the people making me question myself and my judgement.

I had to be clear, concise and convincing. I only had one shot at this and I needed them to believe me.

The two blokes who were interviewing me were not bad fellas. The younger one of the two was career minded, I could tell by his interviewing technique. He was very thorough, making sure he covered everything and himself at the same time. It was very professional, very textbook. The way he jumped from open to closed questions was easy for me to spot. He patronised me from time to time, as if I was some tosser he was trying to catch out, and I had to remind him to speak to me with some respect; I wasn't some shitbag he'd just nicked. Mike gave me a look as if to say, 'You've told him now, so move on.' My brief gave me a respectful nod, showing that he thought I was handling myself well. Thankfully, this young copper wound his neck in and stopped treating me like a mug.

They questioned me thoroughly, going over everything. They asked me if I saw Bob provoking the inmate, or whether I saw the inmate provoking Bob? Was it necessary for me to restrain the con? How did I do it? Why did I do it? Was it carried out correctly? They asked everything other than the colour of my fucking socks.

I was in there for three hours. From the minute we escorted that scroat from the Visits Hall to the point when Frankie was relieved by Miss Neil, the incident lasted five or six minutes, with half of it on camera. It was a fucking joke. The whole thing was a waste of time and money. They wanted their man and they were going to get him. That's all the Prison Service was bothered about.

Finally, they thanked me for helping them with their enquiries and released me. They didn't charge me but said that they might need to talk to me again. My brief said that this was good news. However, he also said that I was not in the clear until they officially stated that I was exonerated from their investigations and was only a witness.

I had told them exactly how it was and I didn't incriminate anyone. Frankie may have been a dangerous cunt in the past but, on that day, he did nothing other than his correct duties. I wasn't going to point the finger at someone because of their reputation.

Whatever the Governors had said to me, surely they couldn't do anything to me for being honest?

I continued to meet the requirements of my suspension, and rang up religiously every Monday to be told there was no news. Over the course of the next three weeks, Bob, AJ and finally Frankie were also interviewed.

AJ had been questioned and released. They told him there and then there was no charge being brought against him. He didn't give a fuck; he had been in this sort of shit before and nothing fazed him. Bob was a nervous wreck, crying all the time. He was scared stiff. He knew that if he slipped up, he would go down the river and The Well wouldn't help him. He managed to compose himself and say enough for the Old Bill to release him. They realised that he wasn't the brightest spark and had probably done nothing wrong. However, like me, he was not yet completely exonerated.

Before Frankie was interviewed, the Old Bill had to interview both the con and Neil. It was obvious what the con was going to say, but Neil's evidence was what the whole case was based on. Neil said that she saw Frankie punching the con repeatedly in the face. A member of staff testifying against Frankie was all the police needed. They had a case.

It was Frankie's turn to be interviewed. The position of the police was straightforward. Because the prisoner's injuries were so minimal, they didn't have enough to charge Frankie with ABH, but they did have enough to charge him with assaulting a prisoner while under restraint.

He phoned me as soon as he got out of the interview and told me that he'd been charged. My heart sank to the pit of my stomach. He told me not to worry and that things would be OK.

I rang Bob and AJ to tell them. Bob was quite shattered. He and I had still not been told whether or not we were going to be charged. We didn't know what was going to happen to us. We were hoping the CPS would throw the case out, but our brief said that it was unlikely because Miss Neil's statement, implicating Frankie in assault, made the case very strong.

The CPS agreed with the Old Bill, that there was enough to substantiate a court case. Due to the lesser charge, it would be the Magistrates' Court that would deal with it. This meant that he could get a maximum of twelve months in prison. It was better than the possibility of five years for ABH, but it was still disgraceful that he had been charged with anything.

Bob and I were finally told that there would be no criminal charges brought against us. It was hard to feel pleased or even relieved. Rumpole warned us, however, that once the criminal case was finished, the internal investigation would start again. He went on to tell us that, even though we had been cleared by the police of any wrongdoing, the prison could still find us guilty of acting inappropriately, which would result in us losing our jobs. Unbelievable; you can be cleared by the Old Bill but still be fucked over by the disciplinary procedures. How is that fair? Surely they can't do that? Apparently so, Rumpole informed us. The Prison Service works on a balance-of-probability basis. If they think that you probably did something, then that would be enough to discipline or, in our case, sack us.

The Prison Service would not resume their investigations until Frankie had been brought to court. Our brief told us that this would take months and months, especially as papers at the Well kept going missing, or were not sent when requested by

Frankie's brief. It seemed like they were doing everything they could to be arseholes. It got adjourned over and over again. We were far from out of the woods.

We also found out that Bob, AJ and I would be summoned to appear in Frankie's court case. If we slipped up in court, then Frankie was going down, simple as that.

I texted Danielle to tell her that I wasn't charged but that Frankie had been. She phoned me and we had a quick chat. She seemed pleased to talk to me. It ripped my heart out of my chest just speaking to her. Fox and my mate Steve were sitting in my lounge as I spoke to her. I was struggling to contain my emotions. The last thing I wanted was my pals to see me upset.

AJ fucked off abroad. When he'd been suspended before, among other business ventures he had bought a bar in Spain. When he was at work, he sorted his shifts so he could do a week on and a week off. His family lived out in Spain permanently, with AJ coming back every other week. He only stayed in the job for the pension – the one last thing that is good about being a Prison Officer, and the Government are doing their best to make that worse, as well.

Bob was so worried about what was going to happen that he didn't know what to do with himself. He let his missus into what he was going through. He was still with Alison. She was a nice lady; I spoke to her numerous times during my suspension. I didn't really speak to many people from work, to be honest, just Rhys, Garry and Scouse. I discovered my real friends during those times. I know it is difficult to find the time to keep in touch with your mates, but the ones who made contact were my true friends. It wasn't as though I could bump into work colleagues in town. Ninety per cent of the screws I worked with either used to travel in or stay in the quarters while they worked. For most, I was out of sight, out of mind.

I met up with Garry and Rhys a few times for beers, but not often. Rhys had met a bird and was engaged, so he had other commitments. I liked Garry, but I could only handle him in small doses. He came down to stay with me, from time to time, and we would go out on the piss. However, he was an arrogant little cunt and many of my home mates took a dislike to him – something I had to smooth over, or one of them would have belted him.

Garry had this way of getting on everyone's tits but, once you actually got to know him, his heart was in the right place and he could be a good laugh. Thankfully, my mates learned to tolerate him for my sake.

Scouse would make regular trips down. He was supportive throughout. He could see that I was in a bad way. He told me I needed to get a grip of myself but, as soon as he'd finished the lecture, he was ready to get out on the piss!

I was speaking to Frankie regularly and he seemed in good spirits. He was calmer than I would have expected. He was very matter of fact about what could happen and was trying to stay positive, but I think he was preparing himself for the worst. He was also giving me updates on when the case was going to reach court. He had a copy of Neil's statement as well, if that's what you could fucking call it . . .

Nine months had passed and finally the court case had arrived. I got a call from our brief and Rumpole respectively. I was given the dates and times. Rumpole told me to meet him at the front of the Well and catch a cab with him to the court. I decided to go to the nick the night before to stay at the staff quarters, so that I was closer for the morning. I could also have a good drink with a few of my pals. I'd not seen many people from work for the best part of a year. I had kept my fitness up, even though I had been abusing myself with alcohol. I was in shape, although my once-tidy cropped hair had grown into an 'Oasis style' mop top.

I got down to the Well and went out for beers with Scouse. I went round to the club. When I got in there, no one recognised me. They had to look twice to realise that it was me. Bob, Frankie and AJ were there. It was very emotional. Was the nightmare going to be over or get darker? We didn't know.

The next morning I was awake long before my alarm clock went off. I didn't sleep much that night. Tossing and turning, I was waiting for the break of day. I went to the front of the prison ten minutes earlier than Rumpole had specified, but he was already there, puffing on a fag, looking fatter and uglier than ever. First thing he said was, 'Doing too much partying, Ronnie? You look like shit.'

I hadn't seen the moody old fucker for ages but I could tell that he liked me. It was something to with the fact that, if he didn't, he would have fed me to the wolves by now.

AJ and Bob turned up. Frankie was going to meet us at the court. Feelings were already running high when Rumpole dropped a bombshell: he told us that Neil was meeting us to share the taxi. I couldn't believe it. I was fucking fuming. She was the last person I wanted to sit with.

The taxi arrived to take us to court. Neil had more front than Southend pier for getting into that cab. The journey was silent. All you could hear was Rumpole sucking the life out of his Superkings, one after another.

When we finally got to court, I couldn't get out of the cab fast enough. Frankie was already there, smiling, looking surprisingly relaxed. He looked smart, as always. That was when the whole situation suddenly became very real to me. It was happening! We were on our way into court! The support that Frankie had was amazing. So many off-duty screws turned up that they couldn't all fit into the courtroom.

The two coppers who had interviewed me arrived. They couldn't believe that AJ, Bob and I were all still suspended; they couldn't see any reason for it. They couldn't see the reason for it! Thanks to this pile-of-shit suspension and case, I had lost my relationship and my son, had sunk into a depression, and faced the prospect of losing my job and my house. They couldn't see the reason for it! How the fuck did they think I felt?

Court proceedings began. Bob, AJ and I sat outside the courtroom; we weren't allowed to go into the court because we were giving evidence. Neil wasn't allowed in, either; however, she was a part of the prosecution and we were defence, so she sat in another area. The scroat that we bent up that day was there to give his bullshit evidence. He was still in prison, so he was waiting in the cells before being taken to the courtroom. I didn't see him enter the court or give his evidence.

An hour or so later, Neil walked past us and into the courtroom. There was only one way in and one way out (except for cons). I paced up and down the corridor. Soon enough, Neil came out of court looking at the floor. Apparently, as she had left the stand, all the Officers in the gallery started slagging her off and shouting abuse at her for her evidence.

Frankie took the stand next. He was grilled for the rest of the day. He spoke the Queen's English perfectly, throwing aside any challenges from the prosecution. He was one silky smooth operator. The brief said he handled himself perfectly, which was good news. It was an agonising time for everyone. AJ, Bob and I spent the day just staring at each other and the walls. It dragged on and on. It gave us all the time in the world to worry. It was horrible. I was pulling my bloody hair out. When the first day in court was over, we went to the pub. It was very depressing, but we were all trying to keep our spirits up.

The morning came round too soon. We made our way to court, this time without Neil. The journey went too quickly; it didn't seem long enough to get my thoughts together. I had the worst butterflies; I felt sick and it wasn't from the booze. It was time for us to receive a grilling: it was make or break now.

AJ was called into court first. He seemed to be in and out of there quick as fuck. Scouse came out and told me that it went fine for him, which was good news. It was now Bob's turn to take the stand, leaving me sitting outside the court alone. I was beginning to sweat, knowing it wouldn't be long until I was called. Bob isn't the cleverest person you'll meet; and he proved that perfectly here. The prosecution could see his weaknesses, and they almost managed to get him to commit perjury by confusing him and tripping him up. He was sent out of court halfway through his time on the stand. A copper came out with him, to make sure that he didn't talk to me, since I was going to take the stand next, so I had no fucking idea why he was sent out and then called back; but I knew that it wasn't good. Twenty minutes after he was called back in, he finished and went and joined the other screws in the gallery.

There was a fifteen-minute break and everyone spilled out of the courtroom. My evidence was going to be the last piece to be heard in court. Frankie came over to me and told me to not worry.

His spirits were good considering his brief had told him it was fifty-fifty after Neil's performance. Everyone piled back into court and I heard a chorus of 'Good luck, mate' from those who walked past me.

I started to pace up and down the corridor, desperate to get on with it. 'What the fuck are they doing in there?' I was thinking. I finally heard 'Mr Thompson'. As I entered, I looked over to the gallery, and saw the phenomenal amount of support that Frankie had. The sea of heads facing me looked like an audience at the Albert Hall. I took deep breaths before stepping up to the box and swearing to tell the truth.

I had to go through the whole incident from start to finish, explaining it in fine detail. I had this down to a fine art, as if it were lines that I'd learnt for a play, only this was the truth and no act. I found my stride and stayed articulate. I was in over-drive; it was like it wasn't really happening. The prosecution fired some questions at me, putting forward their theories of what happened. I quickly dismissed them, informing everyone that they were bollocks, but in the most professional manner I could. They tried to make me slip up, but I just stuck to telling the truth.

Almost before I knew it, I heard, 'Thank you, Mr Thompson, there are no further questions. You may step down.'

Had I done enough, did I say the right thing? I just didn't know. The court broke while the Magistrate left to make his decision.

This wasn't like a normal Magistrates' Court; instead of having three magistrates, it only had one. From what I've heard, it's like this when a Barrister or QC is training to be a Judge, so he takes sole control. This could be seen as good or bad. Good, as you only have one person to convince; but bad, as there weren't two others there to convince him if he was unsure.

We all sat around the court, nervous as fuck. Was Frankie going to be sent down or walk free? It really was fifty-fifty; even his brief didn't want to call it.

I spoke to Frankie and he thanked me profusely, saying I couldn't have done more than I did, and his brief agreed. It was good to know I didn't cock it up. I went to Bob and threw my arms around him (he was still crying his eyes out). Everyone was talking to each other in whispers, anxious about what they were going to hear. The tension was incredible. Everything was resting on these precious minutes. I was fidgeting, unable to relax. Enough was enough; we had to know. Then suddenly, 'All rise.'

We stood up. Then, as we sat down, Frankie was told to remain standing. All of us in the gallery were holding hands, praying that Frankie was not going to be found guilty for something that he hadn't done. It was painful, wrong, horrible, all these feelings were running through my veins. You could have cut the atmosphere with a knife. I noticed a couple of the court security guards by the door. That put my imagination into overdrive. Were they here to take Frankie down to the cells? Did they know the outcome? Had they come to take him away?

The Magistrate took a minute to get his paperwork together. He coughed loudly, clearing his throat, 'I find the charge . . . Not proved.'

It took a second for everyone to realise what he had said. Once it had sunk in, it was like England scoring the winning goal in the World Cup. There were cheers of joy throughout the whole place! 'COME ON!' I screamed with pure emotion. Frankie was clenching his fist, shaking it like a madman with a tear rolling down his cheek. Bob was in the corner, still crying. Even AJ let a small smile break across that strong weathered face of his. Everyone was standing, everyone was smiling. Elation, happiness and relief all flooded over me.

The Magistrate told us to quieten down. We all sat back down to listen to his words as he explained the reasons for the decision. He went on to defend Frankie, saying that he had acted professionally throughout the incident. Frankie had said from day one that he had moved the prisoner's face away from him, with force, to prevent the prisoner from continuing to spit on him. The Magistrate went on to say that being spat on is an assault and, in the light of the situation of restraining a prisoner that possibly had drugs on them – and may well have been under the influence of them – Frankie acted very modestly and would have been completely justified in striking the inmate with a closed hand (a punch) to prevent further assault. Spit can carry all sorts of germs. It is disgusting and unjust. He told the courtroom that, instead of a criminal investigation and suspension, we should have all been commended for our excellent conduct in preventing Class A drugs entering the establishment. He said we should be praised for the way we restrained the inmate in these awful conditions. He could not praise Frankie's conduct enough. He made it quite clear that he thought the whole case was farcical.

We left the courtroom, with everyone congratulating Frankie. Finally, the criminal case was over. We streamed out in double time, eager to celebrate. Rumpole spoke to Frankie outside court, reminding him that we still had the internal investigation to deal with. Rumpole wasn't trying to spoil the party: he was just always keeping reality in his sights. Frankie wasn't stupid; he knew that they would not stop until they had him out of the job. He handed Rumpole his letter of resignation there and then. It was hard for him to do as he had been a screw for well over fifteen years, but he felt he had to do it. During his whole time on suspension he had been going through a series of interviews for another job with a local council – and he got it. Good on him.

We went to the pub and got on it – including the two coppers who had interviewed us and charged Frankie. Over many beers they told me that, if Frankie had gone down, Bob would have been in a lot of trouble. He was sent out of court, during the time he was on the stand, because he was tripped up, and said something that didn't tally with his original statement, so they had to listen to the tape of his interview. The prosecution had led him into contradicting himself. I never told him how close he was to being in serious trouble that day. The party went long into the night.

As happy as I was for Frankie that day, the cloud of an internal investigation still loomed over me. There was more shit to come.

BE HERE NOW

Frankie had been cleared of all charges and had resigned, so why the fuck were AJ, Bob and I still suspended? Rumpole told us he was sure we had nothing to worry about; they had achieved their aim of pushing Frankie out, so our forthcoming interviews were only to enable them to close the internal investigation and get us back to work. Every day was agonising for us, and we were all going out of our minds. We couldn't see any reason why we were still suspended unless they wanted to make some sort of example of us.

I wanted to get a grip of myself. I wanted to cut down my drinking and get back to work. I wanted to sort myself out so I could see my son and, as painful as it was, try and see Danielle. I felt like a disgrace. I shut myself away from most of my family. I couldn't handle seeing my mum because she would go on at me all the time, telling me that I was a mess and that I had responsibilities to face up to. Even though she was right, it was the last thing that I wanted to hear. I was still very scared about losing my job. I maxed out every credit card I had in paying for the lavish lifestyle I was living as a way of trying to shut my problems out. If I lost my job, then I would be really fucked.

I couldn't move on or face everything until I knew what was finally going to happen. I felt as if I was cracking up. A further two agonising weeks went past and there was still no indication of when we going to be called in to be interviewed. There was no reason for us still to be suspended. Or maybe there was . . .

Danielle knew that the court case was over and that I was waiting for the internal investigation to be completed. After everything, she obviously still cared for me. I struggled to talk to her; I was grieving about losing her. But I never told her. I buried that like everything else. I was wallowing in my own self pity. I felt I was going to explode.

It was a Monday morning. I was sitting about, wondering how to kill the day till it was time to go to the gym, when my phone rang.

'Hello?'

'You are being interviewed on Thursday at 11:30 hours by the investigations team.' It was Rumpole ringing to tell me the news, still moody, with not as much as a hello.

'Do I need to bring anything?'

'Just yourself, lad.'

'What rep is coming in with me?'

'Me. Be at the gate at 10:30 hours.'

He hung up.

What a week I had before me. As much as it had the possibility of being the end of my career, I suddenly felt a little better. Not much, just a little.

Bob called me, followed by AJ. They told me that they were meeting up at the same time as me. I rang my brother Mark, who then helped me celebrate my relief with a piss-up. I told my mum, and she was delighted that the final meeting had arrived. She had come to the conclusion that, whatever happened, I could put a full stop there and get on with my life.

Thursday came round quickly. I laid off the booze after my session with Mark; so, for the first time in months, I felt clear-headed. I met the other two at the gate and we made our way inside the nick to Rumpole's office. It was nerve-racking. We hadn't been inside the prison since we were first suspended. As we made our way to the office, we saw many familiar faces but there was also lots of new staff who we didn't recognise, as staff retention at the Well was a fucking joke. Always new staff with no experience. All adding to the shitness of the place.

We got to the office and nothing had changed there. It still smelt of fags and burgers. Dirty, stained chair, messy desk, an overflowing bin and shit all over the floor. When we walked in, Rumpole was eating and smoking at the same time! I could hear his arteries hardening. He informed us that the investigation team would be there shortly. He told us that we should all be fine. Should? I wished he'd said would.

The investigation team turned up looking very hurried, as if this meeting was interrupting an important tea break. There were three of them, two blokes and a woman, in their forties or fifties. The thing I do remember clearly is that one of them had a full beard and glasses and bore a striking resemblance to Dr Harold Shipman. It was hard to not laugh out loud.

They told us they would call us in one at a time and then collate their information from the interviews. They would then call us all in together to tell us the decision they had made.

I was summoned first, which was a refreshing change. They got me sat down quicker than was comfortable. It was all very rushed, as if they didn't really give a fuck what I had to say. It seemed merely a formality. They told me to run through the incident, but to keep it brief. I had been in there but five or six minutes, and hadn't even finished, when they said, 'Thank you, Mr Thompson, that's all.'

Fucking hell! I hadn't really started and they'd jogged me on. It was obvious that they had already made their decision. Well, definitely maybe. Bob was next, and he spent less time in there than I had. AJ's interview was amazing: no sooner had he walked in than he was walking out.

I didn't have time to fart, let alone consider the potentially bad decisions that could be made, before the three of us were called back in. Fucking hell, that was quick.

'I find the disciplinary charges not proven. Thank you all for your cooperation.'

The three of us were left standing there in disbelief. Was that it?

'It's over. When can you come back to work?' Rumpole said, after lighting up.

It was over. YES! We were all pleased, but I couldn't help feeling some anguish over the fact that the best part of a year of our lives had been lost and destroyed for nothing. When it came down to it, they had won. Frankie was gone. We were only pawns. Even though there was no reason to sack us, had Frankie not resigned, Rumpole told us they probably would have got rid of the lot of us to avoid him suing for unfair dismissal.

This whole disgraceful, time-consuming, family-damaging investigation took a year and no disciplinary action was taken against any of us. All we got, by way of recompense or apology, was a 'Thank you' from an investigator who didn't know us from Adam. It left a sour taste in my mouth, to say the least. I felt raped by the system. I felt bitter and angry, even though I was relieved.

We walked out of HMP Romwell together as if a huge weight had been lifted from us. It was time for me to try and rebuild my life. I had to get myself back together. Piece by piece.

And it started with going back to work. I agreed to start the next week – and start full time. They offered us a return-to-work schedule, where you begin with less hours and gradually build back up to full time. Fuck that, I'd been off for far too long. Maybe it was too soon, but I needed a bit of normality in my life.

Monday came round and I was tense and excited. I walked on to D Wing, ready for my staff briefing. As I got into the office, the screws started to clap and cheer. It made me feel really good. I was back. And I was happy to be back. I went to the staff toilet where I shed a tear because the occasion had got the better of me.

I was soon into the swing of things, pounding the landings, doing what I did best. Good diet, plenty of exercise and work got me back to the man I was. However, I started suffering from panic attacks – camomile tea, deep breaths and a good sleep helped me on my way. I began to spend a lot of time with my son, which was brilliant, and Danni and I were getting along great, which was perfect. I was still very much in love with her. I was treating her much better then, better than I ever did when we were together. There was still a huge spark between us. We were doing more and more together as a family and, for once in my life, I had my values in the right place. I was putting my boy and Danielle first. And, when we got back together, it felt right. I was back with my family, where I belonged. I needed to be home every night, concentrating on what was important. The only way to do that was for me to leave the Well and be closer to home.

The corruption at the Well was still rife, so getting out was the best option for me. Besides, I had knocked a few Governors' noses out of joint. I put in for a transfer to an open nick a lot closer to where I lived. I spoke to the Governors about transferring. They fucked me about a bit, not letting me, then agreeing, then changing their minds again. Standard Prison Service procedure. After months and months of it, they were still fucking with my life. They still weren't doing anything to help me. I wasn't asking for the earth to be moved. I only wanted a transfer.

Ever since I'd been back, I'd felt that I had to watch everything I did. I knew that they were waiting for me to slip up. I was a marked man.

Rumpole helped me out again and sorted out the transfer. Powerful man; a true legend.

I got my start date at the Cat D holiday camp. It was certainly going to be a lot quieter than the Well . . .

POSTSCRIPT

Further down the line, Keenan, the ex-TA cunt and Noil woro all sacked. Their methods of working 'together' eventually caught up with them. Thank fuck for that.

EPILOGUE

What do you think of when you hear the words 'Prison Officer'? You think of a burly, tough-looking geezer in a military-style uniform with a big bunch of keys and a loud voice who knows how to turn off the surveillance cameras while he has a 'friendly chat' with a con? Of course you do. We've all seen them on TV.

But, in the course of any one day as a Prison Officer, you have to deal with a staggering array of crackheads, smackheads, drug dealers, arse-kickers, pimps, nonces, grasses, troublemakers, meat-heads, knobheads, dickheads, scumbags, shitbags, time-wasters and toe-rags.

'So what's so special about that?' you say.

What's special, is that you are also managing bend-ups, cock-ups, wrap-ups, fuck-ups, rub-downs, strip-searches, barricades, riots, hostages, self-harmers, corruption and ineptitude . . . and what's so special *there* is that the phrase 'life-threatening' wouldn't be inappropriate in front of any of them.

On top of all this, the powers-that-be expect you to manage this alongside paperwork, overwork, donkey work, underpay and understaffing – and all while wearing the most unbelievably, disgustingly scratchy trousers.

So, the next time you think 'Prison Officer', let's hear you think it *with a little RESPECT!!!*

ACKNOWLEDGEMENTS

Every Prison Officer who works in this country, and there are over 40,000 of them, does an extraordinary job that is vastly underrated.

I would like to thank every decent screw I've ever met or had the pleasure of working with: you do a great job. Look after each other and leave safely at the end of your shift.

I have full respect for any man or woman who enters a service or force. It's not just a job: it really is a way of life. There will always be issues of underpayment and bad treatment in this sector – the police, Fire Service, NHS and the military have well-publicised protests over their payment and conditions. While they may not get paid enough, at least these courageous and committed people have the respect and recognition they deserve. Spare a thought for Prison Officers – the unsung heroes – and what they do.

DEDICATION

My partner, my rock, the love of my life. You are a true angel. Being with you provides me with more happiness than you would ever know.

My son, I couldn't have wanted for a better child. Every time I look at you, I'm the proudest father in the world.

Being together as a family is what makes it all worth while. In the darkest times, the pair of you have given me the courage to carry on. I love you with all my heart.

God bless you both.